How to Ruin Your Education and TV Viewing

How to Ruin Your Education and TV Viewing

Five Lessons from John Dominic Crossan

SPENCER D. GEAR

WIPF & STOCK · Eugene, Oregon

HOW TO RUIN YOUR EDUCATION AND TV VIEWING
Five Lessons from John Dominic Crossan

Copyright © 2022 Spencer D. Gear. All rights reserved. Except for brief quotations in critical publications or reviews, no part of this book may be reproduced in any manner without prior written permission from the publisher. Write: Permissions, Wipf and Stock Publishers, 199 W. 8th Ave., Suite 3, Eugene, OR 97401.

Spencer Gear, Department of New Testament and Related Literature, Faculty of Theology and Religion, University of Pretoria, Pretoria, South Africa.

The author declares that the manuscript represents a reworking of about one-third of his obtained PhD. He also declares that there is no plagiarism in the manuscript

Wipf & Stock
An Imprint of Wipf and Stock Publishers
199 W. 8th Ave., Suite 3
Eugene, OR 97401

www.wipfandstock.com

PAPERBACK ISBN: 978-1-6667-3527-7
HARDCOVER ISBN: 978-1-6667-9218-8
EBOOK ISBN: 978-1-6667-9219-5

03/23/22

Contents

Bible Translations Used		vii
List of Abbreviations		ix
One	A Back-to-Front Chapter	1
Two	First Crossan Lesson	6
Three	Second Crossan Lesson	22
Four	Third Crossan Lesson	79
Five	Fourth Crossan Lesson	130
Six	Fifth & Final Crossan Lesson	193
Seven	Conclusion: A Front-to-Back Evaluation	241
Bibliography		243

Bible Translations Used

Unless otherwise stated, all scriptural references are from the NIV, the Holy Bible, New International Version®. Copyright ©1973, 1978, 1984, 2011 by Biblica, Inc.™ Used by permission of Zondervan. All rights reserved worldwide.

Scriptures designated ERV are from the Holy Bible: Easy-to-Read Version, International Edition ©2013, 2016 Bible League International.

Scriptures designated ESV are from the Holy Bible, English Standard Version®. Copyright ©2001 by Crossway, a publishing ministry of Good News Publishers. All rights reserved.

Scriptures designated CCD are from the Confraternity of Christian Doctrine (CCD) who owns the copyright on the New American Bible, revised edition translation (NABRE).

Scriptures designated NASB are from the New American Standard Bible®. Copyright ©1960, 1971, 1977, 1995, 2020 by The Lockman Foundation. Used by permission. All rights reserved, www.lockman.org.

Scriptures designated NET are from the NET Bible®. Copyright ©1996, 2019 by Biblical Studies Press, LLC. http://netbible.com. Used by permission. All rights reserved.

Scriptures designated NLT are from the Holy Bible, New Living Translation. Copyright ©1996, 2004, 2007 by Tyndale House Foundation. Used by permission of Tyndale House Publishers Inc., Carol Stream, IL 60188. All rights reserved.

Scriptures designated NRSV are from the New Revised Standard Version Bible (NRSV). Copyright ©1989 by the Division of Christian Education of the National

Council of the Churches of Christ in the United States of America. Used by permission. All rights reserved.

Scriptures designated RSV are from the Revised Standard Version of the Bible. Copyright © 1946, 1952, and 1971 by the Division of Christian Education of the National Council of the Churches of Christ in the United States of America. Used by permission. All rights reserved.

List of Abbreviations

CD   *Cambridge Dictionary* (https://dictionary.cambridge.org/)
MD   *Macmillan Dictionary* (https://www.macmillandictionary.com/)
M-WD   *Merriam-Webster Dictionary* (https://www.merriam-webster.com/)
OED   *Oxford English Dictionary* (https://www.lexico.com/)

ONE

A Back-to-Front Chapter

You may think this is a strange title for the first chapter—and it is! However, it was meant to be the back (last) chapter of the book, to deal with applications and possible objections to the topics covered in the book. This chapter will ask a number of searching personal questions of you.

HISTORY: CHRISTOPHER COLUMBUS

What will you do as a parent if your fourteen-year-old comes home from school and says, "You and the teachers have been telling me Columbus discovered the Americas. You've lied to me, because that isn't true. There are no such things, as facts and I decide the meaning of what is written in my text books. I'm the one who chooses the interpretation of any writing, including history and the stories of Columbus."

How are you going to answer, especially in light of what the *Encyclopaedia Britannica* states about Columbus?

> Christopher Columbus, Italian Cristoforo Colombo, Spanish Cristóbal Colón (born between August 26 and October 31?, 1451, Genoa [Italy]—died May 20, 1506, Valladolid, Spain), master navigator and admiral whose four transatlantic voyages (1492–93, 1493–96, 1498–1500, and 1502–04) opened the way for European exploration, exploitation, and colonization of the Americas. He has long been called the "discoverer" of the New World, although Vikings such as Leif Eriksson had visited North America five centuries earlier.[1]

---

1. Flint, "Christopher Columbus."

HISTORY: CAPTAIN ARTHUR PHILLIP AND PORT JACKSON

How would you react if your high school student in my home country of Australia returned after school one day with the news that this information was incorrect and that the school teachers had been teaching lies?

> The First Fleet, consisting of 11 vessels, was the largest single contingent of ships to sail into the Pacific Ocean. Its purpose was to find a convict settlement on the east coast of Australia, at Botany Bay.

The First Fleet sailed from England on 13 May 1787 and arrived at Botany Bay eight months later, on 18 January 1788. Governor Arthur Phillip rejected Botany Bay, choosing instead Port Jackson, to the north, as the site for the new colony; they arrived there on 26 January 1788.

> The number of convicts transported in the First Fleet is unclear; there were between 750–780 convicts and around 550 crew, soldiers and family members.[2]

Your youth claims that this information should not be treated as facts, because facts no longer exist but are interpreted the youth's own way. Your youth has a suspicion of facts and depends on reason to deal with reality.

EDUCATION

Your teen is likely to tell your response to her teacher who could counter, "Forget about the State Library information online. There are no such things as facts, only interpreted things, and your interpretation is all that matters." How will you reply if your youth comes home with that kind of response? Language such as "rubbish" or "baloney" are not adequate responses, because they are examples of ad hominem (abusive) logical fallacies.[3]

In searching the internet for more information on reader-response examples to deconstruct any text, I was attracted to Dr Jeremy Koay's brief article "What Is Reader-Response Theory?" (2017). This is an exceptional, brief overview of a method that is overwhelming education, including the reading of documents of any kind, whether narrative, poetry, or interpretation of art in our contemporary world.

2. "Convicts: Bound for Australia."
3. See "Ad Hominem (Abusive)."

Even though the article was published in December 2017, as of 20 July 2021, no comments had been published online. At an earlier date, I forwarded my response to him, but it was not published.

I find that a major problem with reader-response theory is that it cannot consistently interpret literature. Dr Koay replied to me: "The idea of pure literal meaning is contestable because our culture, experiences and worldview shape our understanding of words." I asked him: is that how you want me to read your article? Or do you want a literal reading (which includes figures of speech)? Can I engage in postmodern, deconstructionist, reader-response techniques with your article to make it mean what I decide it means?

Could you imagine the recorded history of Emperor Nero, George Washington, Hitler and the Nazi concentration camps, Captain James Cook circumnavigating New Zealand and sailing up the east coast of Australia being interpreted by reader responses?

Did Emperor Nero, George Washington, Hitler, and James Cook say and do what is recorded in their journals and history about them, or is that open to the readers' interactive deconstruction with your kind of reader—responses from our century and cultures?

Dr. Koay chose to reply by email rather than publishing my letter on the EduMaxi website. His targeted readers are primarily language teachers (not philosophers), he said. So he considered my reply was philosophical.

I won't publish his email (I've given a hint about what he said), because he has not given me permission to supply the detail in his email. However, you'll pick up some of his content in my response, sent by email on 13 September 2018. I use "you" and "your" in referring to Dr Koay.

> For my breakfast devotions with the three children, my wife and I used to pray, "May the children have a safe day at school and while they travel to and from school." How would you respond if one of your teens said, "Praying for a safe day is a waste of space because there is no 'god' to guide us as we run our own lives and decide if our day will be good or bad?"

Can you imagine engaging in any personal conversation or reading *The New York Times* through a reader-response worldview?

THEOLOGY

What would you do if you encountered either of the following statements?

"Jesus was not born of a virgin, but, like all other children, he was born of a woman after sexual union between a man and a woman."

"Don't believe what the Bible states about Jesus's resurrection, because nobody was at the tomb to see the alleged rising from the dead. They only saw him after the rising, and it could not be resuscitation, because dead people, in normal life situations, are not resuscitated. Miracles do not happen."

A Christian will encounter many rational explanations that are claimed to be better vindications than the miraculous.

Have you heard of ontotheology that is flooding some churches and our world? Ontotheology is "a branch or system of theology in which God is regarded as a being, especially the supreme being."[4] According to ontotheology, he is not the Supreme, Almighty, Creator, and Magnificent God, and we human beings have made our attempts to reach this god by our own efforts. Don't be surprised if the term ontotheology makes it into mainstream language to mean reaching a self-made god by human reason.

CHRISTIAN TEACHING

This book should prepare you to analyze a deluge of information that is flooding liberal and even some evangelical churches. Can you trust the Bible? Is it a Bible that contains only sixty-six books, or are there books outside the canonical Bible that need to be investigated for their worth? Does the Bible contain myths?

Are you prepared for a teenage youth who comes home from youth group to tell you: "What I've heard from our church's pulpit and youth group is only one view, but Scripture has many interpretations and one is no better than the other." How would you reply?

Would you agree or disagree with my statement? "The normal interpretation of literature is essentially literal. If we can't trust words to mean what they say, then writing ceases to be a useful means of communication. Only when Scripture itself indicates a text is other than literal should we interpret it non-literally."

Have you read books such as the Gospel of Peter[5] and the Gospel of Thomas[6] online to understand how the content varies from books of the Bible? Take a read of the books in the Apocrypha and Pseudepigrapha.[7]

---

4. "Ontotheology," in *OED*.
5. Quarles, "Gospel of Peter."
6. Lambdin, "Gospel of Thomas."
7. Evans, *Ancient Texts*.

Why aren't they considered worthy of being included in the Christian canon of Scripture, although the Apocrypha is in some Bibles?[8]

How would you respond if your primary school aged child came home after a religious education class at school and told you, "Jesus wasn't buried in the garden tomb but in a shallow grave like most other people. His body was placed in this grave to be dug up by dogs looking for a feed. The cross Jesus died on began talking." What would your comeback be?

This chapter introduces you to these kinds of teachings that are covered in the remainder of this book and a future book. Are you ready to take the plunge?

---

8. See the NRSV for the Apocrypha.

TWO

First Crossan Lesson

Quit adding extra interpretations to your books and news.[1]

PREFACE: THIS IS THE FIRST CROSSAN LESSON.

When I studied history in a Queensland, Australia, high school (secondary school) in the 1960s, it was straightforward—so I thought. I learned that on 12 October 1492, the Italian explorer Christopher Columbus officially set foot in the Americas and claimed the land for Spain. This is commonly known as "Columbus discovered America," but a more accurate description would be that he introduced the Americas to Western Europe. He made four visits to America between 1492 and 1502 in the ships the *Nina*, the *Pinta*, and the *Santa Maria*.[2] Are these facts true about Columbus, or are they myth?

These are some of the historical facts I learned about Australia. Captain James Cook (1728–1779) volunteered for service in the British Royal Navy. Thereafter, he made three voyages to the South Pacific Ocean.[3] The first trip on the *Endeavour* was to sail to Tahiti and to check if there was any large land mass to the south. He did not locate it but found New Zealand and circumnavigated it.

---

1. These subheadings are lessons I've learned from analyzing Crossan, of what *not* to do with historical Jesus investigations.
2. Enochs, "Real Story."
3. The details about Cook's voyages are from "James Cook."

From there, he sailed up the east coast of New Holland (later to become Australia).[4] The *Endeavour* almost met disaster when it hit the Great Barrier Reef off the Australian northeast coast near what is now known as Cooktown.

The second voyage was on the sloops *Resolution* and *Adventure*. The latter was commanded by Tobias Furneaux and left Sheerness in Britain in June 1772, sailing for Cape Town, before moving on to New Zealand where ten of the crew of *Adventure* were killed by the Maoris.

The third was for Cook to explore a northwest passage from England. On his two ships *Resolution* and *Discovery*, he sailed towards Cape Town, Kerguelen Island in the southern Indian Ocean, Adventure Bay in Van Diemen's Land (Australia), and Queen Charlotte Sound in New Zealand, before he travelled north to the Sandwich Islands (Hawaii), reaching the North American coast in 1778. He discovered Alaska before returning to the Sandwich Islands where Cook was killed by Hawaiians at Kealakekua Bay on 14 February 1779.

It was English explorer Matthew Flinders who made the suggestion the name of New Holland should be Australia. This is appropriate, as Flinders was the first to circumnavigate the country in 1803. He produced a hand drawn map in 1804, and the Australian National Library holds a reproduction of that map.[5]

HISTORY OR FICTION

Are these details fact or fiction? Can we create other versions of these incidents that are as valid as the information above, by introducing deconstructionist free play? This book investigates why this traditional model of history is being questioned and pursues an alternate view that some denounce as outdated. The key question is: should historical evidence be deconstructed?

---

4. The name *Australia* emerged from the view by Europeans that there was a gigantic land in the Southern Hemisphere that was described alternatively as "Terra Australis Incognita" or "Unknown South Land" (see "How Was Australia Named"). However, the specific name Australia was given to the continent by explorer Matthew Flinders.

5. "How Was Australia Named?"

Queensland History Curriculum for High Schools

The Australian Curriculum Version 8 for years seven to ten, Humanities and Social Sciences (HASS), states that the key ideas of these subjects are "who we are, who came before us and traditions and values that have shaped us."[6]

The rationale of history is for "promoting an understanding of societies, events, movements and developments that have shaped humanity.... [It is also for] developing knowledge, understanding and appreciation of the past and forces that shape societies."[7]

These relate exactly to what happened in our past, involving traditions and values, acquiring knowledge, and understanding how the past has influenced and shaped our societies. What was taught to me in grades nine and ten in the 1960s seems to harmonize with the Queensland curriculum of 2021.

However, there is a new wind blowing in history and literature that does not resemble what the Queensland curriculum teaches. The wind creates personal interpretations that add to the speech acts.[8]

University Curricula for History

The University of California at San Francisco (UCSF) adopts the view that history involves "connecting the past with the present" and encourages students and faculty to

> resist the idea that history is static or confined to the past. Examining current events within the context of history, you'll gain a deep understanding of how the past informs present-day issues at local and global levels. We encourage you to think critically about your place in the world and to become an active and engaged citizen.[9]

Katie Hanks of UCSF leans towards a deconstructionist view: "History is not black and white, it is not the memorization of dates; it is the endless possibilities of interpretations of one single event."[10] So, are Christopher Columbus's oceanic ventures not black and white? Are they factual events that

---

6. "Australian Curriculum in Queensland."
7. "Australian Curriculum in Queensland."
8. A speech act is "an utterance considered as an action, particularly with regard to its intention, purpose, or effect" ("Speech Act," in *OED*). See Allison, "Speech Act Theory," for a discussion of speech acts.
9. "History: Connecting the Past."
10. "History: Connecting the Past."

happened at some times in the past that are associated with particular dates? Or are there endless possibilities of Columbus's voyages from Spain to the Americas to open up this continent to the Europeans?

The *Oxford English Dictionary* provides one definition of history as "a continuous, typically chronological, record of important or public events or of a particular trend or institution."[11] If a trend is noted, an interpretation is necessary. The University of Nottingham UK explains. "There has never been a more important time to study the past. An understanding of how we got here is vital to navigating the future."[12]

The history department of Macquarie University in Sydney, Australia, encourages students of history to pursue a traditional approach. It explains that students should

> explore civilisations from Ancient Greece and Rome to Egypt, and also the archaeology of Australasia's Indigenous past. With almost no limit to its interdisciplinarity, you'll engage with archaeological evidence and the science that is re-shaping the study of the past—whether skeletons or ancient coins.[13]

FURTHER HISTORICAL EXAMPLES

SS *Maheno* Shipwreck, Fraser Island, Qld., Australia[14]

11. "History," in *OED*.
12. "Welcome to Department of History."
13. "Ancient Greece, Rome, Egypt."
14. Image licensed by Creative Commons for commercial and personal use, pxhere.com.

Fraser Island, the Great Sandy island off the Queensland coast at Hervey Bay, Australia, has a tourist attraction of a rusted shipwreck. The *Maheno* was a World War I hospital ship from New Zealand that was being towed to Japan to be scrapped in July 1935 when it ran aground on Fraser Island. Built in 1905, it was among the first turbine-driven steamers.

Hand-colored postcard of the SS *Maheno*[15]

The *Maheno* and a sister ship, the *Oonah*, were sold as scrap to Japan. Before the boats were towed to Japan, their rudders were removed. A cyclonic storm stuck them in Queensland waters that caused the tow chain to snap. This left the *Maheno* adrift and the powerful winds drove the ship to the ocean side of the sandy beach of Fraser Island.[16] How can we be confident the *Maheno* wreck belongs to that actual ship?

How do we know these were Roman emperors of the first century? They were Tiberius (AD 14–37), Caligula (AD 37–41), Claudius (AD 41–54), Nero (AD 54–68), Galba (AD 68–69), Otho (AD Jan.–Apr. 69), and Aulus Vitellius (AD July–Dec. 69).[17]

Let us become more current. Did the terrorist attacks on 11 September 2001 actually happen, with two planes flown into the twin towers of New York City; another striking the Pentagon outside Washington, DC; and a

---

15. Author unknown; image copied and digitized from a postcard (https://en.wikipedia.org/wiki/SS_Maheno).

16. "Fraser Island Shipwrecks."

17. Britannica et al., "List of Roman Emperors."

fourth plane crashing into a field near Shanksville, Pennsylvania? Almost three thousand people were killed.[18] Were they actual historical events that took place in three different locations in 2001, or were they some illusion, phantom, or parable?

You may think these are dimwit questions in light of eyewitness reports and mass media coverage of the events.

How do these historical illustrations relate to the theme of this book on ways to wreck any communication?

Up to a certain point in time, history was the investigation of events or facts from the past and the interpretation of those facts in the light of historical knowledge.

But below is the First Crossan Lesson to Ruin your Education.

ENTER JOHN DOMINIC CROSSAN

Crossan has spent much of his professional life writing on the historical Jesus, but his definition of history diverges widely from the descriptions of history from the curricula of the education departments in Queensland and in universities around the world.

This is Crossan's reconstruction or deconstruction of history. His working definition is: "*History is the past reconstructed interactively by the present through argued evidence in public discourse.*"[19]

According to Crossan, Jesus's burial by his friends was not a historical event. It was probably done by his enemies. If he was buried at all—and there are doubts—he was possibly not buried in a tomb hewn out of stone but was put in a shallow grave to be eaten by scavenging dogs. The Easter events do not relate to actions that happened on a given day, but the story is about Jesus's followers struggling to make sense of his death and how they were experiencing his empowerment in their lives as a result of his resurrection. Jesus's resurrection was not in bodily form where one could touch and feel the physical Jesus. His resurrection was an apparition.[20]

Those are the views of John Dominic Crossan.[21] In the *New Yorker* of 24 May 2010, in a popular piece on those who are reconstructing the historical Jesus, Adam Gopnik wrote of complexities of fact that produce

---

18. Editors. "September 11 Attacks."
19. Crossan, "Historical Jesus as Risen Lord," 3 (emphasis in original).
20. An apparition is a ghost or ghostlike appearance of a person or "a remarkable or unexpected appearance of someone or something" ("Apparition," in *OED*).
21. Crossan, *Historical Jesus*, 395–400; Crossan, *Birth of Christianity*, 550; Crossan and Watts, *Who Is Jesus*, 152–53.

ambiguities of faith as one pursues knowledge. He observes that in Gospel study, one of the curious criteria of historical criticism is that the more difficult a remark is to understand, the more likely it is to be true. As applied to Jesus, the more "nasty" a saying by him, the more probable it is true. The contrast is that if Jesus says something that sounds "nice," historical criticism is more likely to attribute it to somebody else. Gopnik uses Crossan's research to report some of his own views on the historical Jesus.[22]

By contrast, church historian Kenneth Scott Latourette states that, based on "the records that have reached us," Jesus's body was laid sorrowfully in the rock tomb and sealed with a large stone, by direct statement or inference, thus indicating that his body was not found in the tomb the next morning. The boulder had been removed, and the tomb was empty. Jesus's disciples were "profoundly convinced that they had seen the risen Jesus" by talking with him, watching him and viewing the wounds in his hands and side. The one who had been a doubter was convinced by touching these wounds. The biographer, almost certainly Luke, a companion of Paul, told of how he had obtained all of the information from *eyewitnesses*, and the narratives were written based on this *eyewitness* information. Latourette's understanding as a historian was that this information was written less than a generation after the events described.[23]

Other supporters of eyewitness testimony (autopsy) do not provide evidence to endorse Crossan's reconstruction of what happened to the body of Jesus. Samuel Byrskog writes that "the enthusiastic resurrection belief was not opposed to a real historical sensitivity."[24] For Richard Bauckham, three of the four Gospels (the exception being Matthew) "must embody the testimony of witnesses who were participants in the story from beginning to end—from the time of John the Baptist's ministry to the time of the resurrection appearances." These witnesses did not provide evidence from the intracanonical Gospels that are compatible with Crossan's specific details of the death, burial, and resurrection of Jesus.[25]

Another eminent historical Jesus scholar, N. T. Wright, concludes that Crossan's "explaining away the evidence" is applying "to the texts a ruthless hermeneutic of suspicion," where the resurrection accounts are "declared worthless as history" and "trivialize Christianity."[26] Wright does consider that "all history involves imaginative reconstruction" and that "there is

22. Gopnik, "What Did Jesus Do," 1.
23. Latourette, *To A.D. 1500*, 57–58.
24. Byrskog, *Story as History*, 138.
25. Bauckham, *Jesus and the Eyewitnesses*, 131.
26. Wright, *Resurrection of the Son*, 19.

always a leap to be made between the actual evidence and the fully-blown reconstruction." However, Wright's assessment of Crossan's *The Historical Jesus* (1991) was that "the book is almost entirely wrong."[27] Is this an accurate assessment or not?

Ben Meyer's review of Crossan's *The Historical Jesus* concludes that the book is "unsalvageable" as historical Jesus research, because it does not include a struggle with the evidence. Instead of wrestling with the data, Meyer judges that Crossan had given prepackaged material with literary finesse, but it was only "the proposal of a bright idea."[28]

It is nonnegotiable that the New Testament Gospels are rooted in historical events that actually happened, according to Wright.[29] I ask: if Jesus's passion accounts did not happen in Jerusalem in the first century, what is the point of salvation? The apostle Paul's assessment of the events in the passion accounts and their necessity for the gospel he preached was:

> By this gospel you are saved, if you hold firmly to the word I preached to you. Otherwise, you have believed in vain. For what I received I passed on to you as of first importance:[30] that Christ died for our sins according to the Scriptures, that he was buried, that he was raised on the third day according to the Scriptures, and that he appeared to Cephas,[31] and then to the Twelve. After that, he appeared to more than five hundred of the brothers and sisters at the same time, most of whom are still living, though some have fallen asleep. Then he appeared to James, then to all the apostles, and last of all he appeared to me also, as to one abnormally born. (1 Cor 15:2–8 NIV)

Why do Crossan's views on the death, burial and resurrection of Jesus diverge from the understanding of Easter as recorded in the four intracanonical Gospels? This study examines Crossan's teaching and investigates whether his contradictory conclusions are related to the presuppositions that underlie his views of the resurrection accounts in the Gospels.

They emerge from Crossan's approach to history and hermeneutics of the historical Jesus:

> Christianity is historical reconstruction interpreted as divine manifestation. It is not (in a postmodern world) that we find once and for all who the historical Jesus was way back then. It

---

27. Wright, *Jesus and the Victory*, 44.
28. Meyer, "Review of *Historical Jesus*," 576.
29. Wright, *New Testament*, 9.
30. NIV footnote: "Or *you at the first*."
31. NIV footnote: "That is, Peter."

is that each generation and century must redo that historical work and establish its best reconstruction, a reconstruction that will be and must be in some creative interaction with its own particular needs, visions, and programs.... The historical Jesus (fact) is the manifestation of God for us here and now (interpretation). *You cannot believe in a fact, only in an interpretation.*[32]

CROSSAN'S DEFINITION OF HISTORY

Crossan's position is straightforward but with severe complications. He explains: "This is my working definition of history: *History is the past reconstructed interactively by the present through argued evidence in public discourse*.... History as argued public reconstruction is necessary to reconstruct our past in order to project our future."[33] This is a question-begging view of historiography, especially in light of the consensus of historians. A begging the question fallacy is "any form of argument where the conclusion is assumed in one of the premises. Many people use the phrase 'begging the question' incorrectly when they use it to mean, 'prompts one to ask the question,' that is *not* the correct usage." It is also called circular reasoning.[34]

DECONSTRUCTIONIST VIEW APPLIED TO CROSSAN'S OWN LIFE

Let's apply this meaning of history to Crossan's life: "While I was born in Nenagh, County Tipperary, Ireland, I needed to reconstruct this to show it was really Belfast, Northern Ireland, and to engage in argued evidence that I'm really a Protestant, disguised as a Servite monk. My writing *The Birth of Christianity* (1998) was as a liberal, deconstructionist Protestant. I became a Protestant pastor in the Chicago area. While in that city, I began teaching at Moody Bible Institute, an eminent, conservative, evangelical Bible college. The Institute knew my reputation as a historical Jesus scholar and my postmodern theology but nevertheless invited me to join the faculty. This allowed me to further my academic activities by also teaching at the conservative, evangelical Wheaton College, Wheaton, Illinois, while I remained in the Servite order. Both Moody and Wheaton gave me full permission

---

32. Crossan, *Who Killed Jesus*, 217 (emphasis added).
33. Crossan, *Birth of Christianity*, 22 (emphasis added).
34. "Begging the Question."

to challenge students to join a Roman Catholic order of monks. There was encouragement from both colleges to allow me to proselytize students."

Crossan should have no objection to my above reconstruction of his life's story, as he believes in textual free play. As early as 1985, Lynn Poland had isolated what she considered were the main literary influences on Crossan, which were the New Criticism as well as two methodological issues. One was subsuming history within language and the other diminished the cognitive content at the expense of form and function. Because Crossan says that the term "historical Jesus" really "means the language of Jesus and most especially the parables themselves,"[35] Poland notes that Crossan's focus is on "structure and function at the expense of the content of the meanings and beliefs embodied in the story." Her observation is that Crossan does not seem to understand that specific content and function of a metaphor are dependent on "the concrete situation that the narrative depicts and the auditors recognize." She rightly sees that metaphor is an extension of ordinary meaning. Free play has application both to linguistics and history.[36]

My discussion about Crossan and Protestant colleges in Chicago was my Protestant deconstruction and free play. You would have every reason to regard me as having a bizarre experience of dysphoria if that paragraph were true to reality. Please be assured it wasn't factual but is an example of how I reconstructed Crossan's academic activities in the Chicago area. However, that kind of story created as free play from his autobiography is what Crossan wants to do with the passion account of Jesus with his postmodern reconstruction.

Could you imagine Crossan promoting a postmodern, deconstructed experience of his own life that needs to be argued interactively in public discourse in Chicago? This means Crossan, who was born in Ireland, has a line of evidence through leaving the priesthood; marrying twice (his first wife died); and teaching for many years at DePaul University, Chicago. But Crossan should have no need to object to my veering from the line of evidence to reconstruct his life story, as that is what he does in his own writing about the historical Jesus.

If postmodern deconstruction applies historically to Jesus's life, death, and resurrection, it is as relevant to Crossan's life and ministry as for Jesus's passion account. As we will see, a better method is to pursue traditional historiography of facts and interpretation, so we are not inventing details in Jesus's life, such as Jesus being buried in a shallow grave to be eaten by dogs scratching about for food or the resurrection being an apparition (ghost).

35. Crossan, *In Parables*, xiii.
36. Poland, in Thiselton, *New Horizons in Hermeneutics*, 116.

There are some foundational needs to be defined to explain the dynamic of this methodology.

DEFINITION OF TERMS

To better understand this book's focus, we need a definition of terms used.

THE HISTORICAL JESUS

Who is the historical Jesus? Wright considers that theologians and others are unsure which Jesus to include in their work, because historical Jesus scholars "choose a Jesus who just happens to fit the programme that was desired on other grounds." For Wright, the Jesus of theology is "the Jesus who lived and died as a Jew of the first century."[37]

Robert Funk, by contrast, claims that "what we need is *a new fiction* that takes as its starting point the central event in the Judeo-Christian drama and reconciles that middle with a new story that reaches beyond old beginnings and endings."[38] Rather than pointing to the need for a new fiction about the historical Jesus, Luke Johnson writes that the "real Jesus" for Christian faith is the resurrected Jesus, who is "the truly uncomfortable Jesus," the genuinely "counter-cultural" Jesus, not the reconstructed Jesus (the politically correct revolutionary Jesus of Crossan) but "the one inscribed in the canonical Gospels."[39]

Albert Schweitzer contends that Jesus of Nazareth, who was Messiah, who preached the kingdom of God and died to give his work its final consecration, *never had any existence.*[40] This historical Jesus should be replaced by "the Jesus who is a spiritual power in the present . . . . It is not Jesus as historically known, but Jesus as spiritually arisen within men, who is significant for our time and can help us."[41] This overthrow of the historical Jesus of Nazareth is by the one who "comes to us as One unknown"; people "shall learn in their own experience Who He is."[42] Schweitzer allegedly prepared the way for the Christ of faith, the modern Jesus, thus confirming Rudolph

---

37. Wright, *New Testament*, 139.
38. Funk, "Jesus Seminar Opening Remarks" (emphasis added).
39. Johnson, *Real Jesus*, 142, 177.
40. Schweitzer, *Quest of Historical Jesus*, 396 (emphasis added).
41. Schweitzer, *Quest of Historical Jesus*, 298, 399.
42. Schweitzer, *Quest of Historical Jesus*, 403.

Bultmann's (*Faith and Understanding*, 1969; *New Testament and Mythology*, 1984) disjunction between the Christ of faith and the Jesus of history.

For Crossan, "the term 'historical' Jesus means the language of Jesus and most especially the parables themselves . . . . We have literally no language and no parables of Jesus except and insofar as such can be retrieved and reconstructed from within the language of their earliest interpreters."[43] Crossan explains that he has "always thought of the historical Jesus as a homeland Jew within Judaism within the Roman Empire."[44] Paul Barnett defends the thesis that the historical Jesus was Jesus of Nazareth who, through his death, bodily resurrection, and ascension, became the Christ of faith.[45] Barnett is convinced that "the 'Christ of faith' was one and the same as the 'Jesus of history.'"[46]

Richard Bauckham notes that the phrase "the historical Jesus" is "seriously ambiguous" and has at least three meanings:[47]

1. "Jesus as he really was in his earthly life";

2. "Not all that Jesus was, but Jesus insofar as his historical reality is accessible to us," and

3. "The Jesus not of the Gospels but the person behind the Gospels. This is the Jesus who is reconstructed through a methodology of alleged ruthless objectivity and scrutiny. This Jesus is created by historians who do not believe the story in the Gospels unless it is independently verified."

Crossan's reconstructing the text, choosing extrabiblical material such as the Gospel of Peter and using other methodological issues, have caused him to define the historical Jesus as "the past Jesus reconstructed interactively by the present through argued evidence in public discourse."[48] In his autobiography, he defines the historical Jesus as "the reconstruction of Jesus' life as lived in the first century's first quarter, long before it was creatively recorded and necessarily reinterpreted by the Gospel writers in that century's last quarter." Therefore, research on the historical Jesus "is open-heart surgery on Christianity, and maybe also on civilization itself," says Crossan.[49]

---

43. Crossan, *In Parables*, xiii.
44. Crossan, *God and Empire*, 1.
45. Barnett, *Jesus and the Rise*, 418.
46. Barnett. *Jesus and the Rise*, 10.
47. Bauckham, *Jesus and the Eyewitnesses*, 2–3.
48. Crossan, *Birth of Christianity*, 30.
49. Crossan, *Long Way from Tipperary*, xv.

INTRODUCTION TO CROSSAN'S FIVE WAYS TO WRECK YOUR EDUCATION:

- How this new scheme of historical reconstruction seeps into many areas of our lives; is it healthy or nasty?
- By wrecking, I indicate that people read a book and in some or many places give meanings the author did not state or intend. The readers have invented new senses and imposed them on the text.
- Let us examine a few practical examples of how this ruin happens.

THE NEWSPAPER

As I began writing this chapter, there was a news article in *The Sydney Morning Herald* by James Massola, 24 January 2021, stating that both sides of federal politics

> backed changes to the Order of Australia honours system, suggesting the awards could better reflect modern Australia. Governor-General David Hurley told *The Sydney Morning Herald* and *The Age* that he wanted to change the awards system, acknowledging it had been historically biased against women and had not included enough Indigenous Australians.... News [was leaked] that former tennis champion Margaret Court will be upgraded from an AO (Order of Australia) to an AC (a Companion in the Order of Australia) on Australia Day.[50]

---

50. Massola, "Liberal and Labor MPs." The AC is a higher honor than the AO in the Commonwealth of Australia Queen's honor list.

Margaret Court at the net in 1970[51]

Margaret Court (née Smith) was recognized on Australia Day, 26 January 2021, with a Companion of the Order of Australia, which is an upgrade of the AO. (Margaret Court AO, MBE, is now a Pentecostal pastor/preacher in Perth.) A major uproar came over Court's support of traditional, Christian marriage and refusal to accept and promote homosexual marriage. She has homosexuals in her church, so is not a homophobe, but the media regularly criticize her for homophobia. The decision to upgrade her to Companion attracted strong criticism because of her alleged prejudice towards the LGBTQI community and opposition to same-sex marriage.[52]

Is that what the story means? Is it true that there is an uproar by journalists, the LGBTQ+ promoters, and pro-homosexual supporters who oppose Court because of her outspoken support in favor of traditional marriage and opposition to homosexual marriage?

That is not what the story means! You're barking up the wrong tree if you want me to swallow that one. You are misguided. Now, how could I make such a seemingly outlandish statement? Because this is what that story about Margaret Court means: the author of the article and opponents of Margaret

---

51. Image courtesy of Eric Koch, https://en.wikipedia.org/wiki/Margaret_Court.
52. Massola, "Liberal and Labor MPs."

Court receiving an upgraded AC have a prejudice against her standing up for what she preaches in her pulpit—from the Bible.

She has said over and over she is not opposed to LGBTQ+ people as she has them in her church. Court was asked about her opposition to same-sex marriage and whether it was discriminatory. Her response was she "loved homosexuals . . . . I have them in the church here [in Perth]. I have nothing against homosexual people, but that is my belief on marriage." Court has called for the same recognition that Tennis Australia has given to Rod Laver, who was celebrated that year for his 1969 grand slam.[53]

This article, when properly interpreted, should then mean: the actions against Margaret Court are symbols or parables of political correctness flooding our society. The Australia Day awards system is a sign of depreciating one person so another can be exalted. You'll learn more of this deconstructionist application as the book proceeds.

This worldview is running wild through the market place. It can affect our views of the meaning of news (in print, online, or on TV). There's no reason why it can't affect non-fictional meaning. It could affect the meaning of this book if you adopt this worldview.

Evidence of certain interpretations of history is widespread. Christian studies are full of it; it's being taught in the school class room.

We'll get to this worldview soon.

The testing of this hypothesis reveals that Crossan redefines the nature of history to include his own perception and presuppositions: "*History is the past reconstructed interactively by the present through argued evidence in public discourse.*"[54] Therefore, it could not be expected for Crossan to affirm a traditional approach to historical investigation.

In much of my reading of Crossan's literature, Crossan's presuppositional acceptance of a postmodern definition of history overflows his conclusions with many postmodern examples, but this postmodern reconstruction is not consistently applied.

Readers of Crossan are exposed to his premise as conclusion: instead of reading a historical text inductively (i.e., reading a set of facts or ideas to arrive at a general principle),[55] as one would with the local newspaper or Crossan's actual publications, and allowing the historical text (as with Plato, the Bible, Herodotus, and the Brisbane *Courier-Mail* newspaper) to provide the definition of the nature of history or contemporary issues for themselves,

---

53. Christmass, "Margaret Court Defends Views."

54. Crossan, "Historical Jesus as Risen Lord," 3 (emphasis in original).

55. "For qualitative researchers, concepts and theories are usually inductively arrived at from the data that are collected" ("Inductively," in *OED*).

readers have Crossan's postmodern epistemology of history, which includes the study of the origin, nature, and limits of human knowledge,[56] foisted on the evidence and conclusions by Crossan.

Evidence was provided above demonstrating that an a priori postmodern approach and the historical critical method of applying postmodernism to the data show themselves to have peculiar epistemological problems[57] when applied to the events of Jesus's resurrection.

SUMMARY OF CHAPTER 2

What is history? The preface of this chapter began with discussions from schools in Australia and the Queensland curriculum on the nature of history.

Then I surveyed history as applied to Christopher Columbus's voyages to the Americas and those of Captain James Cook from Great Britain to sail up the east coast of Australia and circumnavigate New Zealand.

As these relate to the theme of this book, I asked readers to consider the provocative question: are these fact or fiction?

Then we examined the content of the Queensland high school history curriculum as well as international university curricula for history, the latter including Nottingham University, Macquarie University, and the University of California at San Francisco.

Historical examples were given, such as the *Maheno* wreck on Fraser Island, Queensland, Australia. Further examples were given of the Roman emperors of the first century and the terrorist attacks on the USA on 11 September 2001. Were these examples of fact, fiction, or deconstruction?

This is the constant question asked in this book because of John Dominic Crossan's definition of history: "*History is the past reconstructed interactively by the present through argued evidence in public discourse.*"[58] That is a peculiar and unnecessary definition.

It is a radical reversal of the standard meaning of history that is articulated by another eminent historical Jesus scholar, N. T. Wright, who concludes that Crossan's "explaining away the evidence" is applying "to the texts a ruthless hermeneutic of suspicion," where the resurrection accounts are "declared worthless as history" and "trivialize Christianity."[59]

56. Stroll et al., "Epistemology."

57. Epistemology is "the theory of knowledge, especially with regard to its methods, validity, and scope. Epistemology is the investigation of what distinguishes justified belief from opinion" ("Epistemology," in *OED*).

58. Crossan, "Historical Jesus as Risen Lord," 3 (emphasis in original).

59. Wright, *Resurrection of the Son*, 19.

THREE

Second Crossan Lesson

I formulate it here as I see it.[1]

INTRODUCTORY MATTERS

Professionals may be boat builders, accountants, medical doctors, fitters and turners, or fishermen working on trawlers, but they all follow different methods in applying their crafts. Methods are built into any discipline's success. The same applies to the pursuit of history or the interpretation of Scripture.

Let's consider the sugarcane industry as an example of the scientific method being applied for a discipline's success. I was introduced to the scientific method in two circumstances as a child and teenager, when I lived on two sugarcane farms near Bundaberg, Queensland, Australia. The methods relate to how to control sugarcane grubs that were damaging stools of sugarcane.[2]

---

1. This is Crossan's approach to an examination of history (Crossan, *Birth of Christianity*, xxx).

2. "All you need to grow your own sugarcane is a cutting from a fresh stalk of cane. A single mature planting can be cut and regrown every year indefinitely, although sugarcane produces the most and best sugar content during its first five to seven mature years" (Turner, "How to Get Sugarcane").

Sugar Industry: Example of the Need for Research Methods

Cane grubs (grub worms)[3]

One of the problems that can happen with the sugarcane stool is that cane grubs attack it and destroy the potential crop.[4] In an attempt to address this problem, the sugar industry introduced the cane toad, which is native to Central and South America.[5]

The cane toad, introduced in 1935, is spreading to more parts of Australia. Australia has no predators or diseases that control cane toad numbers.[6]

---

3. Image courtesy of Holly Chaffin, https://www.publicdomainpictures.net/en/view-image.php?image=230803&picture=grub-worms.

4. "Canegrubs are the larvae of a number of types of cane beetles. There are 19 endemic and one introduced species of canegrubs in Australia. The larvae, or grub, damage sugarcane through their feeding action on plants roots" ("Canegrubs").

5. "Sugarcane . . . production is customarily from a plant crop followed by two or more ratoon crops, which are grown from the underground stubble called the sugarcane stool. Frequently, the stool has to be ploughed out when the yield of a ratoon crop falls below acceptable levels, or as a control measure for sugarcane diseases" (Owende et al., "Comparison of Options").

6. Image courtesy of Australian Government, Department of Agriculture, Water and

Cane toads became pests after having been introduced into Australia in 1935 to control the destructive beetles that became cane grubs in Australia's sugarcane crops. Cane toads are capable of poisoning predators that try to eat them, and they continue to spread across Australia. There is no broad-scale way to control this pest.[7] "All stages of the Cane Toad's life cycle: eggs, tadpoles, toadlets and adult toads, are poisonous" because of the "venom-secreting poison glands (known as parotoid glands) or swellings on each shoulder where poison is released when they are threatened."[8]

New Australian research has "found that the South American tadpoles [baby cane toads] lived peacefully with each other, while the tadpoles from across Australia tried to eat each other." United States researcher Dr. Jayna DeVore and her colleagues "said the cannibalistic behaviour suggested Australian cane toads, long considered a pest, might be trying to regulate their population." In addition, "the researchers found the South American tadpoles (from which Australian cane toads originated) lived peacefully with each other, while the tadpoles from across Australia tried to eat each other."[9] Like controlling a mouse plague with insecticide, the cane toad was meant to be an antidote to replace insecticides.

It was on the cane farm I gained my firsthand experience of the scientific method—without knowing it. My parents had to investigate which insecticides were most effective in controlling cane grubs on our two sugarcane farms in Queensland. They would try one insecticide, and if it did not succeed, another was tried, with research guidance from the Bureau of Sugar Experiment Stations.[10]

After World War II, in which Dad fought, my father came home and earned his living by using a sugarcane knife (see photo) to cut cane that had been burned. It was heavy, sticky, dirty, laborious work. I have a permanent reminder of how sharp the cane knife can be from when my brother swung the knife (with no animosity), accidentally slicing the thumb on my left hand that I held behind my back. Using that knife was part of Dad's steps to earn enough to sustain a living for two parents and three children and then to save up for the purchase of our own small cane farm near Bundaberg.

Environment, https://www.environment.gov.au/biodiversity/invasive-species/publications/factsheet-cane-toad-bufo-marinus.

7. Department of Environment, "Cane Toad (Bufo marinus)."
8. Threatened Species Scientific Committee, "Biological Effects."
9. Layt, "This Is Not Normal."
10. The Bureau of Sugar Experiment Stations was located in Indooroopilly, Qld.

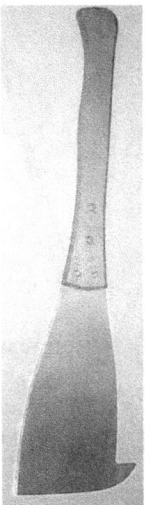

A typical cane knife was used manually for cutting cane and also for cutting down banana trees or other plants.[11]

The sticky cane not only had to be cut, but then it had to have the green tops (leaves) cut off as it lay in rows on the ground before being loaded onto trucks or tram trucks on the railway to be taken to the sugar mill for crushing into sugar, molasses, and syrup (Millaquin Mill at Bundaberg also manufactures rum).

To save the backbreaking task of lifting the cane onto trucks, cane loaders were invented. One of the earliest was created by my late father-in-law, Joseph Alfred Toft, of Bundaberg.

11. Image courtesy of Ratel, https://en.wikipedia.org/wiki/Cane_knife#/media/File:Sugar-cane-knife.jpg.

Joseph Alfred Toft's invention, the first sugarcane loader[12]

The latest model of Austoft/Case International, the 8810/8010[13]

Loaders are no longer needed in contemporary sugarcane harvesting nations as the cane is cut into small lengths by harvesters who can harvest

> an average of 600 acres per day during daylight hours. Using a single-row, combine-style harvester, the cane is cut at the base of the stalk, [then cut into smaller pieces and] transferred into

12. Image supplied by the author.

13. Permission was granted by Ag & CE, Australia and New Zealand, to use this image of a prototype of a new Austoft harvester developed by Case International.

in-field wagons and loaded in semi-trailers for transport to the processing facility. A typical harvesting unit contains three or four harvesters operating in tandem with six to eight tractors and a string of in-field wagons. . . . [In Florida, this scientific development of sugarcane results in] about 70,000 acres [being] harvested each season, producing more than three million tons of sugarcane.[14]

While raised on the farm, I also learned the scientific method in chemistry and physics classes in secondary school. The steps of the scientific method are included in "The Methodological Approach" in this chapter.

Many industries require adoption of certain methods to achieve their goals. As indicated, the sugar industry has pursued the methodology of detailed examination of the use of certain herbicides and insecticides to deal with disease among the sugar crops. Additional methods have been developed to meet . . .

JAPAN'S NEED FOR FUEL: RESEARCH METHODOLOGY REQUIRED

Investigation was made into which means were used to obtain Japan's total energy consumption for 2019, which was petroleum and other liquids (40%), coal (26%), natural gas (21%), hydroelectric (4%), other renewables (6%), and nuclear (3%). "Japan was the fifth-largest oil consumer and fourth-largest crude oil importer in the world in 2019. Japan also ranked as the world's largest importer of liquefied natural gas (LNG) and the third-largest importer of coal behind China and India in 2019."[15]

If we take the two largest needs in Japan for energy supplies, (1) petroleum and other liquids and (2) coal, from where would Japan source these energy needs? Methodologies needed to be developed to acquire this fuel.

---

14. "How Sugar Is Made."
15. "Country Analysis Executive Summary."

Men Landing on the Moon

Buzz Aldrin was part of the first crew to land on the moon.[16]

The Apollo program of NASA resulted in eleven spaceflights with men walking on the moon. The first four flights only tested the equipment that was later used in the Apollo Program. That scientific testing allowed six of the next seven flights to land on the moon and twelve astronauts to walk on the moon.[17]

Pharmaceuticals

According to the US Centers for Disease Control and Prevention (CDC), for the creation of new vaccines, the general stages of the development cycle are: exploratory stage; pre-clinical stage; clinical development; regulatory review and approval; manufacturing; and quality control.[18]

Clinical development is a three-phase process. (1) During phase 1, small groups of people receive the trial vaccine. (2) In phase 2, the clinical study is expanded, and the vaccine is given to people who have characteristics (such as age and physical health) similar to those for whom the new vaccine is intended. (3) In phase 3, the vaccine is given to thousands of people and tested for efficacy and safety.

Many vaccines undergo phase 4 of formal, ongoing studies after the vaccine is approved and licensed. As I write, these phases are being implemented for COVID-19 vaccines around the world.

---

16. Image courtesy of NASA.
17. "What Was Apollo Program."
18. "Vaccine Testing."

How Does Hypothesis Testing Work?

Hypothesis testing is used especially in biological research, but it has a much broader range of applications.

> The purpose of statistical inference is to draw conclusions about a population on the basis of data obtained from a sample of that population. Hypothesis testing is the process used to evaluate the strength of evidence from the sample and provides a framework for making determinations related to the population.[19]

This is a method for assessing the validity of Crossan's views on the historical Jesus when compared with the biblical and other historical data. How strong is Crossan's evidence for the deconstructed historical Jesus, against the Jesus of the first century, as articulated in the New Testament? The challenges of the extracanonical material Crossan uses will need to be evaluated with basic hypothesis testing drawn from the scientific method.

One hypothesis will be tested in this book, based on Crossan's data and tested to determine if his interpretations fit the facts. Talking about facts is not a good fit for the Crossan framework. Crossan doesn't like that language, as he chooses to read his radical conclusions into the life of Jesus, with some creative, far-reaching, free play inventions.

Which Disciplines Use Hypothesis Testing in Research?

This chapter may introduce you to some new concepts concerning hypothesis testing. "A scientific hypothesis [is] an idea that proposes a tentative explanation about a phenomenon or a narrow set of phenomena observed in the natural world." There are two primary features of a hypothesis: it can be falsified, and it can be tested.

When a scientific theory (including history) is based on insufficient evidence, it is known as a null hypothesis (H_0), which requires additional testing to prove whether the observed data is true or false. An example of a null hypothesis statement, given by the Corporate Finance Institute, is "'the rate of plant growth is not affected by sunlight.' It can be tested by measuring the growth of plants in the presence of sunlight and comparing this with the growth of plants in the absence of sunlight."[20]

---

19. Davis and Mukamal, "Hypothesis Testing."
20. "Null Hypothesis."

When the H_O is rejected, researchers can then pursue further experimentation. The scientific community uses two approaches to hypotheses: the null hypothesis and the alternate hypothesis, abbreviated as H_A or H_1. "A significance test is used to establish confidence in a null hypothesis and determine whether the observed data is not due to chance or manipulation of data. . . . Researchers test the hypothesis by examining a random sample of the plants being grown with or without sunlight. If the outcome demonstrates a statistically significant change in the observed change, the null hypothesis is rejected."[21]

Hypothesis testing is used especially in the biological and biomedical sciences but it is employed in other disciplines. "Hypothesis testing is an essential procedure in statistics. A hypothesis test evaluates two mutually exclusive statements about a population to determine which statement is best supported by the sample data. When we say that a finding is statistically significant, it's thanks to a hypothesis test. How do these tests really work and what does statistical significance actually mean?"[22] As a general format, the following five steps need to be used to test any hypothesis.

State your research hypothesis as a null hypothesis (H_O), based on the data from subjects you are investigating, and an alternate (H_A) hypothesis, which is developed by the researcher.
Collect data in a way designed to test the hypothesis.
Perform an appropriate statistical test.
Decide whether the null hypothesis is supported or refuted.
Present the findings of your results along with a discussion section.

The five steps in the above table can be illustrated using the cane grub and the introduction of the cane toad.

1. The H_O could be: "Cane grubs are destroying the cane stool, and some method (H_A) needs to be developed to kill the grubs."

2. It has been noted in Central and South America that the cane toad kills cane grubs, so the toad is introduced to Australia's cane growing regions. Collect data to determine if the toad is achieving its outcome.

3. Design a statistical test of an alternative hypothesis (H_A) to determine if the toad introduction is working. This should become evident, as the cane stool is not being devastated as previously.

4. This H_A will determine whether the H_O or H_A is working.

21. "Null Hypothesis."
22. Minitab Blog Editor, "Understanding Hypothesis Tests."

5. At the appropriate meetings of the Cane Growers' Associations and other sugar industry bodies, the findings of the research are presented.

Though the specific details might vary, the procedure you will use when testing a hypothesis will always follow some version of these steps.[23]

METHODS USED BY HISTORIANS

The Gospel writer Luke consulted eyewitnesses and servants of the word (i.e., one category of Christian eyewitnesses). He "carefully investigated everything" and wrote "an orderly account," which was not a chronological description. This was not based on hearsay evidence or that of sources invented by deconstruction but was from eyewitnesses who were committed to the word of God by being "servants of the word" (see Luke 1:1–4 NIV).

Crossan admits his use of both intracanonical and extracanonical Gospels is controversial.[24] Therefore, in establishing a historical method for this research, textual stratifications involving both canonical and extracanonical material will be examined only as they impact on the resurrection tradition. Crossan's emphasis is that the study of the historical Jesus will stand or fall on how a scholar "handles the literary level of the text itself."[25] I agree.

However, where do we date the Gospel of Peter, Gospel of Thomas, and Gospel of the Hebrews? Crossan has made a deliberate attempt to date these Gospels early—in the first strata, AD 30–60. Crossan's four strata are:[26]

AD 30–60: He places the Gospel of Thomas I, Gospel of the Hebrews, and the Cross Gospel (of the Gospel of Peter) in this first layer, along with 1 Thess, Gal, 1 Cor, the Egerton Gospel, and the Sayings Gospel Q.[27]
AD 60–80
AD 80–120
AD 120–50

Since Crossan places particular emphasis on the Gospel of Peter, that is where I will focus for the moment. The Gospel of Thomas and the Gospel of the Hebrews are of inconsequential importance for Crossan in developing his sources for source criticism.

---

23. Bevans, "Step-by-Step Guide."
24. Crossan, *Birth of Christianity*, 103.
25. Crossan, *Historical Jesus*, xxix.
26. Crossan, *Historical Jesus*, xxxi.
27. Crossan, *Historical Jesus*, 427–29.

Gospel of Peter

Under normal circumstances in dealing with Jesus's resurrection, one would not consign emphasis to the apocryphal Gospel of Peter.[28] However, Crossan places so much stress on this document that he published in 1988, *The Cross That Spoke: The Origins of the Passion Narrative*. That title is drawn from the Gospel of Peter's narrative: "And they [soldiers] heard a voice out of the heavens saying: Hast thou (or Thou hast) preached unto them that sleep? And an answer was heard from the cross, saying: Yea."[29]

Until 1886, only fragmentary evidence was available of the Gospel of Peter. Eusebius of Caesarea discusses it in his *Ecclesiastical History* in the early fourth century.[30] He recorded that the document was debated in the church at Rhossus.[31] Initially, the bishop of Antioch, Serapion, approved it for reading in the church of Rhossus. However, "upon more careful examination of its contents he rejected the work. In a letter to the church, Serapion noted that while the document was generally in accord with the NT Gospels, the Docetists[32] had added some elements in support of their false teaching."[33]

In his commentary on Matthew, Origen writes, "They thought, then, that He [Jesus] was the son of Joseph and Mary. But some say, basing it on a tradition in the Gospel according to Peter, as it is entitled, or The Book of James, that the brethren of Jesus were sons of Joseph by a former wife, whom he married before Mary."[34]

M. R. James, translator of the Gospel of Peter, reached this conclusion about dating in 1924: It "is quoted by writers of the latter end of the second century. It has been contended that Justin Martyr also used it soon after the middle of that century, but the evidence is not demonstrative. I believe it is not safe to date the book much earlier than A. D. 150."[35] Joel Green's more recent research confirms the Gospel of Peter as having been written "before the end of the second century," as it was a source of controversy in Rhossus.

---

28. I use apocryphal as defined by the *M-WD*, where apocryphal means "of doubtful authenticity: spurious."

29. James, "Gospel of Peter," vv 41b–42.

30. See Eusebius, *Hist. eccl.*, 3.3.1–4.

31. See Eusebius, *Hist. eccl.*, 6.12.3–6.

32. The name is based on the Greek *dokeō* ("I seem; I appear"); so Jesus seemed to have a real body, but the Docetists denied it was a material body. This was one variety of Gnosticism that threatened the church in its early centuries.

33. Quarles, "Gospel of Peter."

34. Origen, *Commentary on Gospel*, 10:17.

35. James, "Gospel of Peter," introductory issues.

Green considers the evidence points to it being "more likely" to be "dated after 100, probably in the first half of the second century."[36]

In 1886–1887, at Akhmim, Egypt, a French archaeological team found a small codex while they were excavating a cemetery. It was fragmentary, as the codex began in mid-sentence with the words describing Jesus's trial and "ends mid-sentence with Simon Peter and others at the sea, where, presumably, it would be recorded that the risen Lord appeared to them. Because of the spacing and ornamentation preceding and following the text, it appears that the scribe had access only to this excerpt."[37]

Dating of the Akhmim document "is as early as the fifth century or as late as the ninth. Two small papyrus fragments from Oxyrhnchus (POxy 2949) provide a second witness to the manuscript tradition" of Gospel of Peter 2:3–5, "and these were written ca. 200." Another papyrus (POxy 4009) also has dated the Gospel of Peter to the third century, with a resurrection narrative similar to John 21.[38] Green wraps up his discussion on, stating the Gospel of Peter "must be dated after 100, probably in the first half of the second century."[39]

Richard Bauckham notes, "The Gospel's relationship to the canonical Gospels is disputed. There are parallels to all four canonical Gospels, but remarkably few verbal parallels. Some scholars have thought the *Gospel of Peter* completely independent of the canonical Gospels; most have thought it dependent on all four."[40]

Timothy Henderson's dissertation argues the author of the Gospel of Peter "used all four canonical gospels as sources and that the category of Second Temple Jewish literature known today as 'Rewritten Bible' provides the best analogue for understanding the manner in which the New Testament accounts have been reworked in the noncanonical gospel."[41]

Crossan's prologue to his book supporting the Gospel of Peter was by a sympathetic supporter, Helmut Koester, whose view was he didn't "know what happened to the *Gospel of Peter* between, say, the first or second century when it was originally written and the time when it was copied as an amulet[42] in the eighth century." Koester's difficulty surrounds "the canonical

36. Green, "Peter, Gospel of," 929.
37. Green, "Peter, Gospel of," 927.
38. Green, "Peter, Gospel of," 927.
39. Green, "Peter, Gospel of," 929.
40. Bauckham, "Gospels (Apocryphal)," 288.
41. Henderson, "People Believe."
42. An amulet is "a charm (such as an ornament) often inscribed with a magic incantation or symbol to aid the wearer or protect against evil (such as disease or witchcraft)" ("Amulet," in *M-WD*).

Gospels [that] were fairly well treated after the third century." His call was for scholars to "do text-critical work" on the Gospel of Peter. "One cannot just say this must have been a gospel from the first century." Instead "one would have to sit down and say, now, what is late and what is early."[43]

I find it unusual that Crossan provides a prologue by Koester that does not thoroughly endorse Crossan's views on the Gospel of Peter. Maybe my thinking is in too black-and-white pictures.

Crossan proposes the division of Gospel strata, as the "first major proposition is that the original *Cross Gospel* is the one passion and resurrection narrative from which all four of the intracanonical versions derive."[44] Based on the above information about sources and dating, Crossan's acceptance of the Cross Gospel is based on his presuppositions. He has not provided substantial evidence to back his position.

Ancient historian Paul Barnett dates these extracanonical documents as follows:[45]

AD 120	AD 150	AD 160	AD 180
Gospel of Nazoreans	P Egerton 2	Gospel of Peter	Gospel of Thomas
Gospel of Ebionite	Gospel of Truth?		

Green's comment is that "the modern reaffirmation of the independence of the *Gospel of Peter* is *assumed or asserted more than argued* by its proponents, in particular Crossan's works suffers from his failure to provide any detailed analysis of the text of the apocryphal Gospel that would lead to the conclusion of its early and independent origins."[46]

John Meier provides a penetrating analysis of the Gospel of Peter, placing it as a second-century apocryphal document and refuting Crossan's claim that the Cross Gospel was written mid-first century. Meier states, "Even the hypothetical *Cross Gospel* bears telltale marks of dependence on the Synoptics," noting "both *Gospel of Peter* 30 (included in Crossan's *Cross Gospel*) and Matthew 27:64b read exactly the same phrase: '. . . lest his disciples, coming, steal him and . . .' When it comes to who is dependent on whom, all the signs point to Matthew's priority."[47]

---

43. Koester, "History and Development," 82, as cited in Crossan, *Four Other Gospels*, 124.
44. Crossan, *Cross That Spoke*, 17.
45. Barnett, *Finding the Historical Christ*, 43.
46. Green, "Peter, Gospel of," 928 (emphasis added).
47. Meier, *Marginal Jew*, 1:117.

Meier attributes the following three points to Raymond Brown regarding "extravagant assertions about very early traditions in apocryphal gospels":

1. "The assertions about some apocryphal gospels, while bold and accompanied by a great show of learning, turn out, on close analysis, to be based on rather slim evidence and questionable reasoning."
2. "The radical claims usually overlook the fact that, for all the differences and even conflicts among first-generation Christian leaders, there was a common gospel message on which all of them agreed (cf. Paul's affirmation of a common proclamation by all Christian preachers in 1 Cor 15:11)."
3. 'The exaltation of a gnosticizing form of Christianity ignores the fact that, from the beginning of Christian preaching about Jesus, there was a certain 'biographical' thrust that formed the Jesus tradition in a direction that ultimately produced the canonical Gospels."[48]

For his part, N. T. Wright lists eight elements that he considers most readers would regard as "conclusive evidence" for dating the Gospel of Peter "later and more developed than the canonical parallels"[49] and with additions to the canonical material. Wright particularly mentions that "all the resurrection accounts include exceedingly strange events" in the Gospel of Peter, including the talking cross.[50]

Crossan knows the need to emphasize "method, method, and, once again, method."[51] He issues the challenge to debate his methodology, but he admits method will not guarantee us the truth, because nothing can do that. But method, as self-conscious and self-critical as we can make it, is our only discipline.[52] He claims that when he published *The Historical Jesus* (1991), he intended his reconstruction of the historical Jesus to launch a "full-blown debate on methodology among my peers."[53] By the time of his 1998 publication, his view was that there had been little scholarly discussion of historical Jesus methodology.

---

48. These three points are from Meier, *Marginal Jew*, 1.118.
49. Wright, *Resurrection of the Son*, 594–95.
50. Wright. *Resurrection of the Son*, 594.
51. Crossan, "Historical Jesus as Risen Lord," 5.
52. Crossan, *Birth of Christianity*, 139–40.
53. Crossan, *Birth of Christianity*, 139.

With that kind of statement, Crossan seems to have overlooked methodological issues investigated by N. T. Wright and Ben Meyer.[54] The latter is a reprint of a 1979 edition, written well before Crossan's *The Historical Jesus*, on "Jesus and critical history," which Wright regards as "probably the finest statement on historical method by a practising contemporary New Testament scholar."[55]

Bauckham regards reconstruction (an aspect of Crossan's method) as seriously faulty methodology that results in the accumulation of minimal "uninteresting facts" of a historical figure, Jesus Christ, who has been "stripped of any real significance." Therefore, for authoritative and accurate historical data on Jesus Christ, Bauckham refers to the eyewitness testimony provided by the Gospel writers and not to extra-biblical information.[56] Bauckham's methodology requires that this testimony must *not* be accepted uncritically and is required to be tested for internal consistency and coherence as well as with other relevant historical evidence and context.

Bauckham warns of the need to practice historical methodology that does not prejudice one from accepting "exceptionality in history" and does not reduce the extraordinary to the ordinary. In my investigation of the presuppositions used by Crossan for the resurrection account, one of the issues is an examination of Crossan's preference for extracanonical material such as the Gospel of Peter, with lesser prominence given to intracanonical data, especially when the content of Luke 1:1–4 is considered.

Conclusion: Gospel of Peter

Recent scholarship has shown Crossan's dating of the Cross Gospel to AD 30–60 is way too early and that, more accurately, the Gospel of Peter is dated in the second century. So, Crossan's dating is based on his presuppositions to add extracanonical, apocryphal materials to the canonical accounts and place them on an even footing.

The methodology of the Jesus Seminar, by contrast with Bauckham, led to a conclusion that the evidence in the New Testament Gospels indicates that it is hearsay (secondhand) evidence, and none of the Gospel writers "was an ear or eyewitness of the words and events he records," and the

---

54. Wright, *New Testament*, 3–144; *Jesus and the Victory*, 8–11, 86–89, 122–44, 540–611, 660–62; Meyer, *Aims of Jesus*, 76–94.

55. Wright, *New Testament*, 98n32.

56. Bauckham, *Jesus and the Eyewitnesses*, 506 (emphasis added).

authors of the written Gospels were anonymous; the names now assigned to the Gospels are "pious fictions."[57]

The hypothesis-testing methodology is developed to practice an examination of the parameters of this study. An explanation of the so-called philosophical crusher is in Crossan's book, but you can gain an introduction in Meyer's "The Philosophical Crusher." Meyer learned about it from Alex Tourigny, his teacher in philosophical psychology, whose "version of the crusher was a deadly 'reduction to first principles.'" Meyer expounds one example of a philosophical crusher as referring to "the reduction of implicit to explicit self-contradiction." The nature of this reduction is that it "takes place by making explicit, not the content of an affirmation, but the performance of affirming (or denying)." The self-contradiction of this crusher is that "the actuality of performance belies the all-comprehensive explanation."[58]

On a practical level, this means that Crossan (or any writer) states his method of interpretation (postmodern reconstruction for Crossan) but fails to apply it with consistency throughout all of his writings—thus providing crushers of contradiction. If you want a taste of this, read Crossan's working definition of history and then compare with how he does or does not put this into practice in his publications: "*History is the past reconstructed interactively by the present through argued evidence in public discourse.*"[59] Compare Crossan's hermeneutics in *The Historical Jesus* with those in *A Long Way from Tipperary*. Crossan is a deconstructionist in *Historical Jesus* but a traditional historian in *Tipperary*.

Chew on that tonight with the family over dinner and decide what that kind of definition means for Columbus's visit to the Americas, the terrorist attacks of 9/11, COVID-19's spread around the world in 2020, and Captain Arthur Phillip's sailing into Sydney Cove with the first fleet to establish a convict settlement in what was to become Australia.[60] Try making that happen interactively as you reconstruct details of those historical events. Seems to me Crossan is smashing the ship of the philosophical crusher on the rocks of irrational irrelevance. Thus he violates a fundamental of coherence as a test of a worldview and historical construction.

---

57. Funk et al., *Five Gospels*, 16.
58. Meyer, "Philosophical Crusher."
59. Crossan, "Historical Jesus as Risen Lord," 3 (emphasis in original).
60. "Convict Cargo."

THE METHODOLOGICAL APPROACH DELIMITING THE STUDY

The effects of methodology for Crossan involve a triadic process that synthesizes anthropology, history, and literature.[61] While Crossan views the three elements affecting the integrity and validity of each other in his method, my study will be restricted to an examination of the presuppositions influencing Crossan's teaching on Jesus's resurrection tradition.

DEFINING THE APPROACH

Lewis and Demarest consider that the verification method of research "defines a topic, surveys influential alternative answers in the church, amasses relevant biblical data in their chronological development, formulates a comprehensive conclusion, defends it against competing alternatives, and exhibits its relevance for life and ministry." They state that theological method as a science uses "*interrelated criteria* of truth." These criteria include logical noncontrradiction, empirical adequacy, and existential viability. The only hypotheses accepted are those that are found to be:[62]

1. Noncontrradictory,
2. Supported by adequate evidence, and
3. Affirmable without hypocrisy.

These criteria will be used in this study, with the exceptions of relevance for life and ministry and existential viability.

This research will follow Meyer's suggested sequence of question, hypothesis, and verification,[63] within the framework recommended by Lewis and Demarest.[64] This involves:

1. Defining the topic of examining the presuppositions used by Crossan that led to his conclusions on the resurrection tradition,
2. Assessing the influential alternative answers to these presuppositions in the scholarly literature,

---

61. Crossan, *Historical Jesus*, xxvii–xxxix.
62. Lewis and Demarest, *Integrative Theology*, 1.25.
63. Meyer, *Aims of Jesus*, 80.
64. Lewis and Demarest, *Integrative Theology*, 1.25.

3. Inductively[65] accumulating data from Crossan (Borg and Crossan, *The Last Week*; Crossan, *The Historical Jesus*; Crossan, *Jesus: A Revolutionary Biography*; Crossan, *Who Killed Jesus*; Crossan, "What Victory? What God? A Review Debate with N. T. Wright on Jesus and the Victory of God";[66] Crossan, *The Birth of Christianity*; Crossan, "Historical Jesus as Risen Lord"; Crossan, *A Long Way from Tipperary*; Crossan, *God and Empire*; Crossan, *The Power of Parable*; Crossan and Reed, *Excavating Jesus*; Crossan and Watts, *Who Is Jesus?*), and

4. Formulating a comprehensive conclusion to support or deny the hypothesis. This will be accomplished by defending it against alternatives.

WHICH DATA ARE IMPORTANT?

Crossan emphasizes "the tremendous importance of that first stratum" for historical Jesus studies, which is the period AD 30–60, because it is closest chronologically to the time of the life of Jesus. He believes items written during that time are more accurate historically. Thus, he gives primary, but not exclusive, attention to that stratum.[67]

Bauckham follows Byrskog in arguing that the best historical evidence comes from historians who participated in the events.[68] In examining the presuppositions of Crossan, the methodological information outlined in the following will be used as a strategy of investigation.

The Gospels as primary historical documents will be examined, with consideration of the historical validity or otherwise of the extracanonical material, especially the Gospel of Peter, which Crossan locates in the first stratum (AD 30–60).

PRESUPPOSITIONS

What are presuppositions? How does one objectively identify them in a speech act? Crossan explains his presuppositions in terms of prejudices and ideas from his life experiences and situations that may have influenced his work in historical reconstruction, positively or negatively. He explains that he did not have all these ideas—presuppositions—before he began his work.

---

65. I use "inductive" to mean "reasoning from particular facts or ideas to a general rule or law" ("Inductive," in *MD*).

66. Wright's response is in *Jesus and the Victory*, 359–79.

67. Crossan, *Historical Jesus*, xxxii.

68. Bauckham, *Jesus and the Eyewitnesses*, 479; Byrskog, *Story as History*.

He developed them in interaction with his work, and he "cannot any longer tell which influenced which."[69]

Wright correctly identifies the study of the New Testament as involving literature, history, and theology and states that if presuppositional matters are not explored, "we can expect endless and fruitless debate."[70]

Definition of Presupposition

A presupposition is a phenomenon by which speakers or writers mark linguistically the information that is "taken for granted, rather than being part of the main propositional content of a speech act. Expressions and constructions carrying presuppositions are called 'presupposition triggers,' forming a large class including definites and factive verbs."[71]

Anthony Thiselton considers that the term *presupposition* "conveys the impression of rooted beliefs and doctrines which are not only cognitive and conceptual, but which also can only be changed and revised with pain, or at least with difficulty. Neither element is *necessarily* involved in [using the term] 'horizon.'"[72] He prefers the term *horizon*, explaining that "every reader brings a horizon of expectation to the text. This is a mind-set, or system of references, which characterizes the reader's finite viewpoint amidst his or her situatedness in time and history." He emphasizes that "patterns of habituation in the reader's attitudes, experiences, reading-practices, and life, define and strengthen his or her horizon of expectation." His perspective is that it is easier to change a horizon than a presupposition, because a text "can surprise, contradict, or even reverse such a horizon of expectation."[73]

The Christian-based linguistics organization SIL International defines a presupposition as "background belief, relating to an utterance" that:

---

69. Crossan, *Who Killed Jesus*, 211.

70. Wright, *New Testament*, 31.

71. Beaver et al., "Presupposition." The term *definites* is meant to convey the placing of limits or boundaries on anything. A definite is the antithesis of being imprecise or vague. A factive verb affirms the truth of the following statement or clause. An example is, "I *know* that Crossan's view on the use of redaction by New Testament authors is correct." "Know" is the factive verb. However, sometimes a comparative meaning can be expressed with "This *is* Crossan's view . . ." or some other sentence where "is" functions as the factive (Beaver et al., "Presupposition").

72. Thiselton, *New Horizons*, 45 (emphasis in original).

73. Thiselton, *New Horizons*, 34.

1. Must be known by both the speaker and addressee to be considered appropriate in a given context;
2. Will be a necessary assumption for an utterance, whether the form is an assertion, denial, or question; and
3. Generally can "be associated with a specific lexical item or grammatical feature (presupposition trigger) in the utterance."[74]

Examples of the need to examine presuppositions would be in Crossan's statements such as:

1. "Mark's solution is to create the Barabbas incident in Mk 15:6–15. I do not believe for a second that it actually happened."[75]
2. "I understand, therefore, the story of Lazarus as process incarnated in event and not the reverse. I do not think that anyone, anywhere at any time brings dead people back to life."[76]
3. "Christianity is historical reconstruction interpreted as divine manifestation. It is not (in our postmodern world) that we find once and for all who the historical Jesus was way back then. It is that each generation and century must redo that historical work and establish its best reconstruction."[77]

PRO FORMA FOR IDENTIFYING PRESUPPOSITIONS

Presuppositions by any communicator will be used as a plan for objectively (as much as possible) discovering indicators of Crossan's assumptions. These are based on more objective ways to identify presuppositions and are designed to assist with the recognition of presuppositional triggers. I ask you to be patient as we discuss presuppositional language that seldom makes it to the forefront of language description.

Methodological abduction will be used throughout this investigation in tandem with induction and deduction. Abduction is used here to refer to a procedure that is central to the scientific process of an "inferential step

---

74. "Presupposition" (SIL).
75. Crossan, *Historical Jesus*, 390.
76. Crossan, *Jesus*, 95.
77. Crossan, *Who Killed Jesus*, 217.

from some initial puzzling fact to some theoretical hypothesis which can explain it."[78]

WHY EXAMINE CROSSAN'S PRESUPPOSITIONS?

If historical scholarship is not used to discover absolutes or certitudes but only by its best reconstruction to arrive at a decision "beyond a reasonable doubt,"[79] how does a scholar decide between contradictory conclusions concerning aspects of the historical Jesus by various scholars? It is important to note Crossan's perspective regarding those who offer a contrary opinion: in quoting "*secondary* literature, I spend no time citing other scholars to show how wrong they are." Instead, he quotes only those who "represent my intellectual debts."[80] Why would he want to preserve his opinion and scholarship and retain it in-house? Is there a possible presuppositional bias coming through? Through this study, we will observe Crossan doesn't practice what he preaches, as he has engaged with the teachings of N. T. Wright, Dorothy Sayers, and Luke Timothy Johnson, which have opposed his perspective.

An example of divergence from some scholars is Crossan's conclusion that Barabbas, Simon of Cyrene (father of Alexander and Rufus), and Joseph of Arimathea were the "fictional creation" of Mark.[81] By contrast, Wright regards Barabbas as a *lestes* (Greek word), a revolutionary figure, the leader of a murderous civil uprising in Jerusalem;[82] and although this content in the Gospels in Matthew 27:15–23, Mark 15:6–14, Luke 23:17–23 and John 18:39–40 has been queried, "there is at least as strong a likelihood that it is historical."[83] How can it be nonhistorical, created by Mark (Crossan), and simultaneously likely be historical (Wright)? Another scholar, John Meier, treats the Pharisee Nicodemus, who helped Joseph of Arimathea provide Jesus with an honorable burial, as operating in a historical situation without questioning the historical veracity in John's Gospel.[84]

There could be different presuppositions operating with each scholar that need to be exposed to help discern possible reasons for difference of understanding.

78. Svennevig, "Abduction," 1.
79. Crossan, *Who Killed Jesus*, x.
80. Crossan, *Historical Jesus*, xxxiv (emphasis in original).
81. Mark 15:7, 21, 43; Crossan, *Who Killed Jesus*, 177.
82. Wright, *Jesus and the Victory*, 420.
83. Wright, *Jesus and the Victory*, 546n30.
84. In John 19:39–40; Meier, *Marginal Jew*, 1:346.

Crossan states that his method for the stratified data is to use a "multiplicity of independent attestations," with a key emphasis on "independent attestation" and "the complete avoidance of any unit found only in single attestation even within the first stratum."[85] However, in his single attestation in the first stratum, he uses three sayings that have single attestations in the Gospel of the Hebrews, which is in a book of "disputed writings." These sayings by Crossan are "Spirit as Mother," "Joy in Love," and "Grieving Another."[86] What presuppositions cause the exceptions in the first stratum, when he states that data found with only a single attestation "could have been created by that source itself"?[87] How does his inconsistent insistence on use of greater than single attestation for historical veracity compare with attestations from secular history?

Craig Blomberg notes that the burden of proof that "guides most historians in their work" is the assumption that the burden of proof lies squarely with the person who doubts the reliability of a specified portion of a text, unless there are good reasons for believing otherwise.[88] Historian Neil J. McEleney states, "In the historical research arena, we have already seen that it is both unfounded and not practiced in the scholarly and academic realms. The skeptical criteria for acceptance are simply wrong. If modern historical scholarship would adopt the 'guilty until proven innocent' tack, the vast majority of accepted history would have to be discarded." In McEleney's words, the opposite principle is "a presumption which one exercises in the reading of all history. Without it no historiography, ancient or modern, would win acceptance. Briefly, it is this, that one accepts a statement upon the word of the reporter unless he has reason not to do so."[89] This method has been accepted by both conservative and other scholars.

Therefore, why would Crossan discard this burden of proof used by historians, even if it relates to single attestation? How much of ancient history would be discarded if single attestation were forbidden? What is driving Crossan's push for elimination of single, independent attestation?

HOW CROSSAN VIEWS PRESUPPOSITIONS

How does Crossan understand presuppositions for himself and in his scholarship?

85. Crossan, *Historical Jesus*, xxxi–xxii.
86. Crossan, *Historical Jesus*, 441.
87. Crossan, *Historical Jesus*, xxxiii.
88. Blomberg, *Historical Reliability of Gospels*, 240.
89. McEleney, "Authenticating Criteria," 446.

> By *presuppositions* I do not mean positions beyond current debate or even future change. Neither do I mean theological commitments. Rather, I mean historical judgments based on present evidence and requiring constant future testing against new theory, method, evidence, or experience. I have learned these presuppositions from scholarly tradition, have studied them internally, have tested them externally, and have found them consistently more persuasive than their alternatives. But if they are wrong, then everything based on them is questionable; and if they are *proved* wrong, then everything based on them will have to be redone.[90]

So his presuppositions are from the scholarly tradition that has been tested internally and externally and found to be persuasive. However, by "scholarly tradition," which scholarly judgments does Crossan support? He affirms the view of those who "represent my intellectual debts,"[91] but he excludes most historians and historical Jesus scholars from the evangelical camp.

HOW TO DISCERN PRESUPPOSITIONS

While writing of earlier Bultmannian, post-Bultmannian, neo-orthodox and "new quest" generations, John W. Montgomery observes a trend that could be repeated in Crossan: "presuppositionalism is allowed to reign and the Jesus of the primary documents is subordinated to a priori commitments."[92] How does one discern presuppositional or a priori commitments in a writer's statements using an objective guide?

MORE OBJECTIVE WAYS TO IDENTIFY PRESUPPOSITIONS

Mandy Simons's extensive examination of presuppositional theory investigates the impact of presuppositions on conversations, assessment on formal and informal grounds, and assessment of presuppositions without a common ground.[93] These views were considered before choosing the following model for presuppositional identification in Crossan. William Lane Craig

---

90. Crossan, *Birth of Christianity*, 109 (emphasis in original).
91. Crossan, *Historical Jesus*, xxxiv.
92. Montgomery, Wh*ere Is History Going*, 10.
93. See Simons, "On the Conversational Basis," "Presupposition without Common Ground," and "Presupposition and Cooperation."

raises some specific issues in relation to Crossan, the Jesus Seminar, and their presuppositions, but his language sometimes becomes provocative with statements such as "politically correct religion" and "pretensions of the Jesus Seminar" (of which Crossan is a fellow).[94] While some of his points are valid, his language could be tamed.

Graham Stanton is penetrating in his appraisal that conscious or unconscious presuppositions adopted by an interpreter "are far more influential in New Testament scholarship than disagreements over method."[95] He also points to Carl Braaten's cynical, but correct, comment that onlookers of New Testament scholarship become skeptical when they observe "a convenient correspondence between what scholars claim to prove historically and what they need theologically."[96]

In assessing a model that has some objective strategies for isolating presuppositions, Beaver et al. have been chosen to identify presuppositions, as they summarize some of the identification markers (triggers) for discerning presuppositions.[97] From a lexical perspective, these are agreed upon by philosophers and linguists as examples of some presupposition triggers:[98]

Factives. A factive verb confirms the truth of the following statement or clause. For example, "I *know* Crossan's view of the Cross Gospel was not affected by the Jesus Seminar's assessment of his position." *Know* is a factive verb.

Aspectual verbs have examples such as *stop* or *continue*. An instance could be, "Linnemann has *discontinued* her use of many of the premises of the historical-critical method after her conversion to Christ."[99] Here, *discontinued* is an aspectual verb.

Temporal clauses begin with conjunctions such as *before*, *after*, or *since*.

Manner adverbs. An example could be: "Crossan uses language *deceptively*." *Deceptively* is the manner adverb, which conveys *how* an action is or should be performed.

Sortally restricted predicates of various categories. A sortal is something that takes a numerical modifier. Therefore, something that is sortally restricted means that predicates (or complements after the verb *to be*) have restricted boundaries. An example would be "John was a bachelor monk," restricting the description of John to an adult male.

94. Craig, "Rediscovering the Historical Jesus."
95. Stanton, "Presuppositions," 60.
96. Stanton, "Presuppositions," 64.
97. Beaver et al., "Presupposition."
98. All examples in the table below were developed by the author.
99. See Linnemann, *Biblical Criticism on Trial*.

Cleft sentences have two parts. One part expresses a focus, while the cleft component expresses some kind of presupposition. An example could be: "The prisoners were released from the Gulag, but this freedom had governmental boundaries."
Quantifiers. For example, "I have written to every headmaster in North Lakes and the immediate district." This restricts the statement to headmasters in the North Lakes suburb of outer northern Brisbane, Queensland, Australia.
Definite descriptions. As an example, "The historical Jesus scholar J. D. Crossan wagged his finger at the people when he made his presentation." Thus, Crossan is a Jesus scholar with an idiosyncratic gesture in public speaking.
Names. An example would be "The author was Burton Mack."[100] So, Burton Mack has existed.
Intonation (focus, contrast). For example, "He set me *free*."[101] So, someone set me free.

There are a couple writing or speaking behaviors that distinguish presuppositions from other literary language and statements. Beaver et al. state that this is known as "the hallmark of presuppositions" and is one that has been studied extensively. It is *projection*.[102] Elsewhere, Beaver explains that "the projection problem for presuppositions is the task of stating and explaining the presuppositions of complex sentences in terms of the presuppositions of their parts."[103]

Consider this information from Crossan about his visit to Oberammergau, Bavaria, Germany, to attend the Passion Play. He found the story he "knew so well as a written *text* was so profoundly unconvincing as *drama*." He wondered if "that infamous scene in which the crowd claims responsibility for Jesus's death by shouting, 'His blood be upon us and upon our children,' was fact or fiction. It did not seem convincing as history. What was the reason for the crowd's change of attitude from acceptance to rejection? Could this story function more as parable than history?"[104]

This insight led him to others and if it were parable, "a fictional story, invented for moral or theological purposes, then there were not only parables *by* Jesus—like that of the Good Samaritan—but parables *about* Jesus—like that of the lethal crowd in this passion play." Thus for Crossan, "the factual history of Jesus's crucifixion had become parable—parabolic

---

100. I refer to Burton L. Mack, *Who Wrote the New Testament?*
101. Emphasis added.
102. Beaver et al., "Presupposition."
103. Beaver, "Presupposition," 5.
104. Crossan, *Power of Parable*, 2 (emphasis in original).

history or historical parable."[105] However, elsewhere, Crossan states, "Read the text"[106] and "any study of the historical Jesus stands or falls on how one handles the literary level of the text itself."[107] Is Crossan reading the text or inventing his own text and calling it "parabolic history"?

These presuppositions follow:

(1a) There were results from his study of Oberammergau and the Passion play, the Emmaus road story, and the text of the crucifixion.

(1b) Something infiltrated his thinking.

(1c) Crossan did something that was contrary to another way of thinking about Jesus's passion.

(1d) Crossan, the scholar, is responsible for the change.

Now consider these sentences:

(2a) It was not Crossan, the scholar, whose thinking about the passion was changed (*negation*).

(2b) If Crossan's view of the passion was changed, his view will be exposed as a movement away from orthodoxy (*antecedent of a condition*).

(2c) Is it Crossan, the scholar, whose view of the Passion was infiltrated or changed (*question*)?

(2d) Maybe it is possible that it is the scholar who allowed and encouraged this changed view of the passion (*possibility modal*).

(2e) Presumably/probably it is Crossan, the scholar, who changed his view of the passion—in the name of infiltration (*evidential modal, probability adverb*).

(2f) The chairman and committee of the Orthodox Religious Society endorsed the view that it was Crossan, the scholar, who caused his view of the passion to be changed to become heterodox (*belief operator*).

Crossan's changed view of the orthodox doctrine of the passion is embedded under various "operators."[108] He uses these verbs to embed

---

105. Crossan, *Power of Parable*, 3 (emphasis in original).

106. White and Crossan, *Is Orthodox Biblical Account*; and Crossan, *God and Empire*, 138.

107. Crossan, *Historical Jesus*, xxix.

108. Verbs such as hear, discover, know, see, think, and believe are often used to embed clauses that are indicators of presuppositions. The embedded clause carries the main thought of the presupposition. Beaver et al., "Presupposition," state: "It makes sense to try several such embeddings when testing for presupposition, because it is not

presuppositions in operators: "*knew* so well as a written text" and "*was so profoundly unconvincing* as drama." Elsewhere, he writes, "It is no longer possible in retrospect *to think* of that passion fiction as *relatively benign propaganda*";[109] *I think* I know what happened to their bodies and I have no reason to *think* Jesus' body did not join them";[110] "*the units, sequences, and frames of the passion narrative were derived not from history remembered but from prophecy historicized*;"[111] "recall how, *in my opinion*, the Johannine tradition . . .";[112] that "is how I *imagine* the author's intention; I do not *think* that theological vision is late but early" in the Cross Gospel";[113] "what *really worked for me*" was that *evolution could not contradict reason in Genesis 1*;[114] and "Mark *created* . . . . Matthew *created* . . . . John *copied* . . . . Why are those stories about the women *created* at all?"[115] These are only a few examples of Crossan's use of various presuppositions that are embedded under a range of operators.

What is observed is that the presuppositions in (1a) to (1d) above do not follow from these embeddings, but there are presuppositions that do follow. In these instances, we say that the presuppositions are *projected*. The inference of projection is stronger in some cases than in others.

It would be difficult to imagine stating (2a) without believing some relevant and identifiable scholar, Crossan, existed. However, (2f) could be stated if Crossan were humorously giving a parody on the results of his research. Unless there are special factors, anyone who made statements (2a) to (2f) would be expected to believe the presuppositions in (1a) and (1b).

Projection that emerges from an embedding, especially in the use of negation, is a standard diagnostic tool for uncovering presuppositions. When trying to recognize presuppositions, it is a sensible practice to seek to find many embeddings, because it is not always transparent how to apply any embedding as a diagnostic. In the indicators of Crossan's presuppositions that are listed below, it will be noted that projection of presuppositions is often used by him.

Questions to Ask of Crossan's Presuppositional Model

---

always clear how to apply a given embedding diagnostic."
109. Crossan, *Who Killed Jesus*, xii (emphasis added).
110. Crossan, *Who Killed Jesus*, 188 (emphasis added).
111. Crossan, *Who Killed Jesus*, 4 (emphasis in original).
112. Crossan, *Who Killed Jesus*, 24 (emphasis added).
113. Crossan, *Who Killed Jesus*, 197 (emphasis added).
114. Crossan, *Who Killed Jesus*, 215 (emphasis added).
115. Crossan, *Birth of Christianity*, 552 (emphasis added).

The topics of this research are limited to:

1. The resurrection tradition;
2. Interpretation of the resurrection accounts;
3. Presuppositions acknowledged;
4. Postmodernism and deconstruction; and
5. Mythology, fiction, legend, and magic.

Does the New Testament evidence for the resurrection of Jesus agree with Crossan's data? This study will ask the following questions with regard to Crossan's presuppositional model and its conclusions, based on the above five topics.

THE RESURRECTION TRADITION

(a) Jesus's resurrection was an apparition.[116] Can this be justified from the biblical material? Crossan uses extrabiblical material to support the apparition perspective.

(b) Jesus's resurrection is seen as a communal process for past, present, and future resurrections.[117] What leads to such an interpretation?

(c) Crossan's perspective is that Mark created the empty tomb story as he did the disciples sleeping in Gethsemane.[118] So does that make the empty tomb a fictional invention or something else?

INTERPRETATION OF THE RESURRECTION ACCOUNTS

(a) Why does Crossan accept general conclusions from some critical scholars but not others?[119]

(b) Is it accurate to state that there are discrepancies in Gospel accounts and that these are due to deliberate, premeditated, theological

---

116. Crossan, *Birth of Christianity*, xxviii–xi.
117. Crossan, *God and Empire*, 187.
118. Mark 10:32–42; 16:1–8.
119. Crossan, *Historical Jesus*, xxxiv; *Jesus*, xii.

interpretations, using creative freedom?[120] There is some creative freedom used by Crossan to reach such conclusions.

(c) Could there be possible logical fallacies used to defend Crossan's view of the historical Jesus?[121]

PRESUPPOSITIONS ACKNOWLEDGED

(a) Historical Jesus research methods depend on presuppositions, and if Crossan's are wrong, "then all is delusion."[122] Is this an accurate estimate of Crossan's conclusions?

(b) Is it possible to test presuppositions by waiting for cracks to appear in the structure?[123]

(c) See the examples below of the autobiographical, theological, and historical presuppositions that Crossan acknowledges in his work.

AUTOBIOGRAPHICAL PRESUPPOSITIONS

"Autobiographical presuppositions" is Crossan's language, and by this, he affirms the validity of the content of his previous books on the historical Jesus.[124]

THEOLOGICAL PRESUPPOSITIONS

In his autobiography, Crossan discusses leaving the monastic priesthood and approaching two Roman Catholic universities in Chicago for a teaching position, but he was turned down. His assessment was that "it was never a question of my competence, but only of my ex-priest status and/or my controversial orthodoxy."[125] Controversial orthodoxy? He admits that as "an ex-priest and controversial theologian," he might not be acceptable to a Roman Catholic

---

120. Crossan, *Historical Jesus*, xxx.

121. Crossan, *Jesus*, 160; *Who Killed Jesus*, xi, 159, 184, 188, 202, 220–21; *Birth of Christianity*, 29, 425.

122. Crossan, "What Victory? What God?," 351.

123. Crossan, *Birth of Christianity*, 96; Vanhoozer, *Is There a Meaning*, 204.

124. Crossan, *Who Killed Jesus*, 211.

125. Crossan, *Long Way from Tipperary*, 91.

college or university. However, he was hired in 1969 as an associate professor of biblical studies at DePaul University, Chicago, where what happened between his bishop and him was considered none of the university's business; he was hired "in terms of our need and your competence, nothing else." He remained there for twenty-six years until his retirement in 1995.[126]

His own background is Irish and Roman Catholic. For him, the resurrection of Jesus means that people experienced human empowerment in Lower Galilee in the first century in and through Jesus, which same empowerment is available now. Empty tomb and physical appearance stories about Jesus are parables of faith, parallel to the good Samaritan story. The meaning of the name Jesus Christ is that Jesus is a "fact" open to proof and disproof of his existence; Christ is an "interpretation," which is not open to proof or disproof. The conjunction of Jesus Christ is an act of faith.[127]

An understanding of Christianity is obtained through reconstruction for a postmodern world. Thus, for Crossan, the Gospels are "even more normative as process than as product."[128] The Christian faith does not tell us what we need to know about the historical Jesus but tells us how the detail of the historical Jesus "is the manifestation of God for us here and now (interpretation). You cannot believe in a fact, only in an interpretation." It is a "lethal deceit" to try to turn interpretation into a fact. He considers that Christians and all other human beings "live from out of the depths of myth and metaphor."[129] With that perspective, how can he discover truth through the evidence of Scripture? He can't.

HISTORICAL PRESUPPOSITIONS

For Crossan, these presuppositions include historical reconstruction involving two great religions from the first century—Christianity and rabbinic Judaism[130]. There are three related presuppositions. Firstly, each of these two religions is a legitimate branch of a common trunk. Secondly, each of these two religions has asserted itself as the sole legitimate heir of the past, thus denying the validity of the other's claim. Thirdly, because Christianity was able to obtain the political and military support of the Roman Empire, it was able to promote its claim and persecute Judaism.

---

126. Crossan, *Long Way from Tipperary*, 94–95.
127. Crossan, *Who Killed Jesus*, 217.
128. Crossan, *Who Killed Jesus*, 217.
129. Crossan, *Who Killed Jesus*, 217–18.
130. Crossan, *Who Killed Jesus*, 217.

"The reconstructed historical Jesus must be understood within his contemporary Hellenistic Judaism," and contemporary Judaism, as modern scholarship asserts, is "a richly creative, diverse and variegated one."[131] Other dimensions of Crossan's historical assumptions include:

i. Presuppositions of Gospel traditions must be decided before reconstructing the historical Jesus or earliest Christianity. These presuppositions control the method used for research and include the nature and function of the Gospels and the relationships among them.[132]

ii. The same principles are used to determine the relationships among extracanonical Gospels as with intracanonical Gospels. Crossan's six presuppositions about sources are: (a) the priority of Mark's Gospel, (b) the existence of the Q Gospel,[133] (c) the dependence of John on the Synoptics, (d) the independence of the Gospel of Thomas, (e) the independence of the Didache, and (f) the existence and independence of the Cross Gospel in the Gospel of Peter. He admits that none of these presuppositions is original, infallible, or noncontrroversial, but every scholar who works on reconstructing the historical Jesus and earliest Christianity must make a decision about these matters.[134]

iii. An anthropological and historical presupposition is that the vision of a dead man did not birth Christianity. Instead, the birth of Christianity was an interaction between the historical Jesus, his first companions, and the continuation of that relationship, even though Jesus was crucified. The focus of this problem or presupposition is not on the birth but on the growth of Christianity, so it relates to those who were with Jesus before and after his crucifixion. The apostle Paul is included in the growth of Christianity, but he was not as important in the first century as he was in the sixteenth century.[135] There seem to be some metaphorical and existential presuppositions suggested by those statements.

---

131. Crossan, *Who Killed Jesus*, 218–21.

132. Crossan, *Birth of Christianity*, 100, 103.

133. "The Sayings Gospel Q, or 'Q,' is a hypothetical document posited as the dominant solution to the Synoptic Problem, the Two Document (or Two Source) Hypothesis. According to this hypothesis, Mark was used independently by Matthew and Luke as a source. Since not all of the material that Matthew and Luke have in common comes from Mark, it is necessary to posit a second source, 'Q' (an abbreviation of the German *Quelle*, 'source')" (Kloppenborg, "Sayings Gospel Q").

134. Crossan, *Birth of Christianity*, 114, 119–20.

135. Crossan, *Birth of Christianity*, xxi.

I agree that "the vision of a dead man did not birth Christianity." It was the fact of a crucified, buried, and bodily resurrected God-man, Jesus Christ, that gave birth to Christianity. This is supported by the biblical evidence at the conclusion of each Gospel (Matt 27–28; Mark 15–16; Luke 21–22; Jn 19–21) and 1 Cor 15. Crossan's Jesus is a Crossan-invented, impotent Jesus, based on Crossan's deconstructive free play and unaffected by much of the influence of the intrabiblical text.

POSTMODERNISM AND DECONSTRUCTION

(a) There is a postmodern tone that predominates in Crossan's 1991 publication, according to Wright,[136] and Crossan's historical reconstruction is understood as the interaction of present and past in textual stratification hermeneutics.[137] What presuppositional agenda leads to this kind of hermeneutic?

(b) Has this postmodern epistemology led to the death of the biblical author?[138] That conclusion is inevitable.

---

136. Wright, *Jesus and the Victory*, 50.
137. Crossan, *Who Killed Jesus*, 5.
138. Vanhoozer, *Is There a Meaning*, 66.

FORM CRITICISM AND REDACTION CRITICISM[139]

(a) Crossan's justification of three stages proposed by FC and RC is retention, development, and creation.[140] What influences such an interpretation?

(b) The empty tomb story and sleeping disciples in Gethsemane are creations by the Gospel writers, according to Crossan.[141] Can this be demonstrated from the biblical text? The evidence is not supportive.

---

139. I will use FC as a shortened form of form criticism, RC for redaction criticism, and SC for source criticism throughout this book. This book's focus will not include a critique of FC, RC, and SC, even though I have numerous areas of disagreement. For a brief critique, I recommend Kulikovsky, "Evaluation of Historical-Critical Methods."

FC of the NT refers to "the study of forms that are or have been used in communication." It is based on the German *Formgeschichte*, which literally means "the history of forms" that are "traced to the work of three German scholars who had all studied with H. Gunkel." These scholars are M. Dibelius (1919), K. L. Schmidt (1919), and R. Bultmann. Despite the speculative nature of FC, "it succeeded in stimulating an imaginative engagement with dimensions of life of the early church in a period largely otherwise inaccessible to us" (Nolland, "Form Criticism and the NT").

RC achieved its prominence through NT studies but is utilized in the OT. The literary discipline "studies the way a biblical author/editor altered his sources to develop his unique theological message." G. von Rad used it in his Genesis commentary to determine "the theological threads of what he called the Yahwist editor. . . . The Gospels themselves were seen as the end result of an artificial scissors-and-paste compilation of the traditions." G. Bornkamm considered the stilling of the storm in Matthew "has changed Mark's miracle story into a discipleship episode centering on 'little faith' journey of the disciples in light of the trials of the church (the boat)" (Osborne, "Redaction Criticism").

SC "seeks to identify independent source documents behind the present biblical texts. It is the oldest method of critical biblical study except for textual criticism. It was initially called higher criticism to distinguish it from lower or textual criticism, then called literary criticism because of its emphasis on written documents. It differs from form criticism in its focus on written rather than oral sources and from redaction criticism in its quest to describe independent sources rather than editorial work" (McKenzie, "What Is Source Criticism?").

140. Crossan, *Jesus*, xiii; Crossan and Reed, *Excavating Jesus*, 12.

141. Crossan, *Birth of Christianity*, 557.

SOURCE CRITICISM (INCLUDING EXTRACANONICAL AND Q)[142]

(a) What rationale is given for including extracanonical Gospels in first and second strata?[143] How will these affect Crossan's understanding of Jesus's resurrection, especially in light of Crossan's support of the Gospel of Peter in the first stratum? See the discussion below.

(b) What are the problems associated with Crossan's version of SC that may affect the stratification model and its impact on Jesus's resurrection?[144]

(c) Is the game "fixed" with the use of extracanonical material?[145] "If wrong on sources, wrong on reconstruction" is Crossan's presupposition.[146] Can his view of sources used for the resurrection tradition be affirmed?

(d) In books published in the 1990s, Crossan makes minimal use of the Book of Acts and New Testament epistles.[147] Why?

(e) There are issues with the Q hypothesis.[148] Why is the Q hypothesis elevated to the position of being regarded as the Q Gospel, when no Q document has ever been discovered? It is a hypothesis and not a recognized document. Scholars should understand this.

(f) "Do we have one, two, three, four, or five *independent* [Gospel] sources? And if, as I believe, we have only one independent source in Mark, it all comes down to these two issues: Is there any pre-Markan tradition

---

142. "Q" is from the German word, *Quelle*, which means "source." Q is a hypothesis and not a Gospel. Its concept is that the Synoptic Gospels (Matthew, Mark, and Luke) have many areas of similarity, which seems to indicate they were copied from each other or another source. "When considering the possibility of a Q gospel, it is important to remember that no evidence whatsoever has ever been found for the existence of a Q gospel. Not even a single manuscript fragment of Q has been found" ("What Is Q Gospel").

143. Crossan, *Historical Jesus*, 427–30; Wright, *Jesus and the Victory*, 49.

144. Crossan, *Birth of Christianity*, 482; Crossan and Reed, *Excavating Jesus*, 12; Koester, *Ancient Christian Gospels*, 216; Meier, *Marginal Jew*, 1:116; Wright, *Jesus and the Victory*, 49; Jesus Seminar, "Voting Records"; Evans, *Ancient Texts*; Quarles, "Gospel of Peter," in Stewart, *Resurrection of Jesus*, 106–20.

145. Johnson, *Real Jesus*, 47; Crossan, *Birth of Christianity*, 103.

146. Crossan, *Birth of Christianity*, 482.

147. See Crossan, *Historical Jesus*; Crossan, *Jesus*; Crossan, *Who Killed Jesus*; Crossan, *Birth of Christianity*, 15.

148. Crossan, *Historical Jesus*, 429; Crossan, *Jesus*, xi; Crossan, *Who Killed Jesus*, 44, 192; Crossan, *Birth of Christianity*, 110, 408, 433.

in Mark 16:1–8, and what is Mark's purpose for this incident?"[149] Is this an accurate understanding of the nature of these sources?

MYTHOLOGY, FICTION, LEGEND, AND MAGIC

Christ's resurrection is regarded as fiction that has intermingled history and myth. How is this verified?[150] It is here stated that history and myth need to be defined clearly.

Indicators of Presuppositions Influencing Crossan's Research[151]

1. Is the New Testament evidence for the resurrection of Jesus better interpreted according to the stratification of the Gospels, or is Crossan expressing the outworking of his presuppositions about the resurrection and the Gospels?

2. Based on the questions above, this raises some of the content from Crossan's publications that could point to presuppositions that he brings to the study of the historical Jesus and the analysis of sources. They are possible triggers in Crossan's assumptions.

3. Why is the most difficult vector literary stratification?[152] Could this stratification model be an imposition on the text of the Gospels that demonstrates a presupposition that supports Wright's claim that Crossan's reconstruction[153] of the historical Jesus is "almost completely wrong"?[154]

4. What are the presuppositional elements of Crossan's reconstruction/deconstruction method that could be contributing to the stratification arrangement that Crossan uses for the resurrection tradition?[155] Could

---

149. Crossan, *Birth of Christianity*, 556.

150. Christ's birth (Mattt 1–2 and Luke 1–2) also is symbolical and fictional rather than actual and factual (Crossan, *God and Empire*, 106). Again, how can this be determined and affirmed or denied?

151. Many of these presuppositional indicators are derived from the questions asked above.

152. Crossan, *Who Killed Jesus*, xii.

153. Crossan, *Historical Jesus*, xxxiv.

154. Wright, *Jesus and the Victory*, 44.

155. Crossan, *Historical Jesus*, 424, 426. Here, reconstruction and deconstruction are used as synonymous terms. Crossan prefers the term reconstruction.

this be part of his original research that his university of employment was seeking?

5. Why does Crossan accept the general conclusions from "most critical scholars today"?[156] However, he ignores or minimizes the contrary conclusions of other critical scholars. Is there a presuppositional bias in favor of liberal postmodern scholars who "represent my intellectual debt"?[157] I have provided a list of references below that Crossan has ignored.[158] Why is it so damaging in applying to the biblical texts of Christ's resurrection "a ruthless hermeneutic of suspicion" where the resurrection accounts are "worthless as history"?[159] Why is Crossan so opposed to the historical hermeneutic of Christ's bodily resurrection?[160] There are strong indicators of a presuppositional bias.

6. If Crossan's historical research is "unsalvageable"[161] (and I agree with this assessment), will other models of historical evaluation assist in making recoverable assessments in Gospel research? That's what this book will attempt to uncover.

7. Could there be a presuppositional bias against other historical models in Crossan's assessment? Or does Wright have a presuppositional preference when he states that "in the last few decades," systematic theologians have unsurprisingly chosen "a Jesus who just happens to fit the programme that was desired on other grounds"? Wright states that when one uses the word Jesus in theology, there is no point in using it unless one is referring "to the Jesus who lived and died as a Jew of the first century." To study Jesus, Paul. and the Gospels in the first century, Wright maintains, does not require the adoption of "wholesale and uncritically" an Enlightenment worldview or of any on offer from the contemporary secular environment.[162]

---

156. Crossan, *Jesus*, xii.

157. Crossan, *Historical Jesus*, xxxiv.

158. The following references are in the bibliography. Crossan has not given emphasis to the conclusions reached by historical Jesus scholars, including: Barnett, Blomberg, Bock, Boyd, Bruce, Byrskog, Carson, Carson and Woodbridge, Craig, Craig and Ehrman, Craig and Lüdemann, Davids, Farnell, Gerhardsson, Habermas, Hagner, Hengel, Ingraffia, Johnson, Ladd, Linnemann, Marshall, Montgomery, Thiselton, Thomas, Vanhoozer, Wenham, Wilkins and Moreland, Witherington, and Wright.

159. Wright, *Jesus and the Victory*, 19.

160. Crossan, *Historical Jesus*, 394, 404; *Jesus*, 160–66; *Birth of Christianity*, xxvii–xxxi, 548–50; Borg and Crossan, *Last Week*, 190–216.

161. Meyer, Review of *Historical Jesus*, 576.

162. Wright, *New Testament*, 139.

8. Is it nonsensical to seek a historical rather than a fictional Jesus? Crossan makes fictional claims about the canonical Gospels.[163]

9. Extracanonical Gospels seem to receive an inordinate prominence in Crossan's writings, especially in the first and second strata. Why the emphases and early dates for the Gospel of Peter, Gospel of Thomas, Egerton Gospel, Gospel of the Hebrews, Gospel of the Egyptians, and the Secret Gospel of Mark?[164] Wright regards it as "highly contentious" to have the Gospel of Thomas placed at an earlier stage of the tradition than the canonical Gospels.[165] He stated in 1996 that the Gospel of Peter has "not been accepted yet by any other serious scholar" and that its dating by the AD 50s is "purely imaginary."[166] Paul Barnett dates the Gospels of Peter and Thomas in the Third Century.[167] Postmodern deconstructionist Burton Mack dates the Gospel of Thomas to "the last quarter of the first century,"[168] while evangelical historian Craig Blomberg dates the Gospel of Thomas as "probably in the mid-second century" and views the Gospel of Peter as providing "additions to the canonical accounts."[169]

10. Meier makes the pointed statement that to call the Gospels of Peter and Thomas a supplement to the four intracanonical Gospels "is to broaden out our pool of sources *from the difficult to the incredible*."[170] Is the Gospel of Thomas dependent on or independent of the canonical Gospels?[171] What presuppositions influence Crossan's use of extracanonical Gospels, especially in the first and second strata?[172] Is this pointing to a movement away from a historical Jesus to a postmodern one by which Crossan affirms his presumption that "there will always be divergent historical Jesuses" and divergent Christs, because the structure of Christianity is *"this is how we see Jesus-then as Christ-now"*?[173]

---

163. Crossan, *Jesus*, 160.
164. Crossan, *Historical Jesus*, 427–30.
165. Wright, *Jesus and the Victory*, 32.
166. Wright, *Jesus and the Victory*, 49.
167. Barnett, *Birth of Christianity*, 213.
168. Mack, *Lost Gospel*, 181.
169. Blomberg, *Historical Reliability of Gospels*, 208, 217.
170. Meier, *Marginal Jew*, 1:141 (emphasis added).
171. See Bauckham, *Jesus and the Eyewitnesses*, 236–37.
172. Crossan, *Historical Jesus*, 427–30.
173. Crossan, *Historical Jesus*, 423 (emphasis in original).

11. Could this be a postmodern, presuppositional imposition on the biblical texts? Is an assessment of the impact of reader-response theories instrumental in showing elements of the stratifications that Crossan uses? Other presuppositional indicators in Crossan's writings include the following, but they will be explored in more detail in this chapter and chapter 4, where bibliographic references are included.

Crossan demonstrates these emphases in his writings:

Postmodern epistemology[174]
Reasons for the Gospel of Peter being in the first stratum
Method leads to inventory and then interpretation: which presuppositions influence this trajectory?
Early dating of some extracanonical material
FC: three levels of stratification
Gospels as consummate theological fictions
Starting with context rather than text
Differences and discrepancies in New Testament Gospels are due to deliberate theological interpretations of Jesus.
Gospel of Q rather than hypothesis of Q
Criteria of historicity with dominant influences
Logical fallacies
Presuppositions on the authority of Scripture
Meaning of parable and megaparable and Crossan's use of them
"Read the text" was Crossan's instruction to the producers of a film on Jesus. Does he do this accurately himself?
Diversity in early Christianity and the Bauer-Ehrman hypothesis
Working definition of historical reconstruction
Historicity and assumptions around Jesus's resurrection
Belief that transmitters of Jesus's tradition had creative freedom.
Support for dialectic between history and faith;[175] Jesus's last breath was not history but of faith and a symbol.
Use of the Cross Gospel in the Gospel of Peter as a foundation for passion accounts, with opposition to eyewitness testimony

---

174. Epistemology is "the theory of knowledge, especially with regard to its methods, validity, and scope. Epistemology is the investigation of what distinguishes justified belief from opinion" ("Epistemology," in OED).

175. "Dialectic" means "the art of investigating or discussing the truth of opinions" ("Dialectic," in OED).

These are some of the indicators in Crossan's writings of possible presuppositions that influence his conclusions that lead to unorthodox Christian teachings.

Beaver et al. classify another identifying factor for presuppositions: "cancellability."[176] This is what causes a "projection problem" to become problematic. If part of the meaning of statement α was never affected by the linguistic context in which α is embedded, it would require a theoretical explanation. Presuppositions generally make projections but sometimes do not, and much empirical and theoretical work on presuppositions since the 1970s has involved trying to explain when presuppositions project or do not project.

The classical explanation of when presuppositions are "cancelled" is when presuppositions are denied directly, when the trigger is embedded under another operator. Otherwise, the content of a presupposition is forced to make an adjustment that may not be natural. An example of a trigger embedded under another operator could be "Crossan has an infiltrated and changed view of Jesus's resurrection, but there is no scholar called Crossan" or "Crossan changed his view of Jesus's resurrection, but he did not do anything that was wrong."

Beaver et al. note that because of the ambiguity of the term cancellation in other circumstances, many scholars have ceased to use the term with presuppositions. One reason given is that the language of cancellation appears to suggest that an inference was made and that it has since been removed. They state that "in many cases there are theoretical reasons not to regard this as an apt characterization."[177]

The above explanations of identifying presuppositions are not always watertight, but they are indicators of how presuppositions may be exposed in an author's writings.

As shown later in this chapter, a verification method of research is used in this study that incorporates "interrelated criteria of truth," which are logical noncontradiction, empirical adequacy, and existential viability. The only hypotheses accepted are those that are noncontrradictory, supported by adequate evidence, and able to be affirmed without hypocrisy.[178]

---

176. Beaver et al., "Presupposition."
177. Beaver et al., "Presupposition."
178. Lewis and Demarest, *Integrative Theology*, 1:25.

OTHER MATTERS FOR CONSIDERATION IN IDENTIFYING PRESUPPOSITIONS

As applied to unstated presuppositions or axioms that Crossan seems to use to reach his conclusions, some further areas need to be enumerated in this verification model to help with the identification of presuppositions. The following are adaptations from the antidote to theological subjectivism in hermeneutics proposed by Lewis and Demarest.[179]

When there is conflict with presuppositions, there can be no resolution, if hermeneutical eisegesis is used in reading ideas into the Gospels. Both of those in conflict need to start from the position that their different views are hypotheses that need to be tested. Both need to submit their presuppositions "to the test of standard logical criteria of truth and hermeneutical principles for interpreting literature in general and of the Bible in particular."[180] Further standards of responsible interpretation include:

1. The meaning of any statement, including a biblical statement, depends on the ordinary or normal meaning of a statement, using literal language, incorporating figures of speech, but it needs to be seen in terms of the context and the author's purpose.

2. A biblical statement needs to fit the historical and cultural situation of the original writer and readers.

3. To understand the meaning of a sentence, the meaning must be coherent with the writer's own context. For example, an author's use of a word, when traced through the person's writings, is a stronger indicator of meaning than the etymology of the word.

4. The Scriptures do "not affirm and deny the same thing at the same time in the same respect." The meaning of any biblical statement, taken alone, will not be contradictory with other scriptural teaching on the same subject. This follows the Reformers' "analogy of faith" by which Scripture interprets Scripture.[181]

5. The intended meaning of a statement or sentence is that which is literal,[182] historical, grammatical, and contextual and will not be determined by

---

179. Lewis and Demarest, *Integrative Theology*, 1:29–31.
180. Lewis and Demarest, *Integrative Theology*, 1:30.
181. Lewis and Demarest, *Integrative Theology*, 1:30–31.
182. Here, *literal*, following the School of Antioch, "means the customarily acknowledged meaning of an expression in its particular context." For example, when Christ declared that he was the door, the metaphorical meaning of door in that context would be obvious that it was not referring to a wooden door but to an entrance. "Although

some deeper, secret, or plural meaning. Crossan's writings seem unable to refuse the pull away from the historical-grammatical hermeneutical understanding of the biblical text and its context toward a postmodern hermeneutic or eisegesis of the text. An example would be Crossan's historical reconstruction, which he states was an interaction of present and past, with no "presumption that the historical Jesus and earliest Christianity is something you get once and for all forever."[183]

6. More extensive passages on a topic are given priority over incidental references.

The following points do not come from Lewis and Demarest but from this author.

7. At times, there seems to be a question begging logical fallacy committed when Crossan sneaks his postmodern conclusion into his premise. It is circular reasoning, as the conclusion becomes the premise. An example would be the one of Crossan's historical reconstruction, given in number 5 above.[184]

8. To expose presuppositions, questions need to be asked to uncover strata of thought. However, a prominent question for various Crossan interpretations is "Why does Crossan hold this belief or presuppositional bias?" In attempting to answer these questions, dimensions of Crossan's worldview may emerge. By worldview, reference is made to a fundamental life orientation, a view of reality that is expressed in a set of presuppositions that may be held consciously or subconsciously, consistently or inconsistently. This worldview is used as a foundation for how a life is lived; hence, this also influences one's scholarly decisions in writing for publication.[185] Questioning Crossan's conclusions may lead to the discovery of the crux presupposition of his worldview that has a trickle-down effect on other presuppositions. Is there an antithesis between Crossan's core presupposition and his teaching on Jesus's resurrection, as revealed in Scripture and the inductive view of Scripture's own statements about the nature of its own authority?

---

metaphorical, this obvious meaning is included in the literal meaning." By application to this research, "'literal' refers to the customary and socially acknowledged meaning in an actual, ordinary, earthly situation. 'Figurative' refers to the transfer of the literal, ordinary meaning from one sphere to another so as to convey by analogy or comparison a different or deeper or higher truth" (Mickelsen, *Interpreting the Bible*, 307).

183. Crossan, *Birth of Christianity*, 45.
184. Crossan, *Birth of Christianity*, 45.
185. Sire, *Universe Next Door*, 17.

9. Has Crossan's "method displaced the meaning of the text," and has he failed to make historical method a servant rather than a master of the interpretive task? Dan Stiver notes Wolterstorff's use of the "first hermeneutic," which determines the meaning of a text in view of its time and its author or authors.[186] All scholars operate with some presuppositions, including this researcher.

SOME DANGERS AND BENEFITS OF EXPOSING PRESUPPOSITIONS

Since this project argues for the view that the portrait of the historical Jesus's resurrection in the canonical Gospels is reliable history, and Crossan provides reasons for the fictional nature of some of the canonical data, it may not be clear which presuppositions are influencing both scholars' research. If the claims of historically reliable Gospels are true, the presuppositions undergirding them need to be validated. Can presuppositions be labelled as true, or should some be more reliable than others? How is reliability defined?

While it is true that every researcher uses presuppositions, and these must be uncovered to prevent "endless and fruitless debate,"[187] there is a complicating factor. In speech acts, whether in person or in writing, many presenters or researchers do not overtly make known all of their presuppositions.[188] Therefore, it is the listener's or reader's responsibility to try to discern these hidden presuppositions from what is stated. This depends on the listener's or reader's background in the scholarly task and experience in identifying the manifestations of presuppositions. It is never possible to be absolutely certain of a person's presuppositions. Probability is all that can be achieved, unless a writer is transparent with acknowledging his or her personal presuppositions. But these probable presuppositions may have some major consequences for the conclusions reached in Crossan's writings. The decoding of his presuppositions begins with asking questions of his stated conclusions. My presuppositions are those of an evangelical, Protestant Christian, with a high view of the authority of Scripture.

---

186. Stiver, "Method," 511–12.

187. Wright, *New Testament*, 31.

188. "Christians believe that the Bible is inspired by God and therefore consists of the words of God that are simultaneously the words of human authors. As a result, the Bible can be read as a set of divinely uttered speech acts. There are many fruitful implications for the Christian faith of such an approach to Scripture" (Allison, "Speech Act Theory").

The same applies to Crossan's claims about God and Jesus's resurrection. Presuppositions cannot be ignored for Crossan or any other historical researcher. It will become evident as this process continues that disagreements about presuppositions often trigger different outcomes when data are analyzed.

What are Crossan's and this researcher's presuppositions regarding the following?

Nature of the New Testament as history or non-history (including myth, fiction, allegory, metaphor, and symbol)
Criteria of historicity
Deconstruction as a procedure and its postmodern influences
Validity of extracanonical versus intracanonical data, especially the use of the Gospel of Peter (Cross Gospel) as a very early document that Crossan claims was the foundation of the New Testament Gospel accounts of Jesus's passion-resurrection. See Charles Quarles's article on the Gospel of Peter for an assessment of why it is later than the New Testament Gospels and not in the first stratification of the first century, as Crossan places it. In the Gospel of Peter, we learn "still other features of the *Gospel of Peter* fit best with the historical data if the *Gospel of Peter* was produced in the mid-second century. The *Gospel of Peter* assumes the doctrine of Jesus' descent into Hades to preach to the dead. However, this doctrine first appears in the words of Justin Martyr around AD 150. The talking cross is a feature of other second-century literature. The *Epistula Apostolorum 16* states that during the second coming Jesus will be carried on the wings of the clouds with his cross going on before him."[189]
Legitimacy of the use of FC, RC and SC, including the Q hypothesis being described by Crossan as the Q Gospel
Best method to pursue in analyzing Gospel data
Hermeneutical procedures used
Whether or not the diversity suggested by Crossan in early Christianity, as illustrated by the prominence given to extracanonical works such as the Gospel of Thomas and the Gospel of Peter, supports the Bauer-Ehrman hypothesis[190]
Whether one can speak of true presuppositions or not
Logical fallacies
Crossan's partiality towards certain researchers when he states that he accepted general conclusions from "most critical scholars today" and cites secondary literature of those who "represent my intellectual debt"[191]

189. Quarles, "Gospel of Peter."

190. The Walter Bauer thesis, adopted by Bart Ehrman and other scholars, including some of the Jesus Seminar, was "that heresy preceded orthodoxy" in the early church, which moved from diversity to unity (Köstenberger and Kruger, *Heresy of Orthodoxy*, 38). For an assessment of the Bauer-Ehrman thesis, see Köstenberger and Kruger, *Heresy of Orthodoxy*, 23–40.

191. Crossan, *Jesus*, xii; Crossan, *Historical Jesus*, xxxiv.

The major benefits achieved in tentative assessments of Crossan's presuppositions should be to have a better understanding of the assumptions influencing his worldview that lead to his scholarly conclusions about Jesus's resurrection tradition. These presuppositions may need to be challenged if there is other evidence that can be applied in the hypothesis-verification methodology.

ARE THE GOSPELS HISTORICAL?

What is history? Tudor historian Sir Geoffrey Elton[192] states that since history "deals with events, not states, it investigates things that happen and not things that are;"[193] it may be defined as "those human sayings, thoughts, deeds and sufferings which occurred in the past and have left a present deposit; and it deals with them from the point of view of happening, change and the particular."[194] Elton does not explain history from a Christian perspective, but his understanding of history has application to the Gospels and Christian history; it did not contain facts *and* interpretation. Barnett defines history as dealing with phenomena and how to explain them. His assessment is that the phenomenon of the origin of early Christianity "is well attested. Its sudden emergence is as historically secure as any event in Palestine in that century."[195]

In a study of theological method, Richard Niebuhr examines the link between Christ's resurrection and historical reason. If he were "to sketch a critical concept of history and historical reason," he would rely on the idea of history from biblical scholars of the nineteenth and twentieth centuries.[196] Within a framework of biblical criticism, he considers history speaks with the "voice" of "faithful memory" and "curious reason."[197] Thus, historical reason requires that there cannot be an either/or a priori metaphysical approach to the resurrection of Christ versus the historical critical method.[198]

Instead, "the resurrection tradition continues both to attract and repel our sense of the historical."[199] The "inner history of the interpreter" cannot be separated from the historically natural causalities that are involved in

192. Elton, *Practice of History*, 10–12.
193. Elton, *Practice of History*, 10.
194. Elton, *Practice of History*, 12.
195. Barnett, *Jesus and the Logic*, 19.
196. Niebuhr, *Resurrection and Historical Reason*, 4.
197. Niebuhr, *Resurrection and Historical Reason*, 5.
198. Niebuhr, *Resurrection and Historical Reason*, 23.
199. Niebuhr, *Resurrection and Historical Reason*, 28.

history.²⁰⁰ What "typifies the character of historical reason"? For Niebuhr, Christ's resurrection represents the epitome of historical reason, because it involves a historical event in nature, something more than nature's causal relationships, and interpretation of history that involves critical memory of that event by the Christian community. He states that the historical event is not needed logically to imply what preceded or followed the event, but it is an "indispensable tool for the interpretation of those other events" that includes the Gospels, the Acts of the Apostles, and the letters to the apostolic churches.²⁰¹

This is a confusing analogy, as Niebuhr finds the historical event (based on nature) of the resurrection of Christ logically unnecessary but still needed for the events described in the New Testament.

Which presuppositions will guide the criticism of Christ's resurrection as historical event and replace it with the rewritten resurrection apparition back into the earthy life of Jesus, based on the Cross Gospel from the Gospel of Peter, according to Crossan?²⁰²

Could this fresh appropriation in each generation be a pointer to contemporary reader-response theories in postmodern interpretations of the Scriptures?

DECONSTRUCTION (OR RECONSTRUCTION)

Although the terms deconstruction and reconstruction often are used interchangeably in discussions on postmodern philosophy, Crossan's preferred term for the method he uses in Jesus studies is reconstruction rather than deconstruction. Crossan admits that there is "the problem of reconstruction" and his "book is one scholar's reconstruction.... If you cannot believe in something produced by reconstruction, you may have nothing left to believe in."²⁰³ To address this need for a reconstruction of the New Testament, Crossan's scholarship was associated with the Jesus Seminar that met twice a year for over five years, using colored beads and ballot boxes for disputed New Testament Greek readings. This was a contemporary equivalent, says Crossan, of the grades of disputed readings given in the critical apparatus of the United Bible Societies' third edition of *The Greek New Testament*, as A, B, C, or D.²⁰⁴

200. Niebuhr, *Resurrection and Historical Reason*, 127.
201. Niebuhr, *Resurrection and Historical Reason*, 170–71.
202. Crossan, *Historical Jesus*, 396.
203. Crossan, *Historical Jesus*, 424, 426.
204. Crossan, *Historical Jesus*, 424–25.

Of the Gospels, Crossan writes that they were inaugural models, but each Christian generation needed to rewrite the Gospels to reconstruct its historical Jesus with integrity and say and live this reconstruction. He considers history and faith to be a "dialectic for sacrophilic Christianity."[205] There is no presumption that earliest Christianity's historical Jesus was "something you get once and for all forever."[206] No past activities, in his view, can "avoid repeated reconstruction."[207] Presuppositional postmodernism seems to be emerging like a rocket from a trainee biblical reconstructionist camp.

Therefore, when Crossan states that "within Christianity the Bible is the Word of God made text, just as Jesus is the Word of God made flesh,"[208] he is not speaking of biblical authority relating to an infallible Word of God. His postmodern deconstruction of the text "is a dialectic between history and faith" that is interpreted from his postmodern horizon.[209]

Elsewhere, he writes of the New Testament, including the Gospels, as "inspired by God"; but because this inspiration comes through a human heart and mind, influenced by personal prejudice and the interpretation of the Christian community, along with fear, dislike, hate, faith, hope, and charity, it can come to us "as inspired propaganda, and inspiration does not make it any the less propaganda."[210] Which presuppositions trigger his understanding of the Gospels as propaganda?

For Crossan, the nineteenth-century dream of "uncommitted, objective, dispassionate historical study" is "a methodological screen."[211] Instead, Crossan challenges the readers through his method and historical hermeneutics, as they presume "there will always be divergent historical Jesuses" with resultant "divergent Christs." The structure of Christianity, for Crossan, will be, without variation, "*This is how we see Jesus-then as Christ-now*."[212]

---

205. Crossan, *Birth of Christianity*, 40. A dialectic is "a way of discovering what is true by considering opposite theories" ("Dialectic," in *CD*). I checked seven dictionaries, but no meaning was found for *sacrophilic*. An analysis of etymology of the NT Greek foundation of the word could lead to a meaning of "love (for) the sacred." Since Crossan uses monastic in association with sacrophilic, he possibly means monks in love with the sacred.

206. Crossan, *Birth of Christianity*, 40.

207. Crossan, *Birth of Christianity*, 45.

208. Crossan, *Birth of Christianity*, 45.

209. Crossan, *Birth of Christianity*, 45.

210. Crossan, *Who Killed Jesus*, xi.

211. Crossan, *Historical Jesus*, 423.

212. Crossan, *Historical Jesus*, 423 (emphasis in original).

Thus, Crossan advocates the reconstruction of the biblical text, including the addition of extra-biblical material, to arrive at an accurate picture of the historical Jesus.

Wright, in his historical method regarding Christ's resurrection, recognizes that all knowledge of the past and other matters is mediated through sources, perceptions, and the "personalities of the knowers." Thus, he accepts that there can be "no such thing as detached objectivity." Historical work involves the interactions of the historian with other historians, source materials, and the "worldview-perspectives" of the historian.[213]

By contrast, Crossan's methodology includes Mark creating the women's discovery of the empty tomb and the burial story; Matthew creating the "apparition of Jesus to the women" after his resurrection, to make Mark's ending more positive; and John copying that vision from Matthew.[214]

Within the scholarly community, there is division over the Gospels' historicity. What then is meant, if Christianity is described as a "historical religion"?

THE CONTROVERSY: THE GOSPELS AS HISTORICAL OR NONHISTORICAL DOCUMENTS

Barnett begins his volume on *Jesus and the Logic of History* with the statement that Christianity is a historical religion in two senses: firstly, Christianity has continuously been part of world history, and secondly, Jesus was a real man who lived and died at a particular place and time.[215] I agree, but that does not equate with Crossan's understanding of history. In fact, Crossan opposes such a definition.

Donald Hagner states that "the Bible is after all the story of God acting in history."[216] Darrell Bock's perspective is that both methods and presuppositions influence the study of the New Testament Gospels.[217] Bauckham admits there is a "crucial methodological problem"[218] in pursuing and understanding the historical Jesus amidst alternatives such as a Jesus seen through the needs and interests of various early Christian groups and many Jesuses constructed and verified by many historians. For Bauckham, the

---

213. Described in Wright, *New Testament*, 29–144. See pp. 38–39 for Wright's emphasis on the historicity of ancient times.

214. Crossan, *Birth of Christianity*, 552.

215. Barnett, *Jesus and the Logic*, 11.

216. Hagner, "New Testament, History," 88.

217. Bock, *Studying the Historical Jesus*, 139.

218. Bauckham, *Jesus and the Eyewitnesses*, 2–3.

Gospels present a combination of fact and interpretation that includes both "the empirically observable and the intuited or constructed meaning."[219] For him, the historiography of the Gospels is presented through the verifiable history of testimony, i.e., eyewitnesses.[220] Moisés Silva maintains that "hardly anything is more crucial to the Christian faith than the historicity of Jesus' life, death and resurrection."[221]

However, Crossan sees the "background of Jesus' resurrectional victory over death" as a basis for the "nature" miracles of Jesus being "actually credal statements about ecclesiastical authority."[222] What presuppositions cause him to come to a metaphorical understanding of Jesus's resurrection rather than a bodily resurrection? He is not obtaining the meaning from the text.

Wright sees the need for a creative synthesis of the pre-modern authoritative text, a modern importance of Christianity integrated into history and involved with theology, and the postmodern emphasis on the text and its readers. For him, this involves putting forward hypotheses about the historical situation in which the New Testament writings were developed. Wright's historical reconstruction involves the Judaism and Christianity of the first century.[223]

German philosopher Hans-Georg Gadamer (1900–2002) propounds the view that people understand texts or laws when they project their self-understanding towards the meaning of texts. Those who understand texts, contrary to traditional hermeneutics, are projecting themselves onto texts. He admits that this could be problematical for the self-understanding of faith.[224] Therefore, what is the nature of history and the historical model when applied to the New Testament Gospel texts? Why should it be necessary to discuss the nature of history and of historicity of these texts? Should it not be common sense to understand that the historical Jesus who lived in a given place and time was a person of history and that a reasonable understanding would be to pursue a straightforward historical method in examining the textual stratification reporting on the death, burial, and resurrection of Jesus Christ? That would have been possible if it were not for the last century of the development of literary and hermeneutical phenomena

---

219. Bauckham, *Jesus and the Eyewitnesses*, 3.
220. Bauckham, *Jesus and the Eyewitnesses*, 5.
221. Silva, "Place of Historical Reconstruction," 111.
222. Crossan, *Historical Jesus*, 404.
223. Wright, *New Testament*, 26–27.
224. Gadamer, *Truth and Method*, 251, 253.

in biblical studies of FC and postmodern deconstruction, the latter incorporating a reader-response paradigm.[225]

While reconstruction and deconstruction are often used interchangeably in historical Jesus studies,[226] Silva considers there is a legitimate use of reconstruction among evangelicals when they gather knowledge to fill the gaps of evidence for New Testament studies. As an example, he affirms the historical centrality of Jesus's death, burial, and resurrection, but acknowledges that nobody knows with certainty the exact dates of these events. To search for this information is an acceptable use of reconstruction for Silva.[227]

However, a more radical understanding of the term deconstruction has been used in the last half-century. It is associated with the writings of French philosopher Jacques Derrida (1930–2004). Caputo indicates that Derrida derived the term deconstruction from Heidegger's use of two German words, *Destruktion* and *Abbau*.[228] From *Destruktion*, the meaning of deconstruction is not destruction but "destructuring that dismantles the structural layers in a system and so on." The use of *Abbau* has a similar meaning, but the concept conveyed is "to take apart an edifice in order to see how it is constituted or deconstructed," and Derrida applied this to the whole of Western philosophy. It has since transitioned to many other disciplines, including biblical history and interpretation.

Some of the scholarly debates on methodology for the study of Jesus have involved contrasting approaches based on the paradigms of historical-critical challenges to historicity, reader-response theories, and Christianity's historical origins that are subject to the laws of historical evidence to be verified or falsified. How do these scholars respond to the historicity or otherwise of the New Testament Gospels?

One response has been to regard the Gospels as nonhistorical.

THE GOSPELS AS NONHISTORICAL DOCUMENTS

After describing seven different scholars with divergent images of Jesus, Crossan observes that this "stunning diversity" gives the suspicion "that historical Jesus research is a very safe place to do theology and call it history, to do autobiography and call it biography."[229] Thus, Crossan's historical

---

225. See below for a further discussion of reader-response theories.
226. See previous section, "Deconstruction (or Reconstruction)."
227. Silva, "Place of Historical Reconstruction," 111.
228. Caputo, "Jacques Derrida"; Derrida, *Ear of the Other*, 86–87.
229. Crossan, *Historical Jesus*, xxvii.

Jesus methodology adopts a "triple triadic approach" that embraces social anthropology; Hellenistic or Greco-Roman history; and the literature of Jesus's sayings, deeds, stories or anecdotes, confessions and interpretations.[230] However, this triad needs to cooperate for an equal and effective synthesis. Thus, "the Gospels are neither histories nor biographies, even within the ancient tolerances for those genres." Instead, they are "good newses" which provide some community's opinion or interpretation.[231] Therefore, Crossan does not ground the New Testament Gospels as historically secure as do Barnett, Blomberg, Bock, Wright, and Lewis and Demarest. For Crossan, the resurrection of Christ has nothing to do with bodily resuscitation but is an "apparition" with metaphorical application by which the "*embodied* life and death of the historical Jesus continues to be experienced by believers."[232]

This is parallel to Bultmann's statement about "the incredibility of a mythical event like the resuscitation of a dead person—for that is what the resurrection means, as is shown by the fact that the risen Lord is apprehended by the physical senses," and "an historical fact which involves a resurrection from the dead is utterly inconceivable." Also, the resurrection is "an article of faith because it is far more than the resuscitation of a corpse—it is the eschatological event."[233]

Did Paul see Christ's resurrection as other than a physical event where Christ appeared to others after the resurrection?[234] What did he mean by the statement "Last of all, as to one untimely born, he appeared also to me"?[235] Crossan's view is that "it is obvious that Christ's appearance to Paul himself in [1 Cor] 15:8–11 is not part of his *received* tradition,"[236] and there was some redactional involvement. Crossan follows Koester in affirming that Paul knew the story of Christ's suffering and death, not as historical information but as a story "that made Jesus present for the participants in the celebration of the eucharist."[237] Thus, Christ's passion had spiritual significance for those who participated in the Lord's Supper, but it was not based on historical details. It needs to be remembered that Christ's appearance to the apostle Paul was not in the passion-resurrection-ascension time frame.

---

230. Crossan, *Historical Jesus*, xxvii.
231. Crossan, *Historical Jesus*, xxx.
232. Crossan, *Birth of Christianity*, xxviii–xxxi (emphasis in original).
233. Bultmann et al., "Mythological Element."
234. See 1 Cor 15:5–7.
235. First Cor 15:8.
236. Crossan, *Birth of Christianity*, 546 (emphasis in original).
237. Crossan, *Birth of Christianity*, 547.

What happened to Saul/Paul on the Damascus Road was a unique encounter with the risen and ascended Christ,[238] yet Paul includes this unexpected meeting in sequence with those to whom the risen Christ appeared physically before the ascension.[239] Paul's encounter could not have been received in the tradition from others, but Barnett understands this as Paul experiencing "a revelation of Christ as he will be at the parousia."[240] Barnett sees the parallel with how the Gospel came to Paul through a revelation (*apokalupsisis*) as stated in Galatians 1:11–12, 16.[241]

Crossan proposes that Jesus's first followers "knew almost nothing whatsoever about the details of his crucifixion, death, or burial," but he adds "that Jesus was crucified is as sure as anything historical can ever be," since both Josephus and Tacitus agree with the Christian accounts on this basic fact.[242] With this intracanonical and extracanonical evidence, Crossan takes "it absolutely for granted that Jesus was crucified under Pontius Pilate."[243] Historical facts are assured because the Christian accounts are substantiated by non-Christian witnesses, Josephus (Jewish) and Tacitus (Roman).

THE CROSS GOSPEL AND THE GOSPEL OF PETER

The priority given to the Cross Gospel in the Gospel of Peter is outlined by Crossan: "My working hypothesis is that the *original stratum* or Cross Gospel in *Peter* had only the guards at the tomb and nothing whatsoever about the women at the tomb. It was Mark himself who created the empty tomb story and its failed anointing as a fitting climax to the literary and theological motifs of his gospel."[244]

Therefore, an examination of the place historically of the Gospel of Peter is necessary to determine the legitimacy of this document and the historical position that Crossan gives to it.

The Gospel of Peter 5:15—6:22[245] is for Crossan "from the *original stratum* of Peter," where Jesus's body, based on Deuteronomy 21:22–23, is taken from the cross and buried before sunset. "The Cross Gospel, the

---

238. Acts 9:1–9.
239. First Cor 15:5–8.
240. Barnett, *Jesus and the Rise*, 183.
241. Barnett, *Jesus and the Rise*, 193n11.
242. Crossan, *Jesus*, 145.
243. Crossan, *Historical Jesus*, 372.
244. Crossan, *Who Killed Jesus*, 185 (emphasis in original).
245. For a translation of the Gospel of Peter, see James, "Gospel of Peter."

original passion-resurrection story within Peter, takes it for granted that Jesus was crucified, removed from the cross, and buried by his enemies." Only this text from the Gospel of Peter is from the Cross Gospel's original stratum. Crossan argues, "My working hypothesis is that the original Cross Gospel story had to accommodate itself to the increasing ascendancy of the canonical gospels after the middle of the second century."[246]

An assessment of the Cross Gospel's validity or otherwise for Jesus's resurrection is in the fifth chapter.

Note that when Crossan uses language such as "scholarly consensus"[247] of research over the last two hundred years, he refers to his colleagues who agree with many of his positions, as he cites those who "represent my intellectual debt," and "in quoting *secondary* literature" he does not "spend time citing other scholars to show how wrong they are."[248] However, by the time of his 1998 publication, Crossan had changed that approach with his comments against some of N. T. Wright's writings.[249] Dorothy Sayers also receives a similar negative appraisal,[250] as does Luke Timothy Johnson.[251]

But could the same apply to Crossan? Could there be a possibility that he already decided who Jesus was and he was setting out to bolster his claims, based on the intellectual debt of those with whom he agrees? He is not immune from his own criticism.

On methods, Crossan says he "started with historical criticism, next incorporated literary criticism, and finally added macro-sociological criticism to form an integrated interdisciplinary model."[252] However, literal exegesis of the biblical text was far from his mind.

He claims he cites only scholars who represent his own intellectual debt.[253] However, he breaks that claim with his challenges to Wright's scholarship[254]—even using a Wright epigraph at the beginning of chapter 7.[255] Then add Crossan's own divergence from Dorothy Sayers's views, in which

---

246. Crossan, *Who Killed Jesus*, 170–71.
247. Crossan, *Birth of Christianity*, 149.
248. Crossan, *Historical Jesus*, xxxiv.
249. Crossan, *Birth of Christianity*, 44, 49–50, 95–99, 104, 258.
250. Crossan, *Birth of Christianity*, 91–93, 98–99.
251. See Johnson, *Real Jesus*. See part of Crossan's critique of Johnson in *Birth of Christianity*, 30–31.
252. Crossan, *Birth of Christianity*, 139.
253. Crossan, *Historical Jesus*, xxxiv.
254. Crossan, *Birth of Christianity*, 44, 49, 95–104, 258.
255. Crossan, *Birth of Christianity*, 95.

he also uses a Sayers epigraph.[256] He debates Luke Timothy Johnson's critique of Crossan for Johnson's "accusation" (Crossan's language) that Crossan's method has "fixed" the data by giving "an early date and independent status to 'virtually all apocryphal materials' and a correspondingly late date and dependent status to 'virtually all intracanonical materials'; and that my only arguments are citations from 'like-minded colleagues.'"[257]

Crossan states, "Because I can see no reason for Josephus to have created that Jewish responsibility [Pilate hearing Jesus accused by men of highest standing], I take it as historical that Jesus was executed by some conjunction of Jewish and Roman authority."[258] Note Crossan's presuppositional trigger: "I can see no reason." Why should you or I listen to this personal projection/reason by Crossan? It amounts to his opinion that has no more historical weight than his outlook. He considers the *"fact of the crucifixion"* is secure,[259] based on two pieces of evidence:[260]

1. "The unlikelihood that Christians would have invented it," and

2. "The existence of two early and independent non-Christian witnesses," one a Jew (Josephus),[261] dated ca. AD 93–94, and the other a Roman historian (Tacitus),[262] dated ca. AD 110s or 120s.

In spite of the difficulties with these quotes and the possible partial or total interpolations by Christian editors of Josephus and Tacitus, Crossan states, "I take it absolutely for granted that Jesus was crucified under Pontius Pilate."[263] He has this kind of confidence with Jesus's crucifixion from a Jewish and a secular historian but not with Jesus's resurrection, based on the intracanonical Gospels. Sounds like the crusher of contradiction is working!

---

256. Crossan, *Birth of Christianity*, 91–99.

257. Crossan, *Birth of Christianity*, 30–31, 103, 114.

258. Crossan, *Who Killed Jesus*, 147–48. Crossan writes that "a prudently neutral Jewish historian reported, at the end of the first century, 'When Pilate, upon hearing him accused by men . . . had condemned him to be crucified . . . . And the tribe of Christians, so called after him, has still to this day not disappeared.'" (*Historical Jesus*, xiii). Why does he not mention that this quote is from Josephus, *Antiquities*, 18.3.3? At this point, Crossan also quotes from "an arrogant Roman historian" who wrote of "Christus, the founder of the name [Christian], had undergone the death penalty, in the reign of Tiberius, by sentence of the procurator Pontius Pilatus" (*Historical Jesus*, xiii). The quote is from Tacitus, *Works of Tacitus*, 15.

259. Crossan, *Historical Jesus*, 372, 375 (emphasis in original).

260. Crossan, *Historical Jesus*, 372.

261. Josephus, *Antiquities*, 18:63; 20:200.

262. Tacitus, *Works of Tacitus*, 15.44.

263. Crossan, *Historical Jesus*, 372.

With regard to Jesus's burial and resurrection, Crossan maintains, "Nobody knew what had happened to Jesus' body" and "with regard to the body of Jesus, by Easter Sunday morning, those who cared did not know where it was, and those who knew did not care."[264] That's a nice turn of phrase, based on nothing but Crossan's opinion.

Concerning the Emmaus road incident with Cleopas and another person after Jesus's resurrection (Luke 24:12–53), Borg and Crossan state, "It is difficult to imagine that this story is speaking about events that could have been videotaped.... This story is the metaphoric condensation of several years of early Christian thought into one parabolic afternoon."[265] Again, it's a statement of Crossan's deconstructed opinion.

Elsewhere, Crossan states of the race to the empty tomb by Peter and the beloved disciple (John 20), "I do not think that story was ever intended as a historical event, intended to describe something that first Easter morning. It always looked to me like a calculated and deliberate parable intended to exalt the authority of the Beloved Disciple over that of Peter."[266] Stated another way, "Empty tomb stories and physical appearance stories are perfectly valid parables expressing that faith, akin in their own way to the Good Samaritan story."[267]

Note Crossan's projection triggers of his presuppositions imposed on the reader: "I do not think," "it always looked to me," and they "are perfectly valid parables expressing that faith." Why would you place any weight on Crossan's opinions, without evidence to demonstrate this?

However, Crossan explains that in the resurrection of Jesus, "Matthew created the story of the apparition of Jesus to the women to change Mark's negative ending into a more positive one."[268] Further, his analysis is that "it never occurs to Paul that Jesus' resurrection might be a special or unique privilege given to him because he is Messiah, Lord, and Son of God.... It was not, therefore, about the vision of a dead man but about the vision of a dead man *who begins the general resurrection*. It is an apparition with cosmically apocalyptic consequences."[269] Crossan has overlooked the Jewish Pharisee Paul's belief in the resurrection, based on his Jewish heritage.

He projects again: "Matthew created the story of the apparition," "it never occurs to Paul." Crossan must be reading a different Bible to mine,

---

264. Crossan, *Historical Jesus*, 394.
265. Borg and Crossan, *Last Week*, 200–201.
266. Crossan, *Long Way from Tipperary*, 164–65.
267. Crossan, *Who Killed Jesus*, 216.
268. Crossan, *Birth of Christianity*, 552.
269. Crossan, "Historical Jesus as Risen Lord," 29 (emphasis in original).

which reads, "If Christ has not been raised, then empty [too] is our preaching; empty, too, your faith . . . . And if Christ has not been raised,[270] your faith is vain; you are still in your sins" (1 Cor 15:14, 17 NABRE).[271] Jesus's resurrection has such an impact for faith and practice that our faith is in vain (or pointless), and we are still in our sins, *if Jesus has not been resurrected*.[272] This again demonstrates how Crossan's presuppositions override the literal interpretation of the biblical text.

Further, Crossan's view is that "the exact sequence of what happened at the end" of Jesus's life "lacks multiple independent accounts," but Christ's death is surer than the few days preceding his death.[273]

Presuppositional triggers take account of:

Factives: "I take it absolutely for granted," "his story is the metaphoric condensation of . . .," "empty tomb stories and physical appearance stories are perfectly valid parables."

- *Aspectual verbs*: "I take it as historical" that Jesus was crucified.
- *Quantifiers*: "exact sequence" and "lacks multiple" attestation.
- *Names*: the Jew Josephus, Roman historian Tacitus, Pontius Pilate, Cleopas, Matthew.
- *Intonation*: "*fact* of the crucifixion."
- *Projection* (emphases added): "*Nobody knew* what had happened to Jesus' body," "*those who cared did not know* where it was [Jesus' body], and *those who knew did not care*." Of the Emmaus road incident with Jesus after his resurrection, "*it is difficult to imagine* that this story is speaking about events that could have been videotaped"; "*I do not think* that story was ever *intended as a historical event*"; "*Matthew created the story of the apparition* of Jesus to the women"; "*it never occurs to Paul* that Jesus' resurrection *might be a special or unique privilege given to him*"; "*it was not*, therefore, about the vision of a dead man but about the vision of a dead man who begins the general resurrection. It is an apparition."

Therefore, presuppositional dimensions include:

---

270. The NAB's footnote was: "The consequences for the Corinthians are grave: both forgiveness of sins and salvation are an illusion, despite their strong convictions about both. Unless Christ is risen, their faith does not save."

271. The NAB (New American Bible) is a Roman Catholic translation and must not be confused with the Protestant NASB (New American Standard Bible).

272. Emphasis added.

273. Crossan, *Historical Jesus*, xii.

- Crossan has no problem with the death of Jesus, but he dissociates it from any construct that includes the supernatural bodily resurrection, as he opposes a belief in miracles.
- Empty tomb stories and physical appearance stories after Jesus's resurrection are parables.
- The Emmaus road incident was not a historical event.
- The apparition of Jesus to the women after his resurrection was a product of FC, created by Matthew.
- The resurrection of Jesus was about a vision of a dead man who began the general resurrection, but it was not valid historically; it was an apparition.
- To know the exact sequence of what happened at the end of Jesus's life, the criterion of historicity of multiple attestation must be affirmed, even though criteria of historicity have created no consensus among scholars, and the criteria are weak and vague.

The Jesus Seminar's warning, endorsed by Crossan as a prominent fellow of the Seminar, is: "Beware of finding a Jesus entirely congenial to you."[274] Could this also apply to the Jesus Seminar's view of Jesus?

In articulating their seven presuppositions of scholarly wisdom, the Jesus Seminar uses language that includes these presuppositional triggers:[275]

- *Factives*: "The gospel writers overlaid the tradition," "the Jesus of the gospels is an imaginative theological construct."
- *Aspectual verbs*: "two pillars were now in place," "was the identification of."
- *Intonation*: "consists of the recognition of the fundamental contrast" of oral and print cultures.
- *Projection*: "Supports the edifice of contemporary gospel scholarship," "is embellished by mythic elements . . . and by plausible fictions that enhance the telling of the gospel story."

Therefore, presuppositional intonation concludes: the assumptions of the historical-critical method are one of the fundamentals in understanding Crossan's and the Jesus Seminar's views of the historical Jesus.

---

274. Funk et al., *Five Gospels*, 5.
275. Funk et al., *Five Gospels*, 3–5.

SUMMARY OF CHAPTER 3

There was an introduction to the need for use of methodology in many disciplines. It was shown the most suitable method is hypothesis testing for historical data. This involves choosing a null hypothesis (H_O), based on the data from the scholar being examined. Then, an alternate hypothesis (H_A) is proposed to test the data, created by the researcher. This will be applied to Crossan's data, with one hypothesis tested later in this book.

Presuppositions were defined and criteria for isolation of presuppositions were indicated. The model chosen by Beaver et al. demonstrates how any researcher can choose more objective measures to isolate presuppositional triggers.[276] Examples were shown from Crossan's writings of the regular use of diverse presuppositional triggers.

One of the challenges to be addressed is Crossan's view that the Gospels in the New Testament are nonhistorical documents. This analysis will be examined in the next chapter.

Crossan places the Gospel of Peter in the early first stratum of AD 30–60. It was asserted by me that it is a second-century document depending on the canonical books for some content. This has to be demonstrated with evidence.

---

276. Beaver et al., "Presupposition."

FOUR

Third Crossan Lesson

The best context for locating Jesus is through text-based historical inquiry and not through sociological analysis.[1]

HOW TO RECOGNIZE HISTORY IN THE NEW TESTAMENT TEXTS

Some of the primary challenges to New Testament historicity come from the association of the Gospels with mythology and its various meanings, FC assessments, and postmodern reader-response theories. Remember some of the application points made in chapter 1. How will you respond if your teen comes home from youth group with the profound news that the Bible contains myths? "No, it doesn't," is not likely to satisfy the youth's announcement. You will need to give reasons (a defence), and this chapter should help.

The chapter will provide some of the main indices for assessing history in the NT.

THE GOSPELS AS MYTHOLOGY

What is myth when applied to the Gospels? Crossan asks of the death, burial, empty tomb, and post-resurrection appearances of Jesus: "Is this fact

---

1. Barnett, *Jesus and the Logic*, 164.

or fiction, history or mythology? Do fiction and mythology crowd closely around the end of the story just as they did around its beginning? And if there is fiction or mythology, on what is it based?" He answers that Jesus's burial by friends "was totally fictional and unhistorical"; and the burial, probably by enemies, was in a shallow grave accessed by "scavenging animals"; and the text has "fictional overlays" designed to hide information. Is what happened on Easter Sunday the story of one day or of several years? Is it the story of a single group of *all* Christians gathered, or is it "one group who claimed to be the whole"?[2] What presuppositions underlie this metaphorical understanding of the events of resurrection Sunday?

For Crossan, the Gospels as myth means that they are fictional and unhistorical. The birth of Jesus in Bethlehem, according to both Matthew and Luke, is "in mythology rather than history."[3] Jesus's burial is mythological fiction, and the Easter story is "so engraved in our imagination as factual history rather than fictional mythology."[4] In this regard, Marcus Borg offers a parallel to Crossan's explanation, where he uses the term myth not as untruth but as a story about God and human beings that can be true and powerful as a symbolic narrative that is unlike uncomplicated historical reports. Borg's statement of the Gospel myths is that "though not literally true, they can be really true; though not factually true, they can be actually true."[5] What puzzling language! Which presuppositions could Crossan and Borg, writing associates and fellows of the Jesus Seminar, be disguising with their use of semiotics rather than semantics?[6]

While John Rogerson admits the study of myth may be of advantage to biblical interpretation, he also acknowledges that the definition of myth has so many opinions that it is not possible to have one definition.[7] Since this assessment is accurate, John Oswalt rightly concludes that no further discussion is possible, as each person provides his or her own distinct definition with the multiplicity of meanings of myth. However, Oswalt concludes that it is possible to state that a myth is A and not B, based on the evidence.[8] There will be further discussion of Oswalt's assessment of myth later in the book.

2. Crossan, *Jesus*, 160 (emphasis in original).
3. Crossan, *Jesus*, 18.
4. Crossan, *Jesus*, 161.
5. Borg, *God We Never Knew*, 101.
6. Semiotics is "the study of the way in which people communicate through signs and symbols" ("Semiotics," in *MD*). Semantics is "the study of words and their meanings" ("Semantics," in *MD*).
7. Rogerson, "Slippery Words," 31.
8. Oswalt, *Bible among the Myths*, 31.

Crossan states that "possibly the key chapter" of his seminal publication, *The Historical Jesus*, is chapter 13, "Magic and Meal."[9] Here, he claims that "religion is official and approved magic"; that Jesus of Nazareth was a magician like Elijah, Elisha, Honi, and Hanina;[10] that he does not think he can distinguish miracle from magic; and that Jesus, as magician and miracle worker, was a "very problematic and controversial phenomenon."[11] How does this relate to myth? Crossan states that the Easter story at the end of Jesus's life, like the nativity at the beginning, is "so engraved on our imagination as factual history rather than fictional mythology."[12] For him, the miracle of Christ's resurrection is regarded as fictional mythology, as "Jesus' burial by his friends was unhistorical and the fiction was 'created to hide.' Therefore, what happened on that first Easter Sunday morning was not the story of one day but of several years, and instead was the story of all Christians gathered together as one group in Jerusalem or of one group that claimed to be the whole."[13] In addition, Crossan regards Jesus's resurrection as an apparition.

Mack uses the term myth in two senses: the first as a created invention[14] and the second as an interpretation and denial of the supernatural events surrounding the symbols of Christ's crucifixion and resurrection, with the Gospels containing "too many miracles for comfort."[15] This demonstrates a presuppositional bias against the supernatural.

Wright supports the use of myth in the Gospels when it describes "foundational stories for the early Christian worldview," when mythological language is used, and when historians decode it as compared with other apocalyptic writings of that era.[16] His view is that the Gospels have this kind of mythological quality because of the underlying Jewish worldview. However, he does note that creational and covenantal monotheism "demands that actual history be the sphere" in which Israel's God reveals himself.

---

9. Crossan, *Historical Jesus*, xxix.

10. In "Jesus: Just Another Wonder-Worker?" Belief.net reports: "As the Mishnah relates, Honi got his name by bringing down miraculously huge quantities of rain during a time of drought. He first prayed to God, but when his prayer went unanswered he drew a circle on the ground and swore he would stand in it until rain fell." Josephus relates a brief version of this story in the *Antiquities*. This article added: 'Hanina was one of a category of wonder-workers called "men of deeds."'

11. Crossan, *Historical Jesus*, 305–6, 311.

12. Crossan, *Jesus*, 160–61.

13. Crossan, *Jesus*, 161.

14. Mack, *Lost Gospel*, 2–3.

15. Mack, *Lost Gospel*, 17.

16. Wright, *New Testament*, 426.

The Oxford English Dictionary defines the primary meaning of myth as to conform to the "foundational stories" of a worldview, "a traditional story, especially one concerning the early history of a people or explaining a natural or social phenomenon, and typically involving supernatural beings or events." However, I will not use myth in this book to refer to the foundational stories for any culture because of the supplementary meanings of myth that could lead to confusion, meanings such as:

(a) "A widely held but false belief or idea"

(b) "A misrepresentation of the truth"

(c) "A fictitious or imaginary person or thing"

(d) "An exaggerated or idealized conception of a person or thing"[17]

Crossan's use of fiction, mythology, legend, and magic in relation to the historical Jesus's resurrection will need to be investigated for possible presuppositional influence.

(A) Form Criticism and Historicity of the Gospels

Form criticism refers to the oral, pre-literary forms prior to the written biblical material. David Aune describes FC, based on the German term *Formgeschichte* (form history), as representing a critical method that was developed to "identify and analyse units of originally oral discourse" in texts of ancient Israel and early Christianity. With the Gospel texts, form critics attempt "to identify individual pericopes that may have had an oral origin." Then they assign "each form to a particular *Sitz im Leben* ('situation in life') in the early church."[18]

Crossan places SC, FC, and RC under the general heading of "*tradition-criticism* (or *transmissional analysis*)," and this "attempts to trace the genetic relationship and historical trajectory of large and small units of the tradition about Jesus." His conclusion is "I do not think, however, that we can *bypass* it."[19] Here he is referring to the necessity of the use of tradition criticism in Jesus studies. "I do not think" is a presuppositional trigger that needs to be investigated. Wright, in contrast, considers that the critical tool of FC needs to be bypassed in the search for Jesus and replaced with the method of hypothesis and verification.[20] Crossan objects to Wright's claim

---

17. "Myth," in *OED*.
18. Aune, *Blackwell Companion*, 140.
19. Crossan, *Birth of Christianity*, 97 (emphasis in original).
20. Wright, *Jesus*, 87.

that these procedures are illegitimate, and he accuses Wright of being "flatly incorrect."[21] Which presuppositions by Wright or Crossan can be supported? An accusation like this is of no value unless Crossan proves the "flatly incorrect" by providing evidence to confirm it.

Crossan describes FC as the search to find the forms in which oral units were transmitted and to correlate these forms "with the situations that produced and used them."[22] Wright notes that instead of "historical study of Jesus *via* the text" of the New Testament Gospels, the FC emphasis has given way to study of the communities presumed to stand behind the text who transmitted the traditions and to study of the evangelists.[23]

Within FC ranks, there is a tendency to deny or downplay the historicity of the Gospels. Soulen and Soulen note that FC's initial thrust "weakened the Gospels as historical sources for biography."[24] Meyer's view is that form critics may have "underestimated" the historical, literary, and theological worth of redactions and, in the process, could have "dismembered gospel traditions."[25] Wright notes that FC was not designed as a tool to discover more about the historical Jesus, but in the hands of FC exponents such as Bultmann, it was a tool to discover more about the early church.[26]

It is not one of the significant emphases of this project to include an assessment of FC and RC, but it will be necessary at certain points to pursue these methods, especially in light of Crossan's views about the resurrection tradition: "Mark created the empty tomb story just as he created the sleeping disciples in Gethsemane . . . . The empty tomb story is neither an early historical event nor a late legendary narrative but a deliberate Markan creation . . . . Mark created the empty tomb narrative to replace any risen apparition story as the conclusion of the gospel."[27]

(B) Reader-Response Theories of Gospel Interpretation

Thiselton, in his hermeneutical reflections on the New Testament, contends that two horizons are presented. By horizon, he means that, metaphorically, there are limits of thought to a given perspective. The goal of biblical

21. Crossan, *Birth of Christianity*, 97.
22. Crossan, *Birth of Christianity*, 97.
23. Wright, *New Testament*, 52–53 (emphasis in original).
24. Soulen and Soulen, *Handbook of Biblical Criticism*, 63.
25. Meyer, *Aims of Jesus*, 112.
26. Wright, *New Testament*, 420.
27. Crossan, "Historical Jesus as Risen Lord," 11–12, 16.

hermeneutics, he states, is "to bring about an active and meaningful engagement between the interpreter and text, in such a way that the interpreter's own horizon is re-shaped and enlarged." He sees this as parallel to Gadamer's goal of hermeneutics as the fusion of horizons. Thiselton regards the two horizons as "separate but close" and acknowledges that "the most distinctive contribution" of his 1980 publication involves the work of Heidegger, Bultmann, Gadamer, and Wittgenstein especially.[28] However, his aim is "not to impose certain philosophical categories onto the biblical text," and "the distinctive horizon of the text must be respected and differentiated . . . from the horizon of the interpreter.[29]

While deconstruction is associated with Derrida's postmodern philosophy and Derrida acknowledges his indebtedness to Heidegger,[30] Bartholomew recognizes Paul de Man as another major figure in deconstruction philosophy and that the roots of deconstruction were in the soil of phenomenology, structuralism, Derrida and Nietzsche.[31] Brian Ingraffia regards Nietzsche, Heidegger, and Derrida as "the three figures I consider to be the founders of postmodern theory."[32] He seeks "to separate the God of the Bible from the god of the philosophers" and sees "the confusion between these two Gods which has caused Christianity to be uncritically equated with ontotheology."[33] Ingraffia considers that this quotation from Heidegger should be placed as an epitaph over all attempts to "use metaphysical concepts to articulate the faith":[34] "Only epochs which no longer fully believe in the true greatness of the task of theology arrive at the disastrous notion that philosophy can help to provide a refurbished theology if not a substitute for theology, which will satisfy the needs and tastes of time."[35]

28. Thiselton, *Two Horizons*, xix.

29. Thiselton, *Two Horizons*, xx.

30. Derrida, *Ear of the Other*, 86–87.

31. Bartholomew, "Deconstruction," 163. David Smith defines phenomenology as the philosophical movement that studies the structures of human experience through the phenomena or appearance of things as they are. It studies experience from the subjective point of view (Smith, "Phenomenology"). Bruce Benson describes structuralism as "the view that meaning in language and culture is based upon internal relations within the linguistic or cultural system as a whole" and not substantially from outside of the system. It can be applied to cultural phenomena such as language, individual texts, and practices in society (Benson, "Structuralism").

32. Ingraffia, *Postmodern Theory*, 14.

33. Ingraffia, *Postmodern Theory*, 14. Westphal defines onto-theology as "*the affirmation and articulation of the Highest Being, who is the ultimate explanation of the whole of being*" (Westphal, "Onto-Theology," 548 [emphasis in original]).

34. Ingraffia, *Postmodern Theory*, 236.

35. Heidegger, *Introduction to Metaphysics*, 7.

Ingraffia's conclusion is that this statement by Heidegger can be applied with accuracy to the ontotheologies of the postmodern theories of Nietzsche, Derrida, and Heidegger. Yet Heidegger can seek an application by alluding to the apostle Paul for Paul's rejection of worldly philosophy: "For the original Christian faith philosophy is foolishness."[36] Ingraffia concludes that ontotheology is humanity's attempt "to think its way to God."[37] Elsewhere, he states ontotheology "is always the result of humanity's attempt to formulate an understanding of god rather than the result of God's revelation towards us."[38]

Crossan writes of "the necessity of a break-out from ontotheology."[39] However, could Crossan's postmodern theology be a variety of ontotheology, if compared with biblical theology, when Crossan makes statements such as these?

1. "I argue, above all, that the structure of a Christianity will always be: *this is how we see Jesus-then as Christ-now*. Christianity must repeatedly, generation after generation, make its best historical judgment about who Jesus was then and, on that basis, decide what that reconstruction means as *Christ* now."

2. "There is not in my work any presumption that the historical Jesus or earliest Christianity is something you get once and for all forever."[40]

In my understanding, ontotheology is an academic term for what my fellow Aussies call "secular" Christianity or generic, liberal, modernist Christianity.

Crossan understands postmodernism as the past and the present interacting "with one another, each changing and challenging the other and the ideal is an absolutely fair and equal reaction between one another."[41] For him, "as a Christian," he believes "in the Word of God, not in the words of specific papyri or the votes of specific committees. But fact and faith, history and theology intertwine together in that process and cannot ever be totally separated."[42]

---

36. Heidegger, *Introduction to Metaphysics*, 7.
37. Ingraffia, *Postmodern Theory*, 236–37.
38. Ingraffia, *Postmodern Theory*, 4.
39. As cited in Kendall and O'Collins, *Resurrection*, 285.
40. Crossan, *Birth of Christianity*, 45.
41. Crossan, *Birth of Christianity*, 42.
42. Crossan, *Birth of Christianity*, 46. The context of Crossan's statement refers to the compilation of a Greek New Testament such as the United Bible Societies text.

How does Crossan favor the New Testament as mythology, use of FC, and reader-response approaches to understanding? Some of Crossan's presuppositions underlying these issues will be pursued in this study.

Briefly, it is noted that Crossan believes that when Matthew and Luke stated that Jesus was born in Bethlehem, they were "in mythology rather than history";[43] "Jesus' burial by his friends was totally fictional and unhistorical";[44] and Jesus's baptism and passion are linked together mythologically.[45]

Crossan explains that FC "seeks to determine the forms in which oral units are transmitted and to correlate them with the situations that produced and used them."[46] The synthesis of forms, sources, and redactions relates to work done by scholars and presuppositions developed about the Gospels. His assessment is that "I do not think, however, that you can *bypass* it."[47] However, Wright's response is that normal critical tools such as FC "are being tacitly (and in my view rightly) bypassed in the search for Jesus" so that researchers can pursue a clear method that uses hypothesis and verification.[48] Wright accepts that there is a valid use of FC in the materials used in the synoptic Gospels.[49] Language such as "I do not think" is a presuppositional trigger of projection used by Crossan.

The use of metaphor as a reader-response interpretation is seen in Crossan's hermeneutics of narratives such as the Gerasene demoniac,[50] where an individual is cured, but "symbolism is also hard to miss or ignore," an example of the symbol being the "political dialectic between possessed individual and possessed society, between demonic microcosm and demonic macrocosm."[51] Which presuppositions could be driving this assessment?

THE GOSPELS AS HISTORICAL DOCUMENTS

How does one decide if documents from the past are historical? According to Barnett, the best context for locating Jesus is through text-based historical inquiry and not through sociological analysis, as the latter, although

43. Crossan, *Jesus*, 18.
44. Crossan, *Jesus*, 160.
45. Crossan, *Historical Jesus*, 234.
46. Crossan, *Birth of Christianity*, 97.
47. Crossan, *Birth of Christianity*, 97 (emphasis in original).
48. Wright, *Jesus and the Victory*, 87.
49. Wright, *New Testament*, 418–33.
50. Mark 5:1–17.
51. Crossan, *Historical Jesus*, 314–15.

useful, has limitations because of the historical distance from the first century until the present.[52] There also is a distance between the reader and the text, in that a reader's knowledge and environment may impact the reader's ability to read a text with understanding. Barnett rates the Gospels as "self-consciously historical." He writes that the New Testament is simultaneously theology, religion, and history.[53]

Wright argues that Christianity is committed to history[54] but acknowledges that reading of texts and attempts to reconstruct history take place "within particular worldviews."[55]

Craig Evans provides this comparison of dates of origin of the New Testament Gospels and related sources:[56]

AD 60–70: Gospel of Mark
AD 75–80: Gospel of Luke, Acts, Gospel of Matthew
AD 90–95: Gospel of John
AD 120: Gospel of Egyptians, POxy 840, Gospel of Ebionites
AD 140: Gospel of Hebrews
AD 150: Apocryphon of James, Fayyum Fragment, POxy 1224
AD 160: Gospel of Mary
AD 170: Gospel of Peter
AD 180: PEgerton 2, Gospel of Thomas

The dates of origin for these sources have been contradicted by many scholars and will be assessed in a later chapter when evaluating Crossan's presuppositions that are influencing the dating of extracanonical and intracanonical material associated with the resurrection tradition.

THE MODEL HERE PURSUED

It is nonnegotiable that the New Testament Gospels are rooted in historical events that actually happened, according to Wright.[57] In this project, history will be examined by use of hypothesis and verification.[58]

52. Barnett, *Jesus and the Logic*, 164.
53. Barnett, *Jesus and the Logic*, 13.
54. Wright, *New Testament*, 137, 377–78.
55. Barnett, *Is New Testament History*, 137.
56. Evans, *Fabricating Jesus*, 54–55.
57. Wright, *New Testament*, 9.
58. Meyer, *Aims of Jesus*, 19, 72–73.

In assessing Crossan's deconstructionist presuppositions, it will be noted that history often involves evidence left by eyewitness testimony that incorporated Gospel (oral) tradition and interpretation.[59] This eyewitness testimony, although not the primary focus of this research, will be seen to be unsympathetic to the use of deconstruction that is used by a radical reader-response method.[60] It is acknowledged that the interpreter's "inner history" is involved in analyzing the natural causalities that are involved in history.[61] This study will use a critical realist epistemology.

While the Bible is not a textbook on history, "a historical impulse runs through the Bible and although not always evident in every place, this historical influence is 'nonetheless pervasive.'"[62]

Therefore, an eclectic historical model will be pursued that critically examines historical and nonhistorical presuppositions of scholars, using a hypothesis-verification methodology.

THE SPECIFIC METHODOLOGICAL TASK

The various contradictory conclusions concerning the historical Jesus are often related to the methods and presuppositions used by scholars. Crossan notes that "when I finally published *The Historical Jesus* in 1991, I intended not just to present another reconstruction of Jesus but to inaugurate a full-blown debate on methodology among my peers,"[63] but such did not happen, in his view. Which presuppositions influenced Crossan's choice of methodology?

Wright, in his chapter on "Easter and History," develops his own extended treatment of a historical method used to historically evaluate Christ's resurrection.[64] He admits that his method is in contrast to that of Crossan,[65] who states, "Emmaus never happened; Emmaus always happens."[66] Wright regards this kind of statement as "a typical combination of provocative denial and winsome appeal" that is a summary of what is happening in scholarship and other circles. This promotes the view that the resurrection stories in the Gospels and especially those in Luke "have nothing to

---

59. Byrskog, *Story as History*, 252, 305.
60. See Vanhoozer, *First Theology*, 259.
61. Niebuhr, *Resurrection and Historical Reason*, 127.
62. Long, "Generating Hope," 57.
63. Crossan, *Birth of Christianity*, 139.
64. Wright, *Resurrection of the Son*, 686–718.
65. Wright, *Resurrection of the Son*, 656.
66. Crossan, *Jesus*, 197.

do with things that actually took place in the real world of space and time," but they have "everything to do with what goes on in an invisible reality," that Jesus is "alive" in some kind of sense, the tomb is empty, and the believers are strengthened because they experience Jesus.[67] Wright considers Luke himself would not have agreed with Crossan's judgment.[68] Rather, the resurrection was an event that Luke presented that was a surprise to the women,[69] the eleven,[70] Peter,[71] the two on the road,[72] and to the disciples in the upper room.[73] Wright states that Luke is resolute about "the bodiliness of the risen Jesus," in that Acts 1:3 states that Jesus presented himself alive by "many convincing proofs," and this refutes any proposal that Jesus "was a phantom, a ghost or a hallucination."[74] Wright does not support Lüdemann's conclusion[75] that because dead people do not rise from the dead, therefore neither did Jesus.[76] With his affirmation of the evidence for the physicality of Jesus's risen body,[77] what are the essential elements in Wright's method for examining Christ's resurrection?

Two things are regarded by Wright as "historically secure" concerning Christ's resurrection:

1. the empty tomb and
2. the meetings of people with the risen Christ.[78]

Wright concludes that the "the kind of proof which historians normally accept" for the tomb-plus-appearances presents a combination for early Christian belief that "is as watertight as one is likely to find."[79] The way to disprove this evidence, he says, is to declare a priori that every piece of evidence about early Christianity is "a late fiction."[80] Conversely, Wright concludes historians of various persuasions have no options but to affirm

67. Wright, *Resurrection of the Son*, 656.
68. Wright, *Resurrection of the Son*, 657.
69. Luke 24:1–8.
70. Luke 24:9–11.
71. Luke 24:12.
72. Luke 24:13–35.
73. Luke 24:37, 41.
74. Wright, *Resurrection of the Son*, 657.
75. Lüdemann, *Resurrection of Jesus*.
76. Wright, *Resurrection of the Son*, 685n2.
77. Wright, *Resurrection of the Son*, 658.
78. Wright, *Resurrection of the Son*, 686.
79. Wright, *Resurrection of the Son*, 707.
80. Wright, *Resurrection of the Son*, 708.

that the empty tomb-appearances scenarios deal with real and significant events that are "provable events" about which historians can write, using the double similarity and double dissimilarity criteria (to Judaism on the one hand and early Christianity on the other) for methodological control.[81]

Wright's historical method led him to this understanding: "*The fact that dead people do not ordinarily rise is itself part of early Christian belief, not an objection to it.*"[82] In the resurrection debate, he regards the scholarly view that Christ's resurrection was "the work of the early church" as equivalent to the "mad scientist" hypothesis.[83]

In this study, Crossan's historical Jesus reconstructions are assessed with reference to Ricoeur, Derrida, Rorty, Poirier, Wright (who advocates a critical realist epistemology),[84] Hengel, Koester, Barnett, Bauckham, Vanhoozer, and others. Vanhoozer asks, "Is there a meaning in this text?"[85] in his critique of postmodern epistemology and its influences on historiography, which also requires an examination of extracanonical writings and canonicity. Wright operates within a form of critical realism, which is "a way of describing the process of 'knowing' that acknowledges the reality of the thing known, as something other than the knower (hence realism), whilst also fully acknowledging that the only access we have to this reality lies along the spiralling path of appropriate dialogue or conversation between the knower and thing known (hence critical)."[86]

That is the epistemology adopted by this researcher as well, because it makes the most sense of my world. This study adopts Meyer's perspective that one of the main questions to be addressed in a historical Jesus inquiry is whether the data of the intracanonical Gospels alone are the data for determining the nature of the historical Jesus, or are the data of extracanonical material needed to gain an accurate picture?[87] Meyer believes that scholars must be repeatedly asking, "Is this a potential datum on Jesus?" Which

---

81. Stories such as the resurrection "make the sense they make within first-century Judaism (similarity), but nobody within first-century Judaism was expecting anything like this (dissimilarity)" (Wright, *Resurrection of the Son*, 709).

82. Wright, *Resurrection of the Son*, 712 (emphasis in original).

83. Wright, *Resurrection of the Son*, 716–17. According to the OED, the mad scientist is "a scientist who is mad or eccentric, especially so as to be dangerous or evil: a stock figure of melodramatic horror stories; frequently attributive" ("Mad Scientist").

84. Critical realism "is a way of describing the process of 'knowing' that acknowledges the *reality of the thing known* (hence 'critical')" (Wright, *New Testament*, 35).

85. Vanhoozer, *Is There a Meaning*.

86. Wright, *New Testament*, 35.

87. Meyer, *Aims of Jesus*, 81.

criteria legitimately determine the data used for Crossan's historical Jesus inquiry?

Were the data of the stratification created and edited by the early church, or were they received from eyewitnesses? Is one of Crossan's presuppositional issues associated with his sociological Jesus whose historicity cannot be assured through historical investigation, including that of eyewitnesses?

To answer these questions, the following methodology will be pursued that critically relies on Meyer.[88] Wright regards Meyer's work as one of the best statements on historical method by a New Testament scholar.[89] Meyer agues that "critical history has been unambitious and ambitious history," but there have been some uncritical dimensions to historical study. He names Straussan followers such as William Wrede and Bultmann as not pursuing a reconstruction of history and concludes that "the fearless hypotheses of a Reimarus or a Schweitzer collapse like playing cards."[90]

Meyer judges that historians have divergent presuppositions and methods for interpretation and explanation of historical events and that to understand history, it must be considered not as event but as knowledge of event, with insights into history's actuality and meaning.[91] When measured by the scales of the New Testament Gospels, Meyer concludes that the quest for its historical duration "has been fundamentally if unintentionally un-Christian."[92] Since Meyer's original publication of this work was in 1979, and he died in 1995, would his assessment of the last thirty years of the quest's scholarship receive a more positive Christian appraisal? The evidence from the New Questers would indicate otherwise. This study will pursue the divergent presuppositions used by Crossan in arriving at his conclusions concerning the resurrection accounts of the New Testament. Could Crossan be pursuing unintentionally un-Christian assumptions?

INTERPRETATION AND EXPLANATION

Meyer gives a critical analysis of the integration of history, interpretation, and explanation.[93] He uses interpretation to indicate "mediation of meaning," and meaning relates to the subject's (author's) intention to

88. Meyer, *Aims of Jesus*, 76–110.
89. Wright, *New Testament*, 98n32.
90. Meyer, *Aims of Jesus*, 24.
91. Meyer, *Aims of Jesus*, 76.
92. Meyer, *Aims of Jesus*, 56.
93. Meyer, *Aims of Jesus*, 76–81.

communicate.⁹⁴ Meaning may need to be mediated if, say, there is a language gap between the author and the audience. This gap may include various linguistic, cultural, and time zone usage, but whether the subject be Plato, Caesar, Jesus, or Crossan, this study seeks to clarify which presuppositions are influencing the movement by Crossan away from the Jesus of history to the Jesus of metaphor and sociology, especially as applied to Jesus's resurrection.

Meyer explains that for interpretation to be more comprehensive, other tools may need to be used, as historical agents were not always engaged in autopsy. Some linguistic tools may be needed to engage with the data to explain "an ulterior task" in historical interpretation.⁹⁵ Historians also need to be aware of some unpredictable events that may develop in the boundary between intention and happenings in the midst of the event. The intention of a cocktail party may satisfy the expectation of all concerned, but when this social event unfolds, elements of irregularity may transpire. Similar situations may unfold in events of history. Therefore, meaning may be impacted by various intentions. Could Crossan be disinterested in the world of historical events because of a priori commitments?

The question of why is not answered through historical interpretation but may be discovered through "historical explanation" obtained through historical criticism, involving "pure exegesis," inductive meaning of the text, and consideration of historical context.⁹⁶ The aims of this criticism, in order to arrive at a successful outcome, involve control of data and establishment of facts.

Meyer admits that while the historical method may have parallels with the scientific method, there are divergences, such as with scientists who often do not need to include considerations of times and places, which are important elements in historical investigation.⁹⁷

Empirical science aims for abstract "invariant correlations" as it commences with "concrete data." For historians, however, their aims are to pursue concrete variables through their generalizations. Meyer notes that "history, pre-critical, critical, or 'scientific,' lacks the distinctive note of science, the quest of invariants."⁹⁸ Thus, interpretation and explanation in

---

94. Meyer, *Aims of Jesus*, 76–77.

95. Meyer, *Aims of Jesus*, 77–78. Autopsy means "a critical examination, evaluation, or assessment of someone or something past" ("Autopsy," in *M-WD*).

96. Meyer, *Aims of Jesus*, 78.

97. Meyer, *Aims of Jesus*, 79.

98. Meyer, *Aims of Jesus*, 79.

history do not relate to new proposals but deal with the aims of historians. Such aims include:

1. the history of human actions,
2. the purpose of human actions, and
3. the interaction of purposes with the instruments used. Historical interpretation functions as it relates to explanation, but actions and interactions can also reveal intentions that need to be tested.

Interpretation and explanation reveal historical unknowns for which a known is sought. Meyer rightly sees "the 'critical' phase of history" as precisely "the structured process of finding answers to questions aimed at interpretation and explanation." However, he also sees the historian's "own encounters with the answers" as "a metacritical phase" in which the historian listens and learns through "dialogical reactions, insights, and judgments," thus going beyond the principles of historical criticism.[99] Is Crossan interested in examining the intention of the biblical authors, or do his postmodern suppositions prevent such an investigation?

To obtain knowledge through choosing certain unknowns, Meyer correctly demonstrates that the historian asks questions to convert unknowns into knowns.[100] This is through using the sequence of question, hypothesis, and verification. Verification is used in history in the wider sense of cross-checking. This cross-checking will involve a movement between knowns and unknowns. In critical history, verification operates in combination with controlling the data and establishing the facts (see below). Controlling the data is not an a priori designation but a final achievement. The data to be used will not be obvious until the hypotheses are formed.

CONTROLLING THE DATA[101]

For guidelines on how to control the data in historical inquiry, Meyer provides these valuable pointers.[102] The quest is to discern answers to questions, using unknowns to define knowns. Data for this project will not be understood until this study is complete. The question before us for this

---

99. Meyer, *Aims of Jesus*, 79–80. Metacriticism asks: "*Can we critically rank the different criteria by which we judge what counts as meaningful or productive effects of texts within this or that context in life?*" (Thiselton, *New Horizons*, 6, emphasis in the original).

100. Meyer, *Aims of Jesus*, 80.

101. This heading is used by Meyer, *Aims of Jesus*, 81.

102. Meyer, *Aims of Jesus*, 81–87.

study is whether or not the data of the four Gospels of the New Testament are the only data on Jesus for the resurrection tradition or whether there are extracanonical data to consider. Control of data requires assessment on whether intracanonical and extracanonical literature refer to the Jesus of history (the past). The constant question before the historian is: "Is this a potential datum on Jesus?"[103]

One of the questions is to determine whether the New Testament Gospels and other literature being examined by Crossan to form a picture of the historical Jesus's resurrection tradition is a use of legitimate historical method or is so influenced by Crossan's presuppositions that the New Testament Gospel authors cannot be heard as they were intended.

Meyer's concern is that Gospel literature is "stamped by the confessional concerns of the church" but also that it "was created by the church" to meet the church's concerns. His view is that "the origin and character" of Gospel material must be understood "unless the materials run counter both to the Judaism of the time (a possible source for the church) and to the certainly ascertained tendencies of the church."[104]

The aim of the historical criticism of this study is to generate knowns from suppositions. Are the suppositions of Crossan's stratification model for the reconstruction of the historical Jesus's resurrection verified or not?

Another question to consider is why certain materials have been conserved in the New Testament Gospels and not the extracanonical material of later discoveries such as the Gospel of Thomas, the Gospel of Peter, the Egerton Gospel, and other extracanonical material.

Should extracanonical materials be placed on equal authority with canonical materials? Why has precedence been given to canonical material through the centuries, but some scholarship in the last century places extracanonical writings on an equal footing with intracanonical material?

It is Meyer's view that methodological skepticism has stifled historical investigation from the beginning. Independent verification follows the pattern of intention, being knowledgeable, and truthfulness. However, in biblical criticism, the factor of intention is sometimes indefinable, thus leading the critic to sometimes "concentrate on establishing oblique patterns of inference."[105] One of these oblique patterns has been the use of the "index of discontinuity" by which the historicity of a Jesus tradition is inferred by whether the tradition is "discontinuous with the tendencies of the community which transmits it." Meyer notes that this index is often used by the

---

103. Meyer, *Aims of Jesus*, 81.
104. Meyer, *Aims of Jesus*, 82.
105. Meyer, *Aims of Jesus*, 85.

methodological skeptic, but it can be used as a positive index for historicity. He prefers to call this "the index of originality," a prime example being Jesus's "consorting with publicans and sinners."[106]

ESTABLISHING THE FACTS[107]

Meyer states that there is no criterion of historicity proposed by the critics that "is invariably requisite to the inference of historicity." He prefers the use of the term index rather than criterion for establishing historicity, as the term index proposes a tendency of more modest proportions than the fixed understanding of criterion.[108]

In Crossan's inventory of the Jesus tradition, he places primary emphasis on the need for chronological stratification and independent attestation.[109] Again, the chronological strata are:

1. AD 30–60
2. AD 60–80
3. AD 80–120
4. AD 120–150

Crossan uses "a triple triadic process" that involves an interplay of social anthropology, Greco-Roman history, and the literature of specific sayings. At the literary level, he pays "acute sensitivity to the chronology of stratification, the multiplicity of [independent] attestation, and the interweaving of retention, mutation, and creation within the Jesus tradition."[110] He states one of his presuppositions: "I do presume that one should work in sequence through those strata and that proper method demands an emphasis on the primary stratum that no other stratum can claim."[111] The first stratum is AD 30–60, but the controversial nature of this stratum for Crossan is that he places extracanonical material at that early date, including the

---

106. Meyer, *Aims of Jesus*, 86.
107. This heading is from Meyer, *Aims of Jesus*, 87.
108. Meyer, *Aims of Jesus*, 86.
109. Crossan, *Historical Jesus*, 427–50.
110. Crossan, *Historical Jesus*, xxviii–xxix, xxxi.
111. Crossan, *Historical Jesus*, xxxii.

Gospel of Thomas I,[112] the Egerton Gospel,[113] the Gospel of the Hebrews,[114] Sayings Gospel Q,[115] and the Cross Gospel (in the Gospel of Peter).[116] He warns of the need to "tread very carefully" when there is only "a single independent source."[117]

Meyer considers "the logic of history" to be the organization of data to reach an interpretation and explanation. He objects to historians making their own mind the determinant of historical knowledge, especially when the historians are in "unfamiliar surroundings" and they fall back on "ready-made cognitional theories."[118] Isn't that what Crossan has done? Instead, Meyer favors the work of Collingwood, a historian and philosopher who redefined the way of searching for the historical unknowns by seeking the inside (the purpose) of an event and thus providing meaning and direction for that event. The event is a historical fact, and the facts emerge as the conclusion of an inquiry. Rational principles are used to infer the facts from the data.[119]

---

112. See Lambdin, "Gospel of Thomas."

113. "The Egerton Gospel is also known as Papyrus Egerton 2. It is known from an ancient manuscript that is rivaled only by the John Rylands fragment p52 in its antiquity. Ron Cameron states in his introduction in *The Other Gospels*, 'On paleographical grounds the papyrus has been assigned a date in the first half of the second century C.E. This makes it one of the two earliest preserved papyrus witnesses to the gospel tradition'" ("Egerton Gospel").

114. The Gospel of the Hebrews may have been known to Papias (a church writer who died ca. 130 CE, whose five-volume "Exegesis of the Sayings of the Lord" is now lost, preserved only in a few quotations in the writings of Eusebius). Hegesippus (late in the second century) and Eusebius (early in the fourth century) attest to the existence of this Gospel but do not quote from it. Fragments are preserved in the writings of Clement of Alexandria (late in the second century), Origen (early in the third century), and Cyril (bishop of Jerusalem, ca. 350 CE). Jerome (ca. 400 CE) also preserves several fragments, all of which he probably reproduced from the writings of Origen ("Gospel of the Hebrews").

115. Or, the text of Q, NRSV text, according to "Lost Sayings Gospel Q."

116. Crossan, *Historical Jesus*, 427–29. In *The Birth of Christianity*, Crossan re-iterates an emphasis on methodology in laying out his presuppositions about the Gospel texts as forming the basis for all of his other judgments about the historical Jesus and early Christianity. Among these are the existence of an early Cross Gospel reconstructed from the Gospel of Peter, as elaborated in his tome *The Cross That Spoke*, as well as his belief that the Gospel of John is dependent upon Mark. Crossan also explores the development of two different traditions from the historical Jesus, the Jerusalem tradition in which Jesus is believed to be the resurrected Christ, and the Q Gospel tradition in which Jesus is remembered as the founder of a way of life (Crossan, "Historical Jesus Theories").

117. Crossan, *Who Killed Jesus*, 22.

118. Meyer, *Aims of Jesus*, 87.

119. Collingwood, *Idea of History*.

Meyer agrees with Collingwood's emphasis that "for the historian there is no difference between discovering what happened and discovering why it happened."[120] Could this also be what Crossan attempts to do in his use of presuppositions, based on previous research?[121] Could one of Crossan's major presuppositional handicaps be that he uses his own mind as the determinant of historical knowledge? Could this be seen in his rejection of the Gospel accounts' descriptions of what happened with the empty tomb and the resurrection appearances? This study will attempt to identify and then verify or invalidate some of Crossan's presuppositions on this topic.

Wright affirms Collingwood's idea of history involving the study of what happened combined with "human intentionality."[122] This does not deny the importance of examining data at the beginning of an inquiry to specify the unknowns and set the boundaries for the investigation.

Meyer uses the example of Charles de Gaulle retiring from the presidency of the French Fifth Republic in 1969 as a datum of history, but "why it happened" is the unknown that needs to be converted into a known, thus becoming what Collingwood asserts as "historical fact."[123] This conclusion cannot be reached without an examination of the supply of data available to the historian. In the process of inquiry, data are critiqued to establish facts through the following principles of historical criticism.

HISTORY IS KNOWLEDGE[124]

It is Meyer's assessment that history is not a belief, but he uses the tools of question and hypothesis instead of accepting unquestioned authority.[125] This is in sympathy with the court practice of examining eyewitness testimony, not to provide truth but to examine the data. The advantage of the court hearing testimony is to increase the availability of data to be examined and not to rely on belief. In court, the data from the witness may become probable only if other particulars do not correlate with the witness's testimony. If a court cannot correlate eyewitness testimony with other data, the court may need to move to the next best conclusion of inference.

Meyer's view is that belief needs to be substituted by "supposition under remote control" in court, science, and, by analogy, in history. For

---

120. Meyer, *Aims of Jesus*, 84; cf. Collingwood, *Idea of History*, 176–204.
121. Crossan, *Birth of Christianity*, 96–120.
122. Wright, *New Testament*, 109.
123. Meyer, *Aims of Jesus*, 88.
124. This sentence is from Meyer, *Aims of Jesus*, 88.
125. Meyer, *Aims of Jesus*, 88–89.

history, he states the historian can always know what he is doing through seeking answers to good questions. This also means that the historian can know when he or she is pretending by supposition or belief. The historian is not functioning as a historical researcher when he or she "supposes the unverifiable" and thus is using supposition and belief instead of examining the data.[126] Is this analysis by Meyer coming close to an accurate assessment of Crossan's method? Is Crossan using supposition and belief to disguise an objective examination of data? Are Crossan's theological presuppositions examples of covering up pretension by supposition or belief instead of engaging in accurate examination of the historical data?

Wright affirms that "history . . . is real knowledge, of a particular sort" which studies "what happened" in the sense of "what physical events would a video camera have recorded," but it also studies "*human intentionality*,"[127] which, in Collingwood's language, involves looking at the "inside" of an event to try to discover what human beings involved in the event "were doing, wanted to do, or tried to do."[128] What physical events happened with the empty tomb and resurrection appearances? Crossan's contention is that Jesus's resurrection as resuscitation was a remote possibility but "meant communal resurrection . . . *within* the general resurrection," and it was not unique.[129]

Of those who went to the empty tomb, including the women,[130] Crossan is "not imagining these as historical but fictional units, as competing visualizations about priority and primacy."[131] Also, the stories, based on the empty tomb and appearances "tell nothing whatsoever about the origins of Christian *faith* but quite a lot about the origins of Christian *authority*. They tell us about power and leadership in the earliest Christian communities."[132] "Empty tomb stories and physical appearance stories are perfectly valid parables expressing that faith, akin in their own way to the Good Samaritan story."[133] However, Crossan explains that in the resurrection of Jesus, "Matthew created the story of the apparition of Jesus to the women to change Mark's negative ending into a more positive one."[134] Were

---

126. Meyer, *Aims of Jesus*, 89.
127. Wright, *New Testament*, 109 (emphasis in original).
128. Wright, *New Testament*, 109; see Collingwood, *Idea of History*.
129. Crossan, *Birth of Christianity*, 549 (emphasis in original).
130. See Matt 28:8–10; Luke 24:12; and John 21:1–2.
131. Crossan, *Jesus*, 187.
132. Crossan, *Jesus*, 190 (emphasis in original).
133. Crossan, *Who Killed Jesus*, 216.
134. Crossan, *Birth of Christianity*, 552.

there any uniquely physical events that took place in association with Jesus's empty tomb and the resurrection appearances?

HISTORICAL KNOWLEDGE IS INFERENTIAL[135]

For history, knowledge is mediated, thus remaining inferential.[136] Too often, the indices to historicity have roots in generalizations that are often implicit rather than explicit, an example being the inference "Men are not gratuitously self-contradictory." Inferences are not suppositions or intuitions but are communicable conclusions of history.[137]

Meyer asks a worthy question: "How can the historian know that what he calls a known is more than a guess?"[138] Insights are drawn from questions that have been squarely answered. When no further questions about data are pertinent, then the relevant questions have been answered and inferences can be drawn. There are irrelevant questions such as "But, what if . . .," and this question retreats from the available evidence.

Meyer affirms the value of the conditional syllogism "If A, then B. But A. Therefore B" that reveals the elements in the process of inference. The major and minor propositions permit the conclusion. The inference can be analyzed "in terms of conditioned/conditions," in which a true inference may have limited conditions. By this, Meyer means that truth does not depend on knowledge of all things but on knowledge of some things, requiring specific conditions for fulfilment. However, "historical relativism is not viable as a theory of knowledge."[139]

THE TECHNIQUE OF HISTORY IS THE HYPOTHESIS[140]

Since history revolves around the formation and resolution of certain questions to try to discern unknowns, the procedure for discovering the

---

135. This is a statement from Meyer, *Aims of Jesus*, 89.

136. Inferential is "characterized by or involving conclusions reached on the basis of evidence and reasoning" ("Inferential," in *OED*).

137. See Meyer, *Aims of Jesus*, 81–87.

138. Crossan, *Jesus*, 91.

139. Crossan, *Jesus*, 90. Historical relativism is "the theory that there can be no objective standard of historical truth, as the interpretation of data will be affected by subjective factors characteristic either of the historian or of the period in which the historian lives" ("Historical Relativism," in *OED*).

140. This sentence is from Meyer, *Aims of Jesus*, 90.

unknown is the technique of the hypothesis, which is quite different from discovering unknowns through exegesis.[141]

By contrast, Meyer notes that in the discipline of exegesis, the aims are to discover a writer's questions, data, and answers.[142] The process in understanding an exegetical document may be piecemeal, cumulative, and dialectical.[143] This could involve changing the structure of a hypothesis, partial confirmation of that hypothesis, and reconstructing a revised hypothesis, its presuppositions and other unintended consequences. The unknown in exegesis has been fixed in advance.

Meyer is convinced there is "a quantum leap" to the unknown when compared with exegesis.[144] In history, there is a different approach, in that the unknown comes from the historians' own questions. The answers to these questions from others provide historians with potential data from which they must choose. The historical hypothesis comes with the freedom for the researchers to select whatever unknowns they desire. "Data are dead until they become relevant to the uncovering of unknowns."[145] From a question to discover the unknown, a number of answers need to be considered and discerned. From the range of answers, selections are narrowed. This is the process of using the hypothesis to answer the unknown.

As applied to the quest for the historical Jesus, Meyer considers that it has foundered in two ways. Firstly, for Strauss, Wrede, and Bultmannians, "there were not enough knowns to support hypotheses"; and, secondly, for Reimarus, Holtzmann, and Schweitzer "there were hypotheses galore, but without control of their presupposed knowns."[146]

Wright supports the historical method's use of inquiry that proceeds by establishing hypotheses that need verification.[147] There are three requirements of a good hypothesis in any field:[148]

1. it must include the data,

2. its overall picture must be simple and coherent, and

---

141. Meyer, *Aims of Jesus*, 90.

142. Meyer, *Aims of Jesus*, 90.

143. Dialectical means "relating to the logical discussion of ideas and opinions" ("Dialectical," in *OED*).

144. Meyer, *Aims of Jesus*, 90–91.

145. Meyer, *Aims of Jesus*, 91.

146. Meyer, *Aims of Jesus*, 91.

147. Wright, *New Testament*, 98–104. A hypothesis is a "proposed explanation made on the basis of limited evidence as a starting point for further investigation" ("Hypothesis," in *OED*).

148. Wright, *New Testament*, 99–100.

3. the explanatory story needs to be fruitful in other related areas.

History, like other sciences, proceeds by the use of hypothesis and verification.

Crossan objects to Wright's version of the historical hypothesis.[149] Wright states that nobody would grumble about a book on Alexander the Great if the author harmonized a couple sources, as that would be his or her job, so that the data could produce a coherent, rather than a scattered, framework. Crossan's objection is that Wright's method of hypothesis and verification happens "without any prior judgments about sources and traditions."[150] Wright does write that the serious historian's task is not to reconstruct traditions about Jesus and place them in the history of the early church, but to advance serious historical hypotheses to see how relevant data about Jesus fit.[151] Wright admits this proposal may seem controversial in some quarters of the Third Quest, where he places himself, but he suggests that this is a common sense way of studying Jesus, by placing him with other figures of ancient history and using the same method of hypothesis and verification.[152]

Could Crossan's objection to Wright's method be harmonized with the development of hypotheses (needing verification) that involve investigation of data from sources and traditions? In harmony with this study, are hypotheses such as those possible to examine the nature of Jesus's resurrection? One hypothesis could be "It is valid to include the Gospel of Thomas I, the Gospel of the Hebrews, and the Cross Gospel (embedded in the Gospel of Peter) in the first stratum (AD 30–60) of an inventory of the Jesus tradition."[153] Another hypothesis could be "It is not valid to claim that Matthew created the story of the apparition of Jesus to the women."[154]

HYPOTHESES NEED VERIFICATION OR FALSIFICATION

The hypothesis poses the what or why questions for investigation. Meyer asserts that verification reflects on the questions of whether the hypotheses are true or false. However, the hypotheses and verification questions require a shift from one question to the other in the learning process. Hypotheses,

---

149. Crossan, *Birth of Christianity*, 98–101; Wright, *Jesus and the Victory*, 87–89.
150. Crossan, *Birth of Christianity*, 98.
151. Wright, *Jesus and the Victory*, 87–88.
152. Wright, *Jesus and the Victory*, 87.
153. See Crossan, *Historical Jesus*, 427–29.
154. Crossan, *Birth of Christianity*, 552.

when being refined, are reshaped by judgments that accept or reject some things. "As intelligent insights require judgments, so hypotheses require verification."[155]

How is it possible to conclude that a hypothesis has been verified? The mark of successful historians is that they know the strengths and weaknesses of their arguments. They can go beyond relevant, deduced evidence to secondary questions that remain unanswered.[156]

A pointer to successful verification is found, Meyer asserts, in defining the conditions of the hypothesis as fully as possible, provoked by asking why a historian is sure of the knowns, as they are a way for determining the relevant unknowns. "When all its conditions are known and known to be fulfilled, the hypothesis is invulnerably verified."[157]

This obtuse indicator may seem like a handicap because of the relativist's demand that "everything must be known for anything to be known." Meyer claims that when testing the facts of knowledge, this demand is self-defeating, as every hypothesis comes with limited conditions. There is another indicator that may act as an inhibitor, and that is a historian's understanding that within the limits of the question of the hypothesis, there will be further related questions that have not yet occurred to him or her. This may mean that other scholarly researchers make the hypothesis unassailable or reverse it. "Verification is invulnerable when no further pertinent questions arise."[158]

The problem investigated in this study is delimited to Crossan's presuppositions as they apply to his understanding of the resurrection accounts in extracanonical and intracanonical documents that are used. There also may be hermeneutical issues relating to the choice of documents and interpretation of those documents.

This proposal will be evaluated, arriving at a confirmation or disconfirmation of the hypothesis, through examination of the primary evidence provided by Crossan in his publications. The elements of the proposal will be evaluated by use of three interrelated criteria of truth: logical noncontrradiction, empirical adequacy, and existential viability.[159]

An inductive method will be used to analyze the particular data from Crossan's publications to determine his presuppositions, based on the

---

155. Meyer, *Aims of Jesus*, 91.
156. Meyer, *Aims of Jesus*, 91.
157. Meyer, *Aims of Jesus*, 92.
158. Meyer, *Aims of Jesus*, 92.
159. Lewis and Demarest, *Integrative Theology*, 1:25.

model by Beaver et al.[160] This study will use the inductive principle from the sciences, including theology, "that theory is to be determined by facts, and not facts by theory."[161] However, this inductive reasoning will yield probable conclusions and not absolute certainty, because "induction is always an argument by analogy."[162] For Lewis, the inductive method commences with a supposed "objective" mind that observes specific phenomena to infer "general conclusions with degrees of probability."[163] This is the reasoning of the scientific method, but differences need to be noted. One of these is that the historical enterprise needs to consider times and places that will influence the causes and conditions being examined. Meyer is correct in his analysis that the "structured process" of history is to discover answers to the interpretations and explanations of history.[164]

POTENTIAL PROBLEMS IN THE HYPOTHESIS-VERIFICATION PROCESS

Wright warns of some problems that may arise in working towards verification of a hypothesis.[165]

Firstly, "what precisely counts as inclusion of data" in reaching a verification?[166] Wright observes that hypotheses need to treat the evidence on its own terms, noting the genre and intention of the Gospels as contemporary examples of this need. In the "would-be historical reconstruction of Jesus," he considers that the "tools of thought and criticism" have too often been used in an indiscriminate way, such as dismissing the evidence for Jesus in the Gospels as a production of the early church. He emphasizes that "in history, it is *getting in the data* that really counts."[167] He questions whether it really counts as an example of "getting in the data" if one says this is a creation of the early church. It may be, but a workable hypothesis about this theory needs to be developed to support or refute this theory. It is his view that "such a story has not yet been suggested" and verified.

---

160. Beaver et al., "Presupposition."
161. Hodge, *Systematic Theology*, 1:14.
162. Geisler and Brooks, *Come, Let Us Reason*, 133.
163. Lewis, "Schaeffer's Apologetic Method," 70.
164. Meyer, *Aims of Jesus*, 78–79.
165. Wright, *New Testament*, 104–9.
166. Wright, *New Testament*, 105–6.
167. Wright, *New Testament*, 106 (emphasis in original).

Secondly, a potential problem can develop in "satisfying the criterion of simplicity."[168] Historians who like tidiness can inflict this desire on material when "history is not about tidiness, but, most often about the unrepeatable and the unlikely." Wright adds that "not all forms of simplicity are of equal value," but simplicity can count strongly in areas of human aims and motivation and "in *the continuity of the person*."[169] As an example, Wright raises several hypotheses that are promoted about Paul's thought. They achieve simplicity but at the expense of removing evidence by suggesting passages are self-contradictory, incoherent, or "glossing of old texts." How is one assured that the index of simplicity is satisfied? When striving for simplicity, historians can become guilty of striving for tidiness when such is not there because of the nature of the complexity of human beings. A person's "unusual or abnormal behaviour" calls for "special investigation and explanation." Because actions and events have consequences, looking for simplicity may help in assessing motivation for behavior taking a certain direction. However, with Jesus and Paul, the complexity of many hypotheses can lead to "major undoings" if there is not consistency of thought with the data supplied and the "promise of coherence with wider fields of study." Wright prefers the option of simplicity to a writer vacillating among decisions.[170]

Wright notes "a different sort of simplicity" that attracts some New Testament scholars but is "extremely questionable." A questionable hypothesis is one that claims that in the development of ideas, ideas moved from simplicity to complexity. But "this is just not true of ideas and how they work," as the simpler is more likely to develop after years of hard work in moving from the complex to the simple.[171]

Wright gives the example of F. C. Baur in the nineteenth century in his attempt at a simple, tidy solution of Jewish Christianity developing one way, Gentile Christianity developing another way, and the two combining to make early Catholicism.[172] He says that this scheme "fails as *history*" because of "the havoc it makes of the actual data—history simply does not seem to have moved like this, in neat unilinear patterns." Instead, there were regress, progress, and "downright change." There was not a simple and smooth observable development. He concludes that in trying to deal with a simple hypothesis, "the simplicity of Baur's idealist scheme was deceptive," because the time available for it to develop was "simply too short; there is

168. Wright, *New Testament*, 107–8.
169. Wright, *New Testament*, 107 (emphasis in original).
170. Wright, *New Testament*, 107–8.
171. Wright, *New Testament*, 108–9.
172. Wright, *New Testament*, 108.

too great a multitude of data" as the evidence for Jewish Christianity is late and for Gentile Christianity is very early, thus causing the theories of history-of-religions derivations to collapse. Wright warns that "there is a tidiness proper to full human life. There is also the tidiness of the graveyard."[173]

Thirdly, there is another potential problem with hypotheses and verification. This relates to the possibility that "there may be more than one possible hypothesis which fits the evidence," and this particularly applies when examining ancient history, as there is so little data with which to work.[174] Wright's view is that the theoretical possibility of two or more equally good solutions to a hypothesis is a problem with which most historians are able to grapple satisfactorily. As there often is too much information for one researcher "to hold *all* of the data in his or her head at the one time, we need each other."[175] Therefore, historians should welcome other researchers who draw to our attention the "bits of evidence we have overlooked" that lead to unnecessary complexities in hypotheses.

BEYOND CRITICISM[176]

When a researcher is interpreting and explaining the past when using the above methodology, Meyer contends that the end result is the obtaining of knowledge and perhaps wisdom. Historical explanation releases one from "imprisonment in routine," to present "a cure for the mindless worship of contemporaneity."[177] His view is that historical interpretation and explanation are "proximate and open goals" that "transcend historical criticism." It is a positivist illusion to think that facts speak for themselves. However, the historian's motives, values, and ulterior purposes are not controlled by history but by the historian's intellectual and moral being, thus amounting to meta-critical presuppositions.

---

173. Wright, *New Testament*, 109 (emphasis in original).
174. Wright, *New Testament*, 109.
175. Wright, *New Testament*, 109 (emphasis in original).
176. This heading is from Meyer, *Aims of Jesus*, 92.
177. Meyer, *Aims of Jesus*, 93.

AN EPISTEMOLOGY OF CRITICAL REALISM

It is Darrell Bock's view that a form of critical realism is helpful in the study of history and the historical method, because it assists in avoiding "many of the pitfalls of more skeptical approaches."[178] This may be new language for you.

Critical realism is an epistemology in which, through the process of knowing, two aspects are acknowledged:

1. the thing known is distinct from the knower (hence "realism"), and
2. the only access to this reality is through "appropriate dialogue or conversation between the knower and the thing known (hence 'critical')."[179]

This means that there will be a critical reflection on the objects or products of inquiry into reality. Wright sketches the critical-realist epistemology in action:[180]

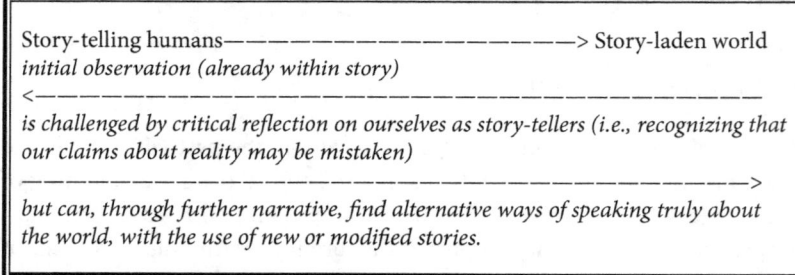

> Story-telling humans————————————> Story-laden world
> initial observation (already within story)
> <————————————————————————
> is challenged by critical reflection on ourselves as story-tellers (i.e., recognizing that our claims about reality may be mistaken)
> ————————————————————————>
> but can, through further narrative, find alternative ways of speaking truly about the world, with the use of new or modified stories.

Wright sees some similarities between critical realism and Paul Ricoeur's hermeneutic of suspicion and retrieval. Thiselton considers critical realism to be a slippery term, because it "denotes the belief that there is more to reality than what we perceive or know" and is a common sense acknowledgment that for finite human beings, "epistemology is unlikely to be necessarily co-extensive with ontology."[181] Wolfe's challenge is addressed by critical realism: "The crucial criticism of a belief system is not whether it involves faith, but if it can survive testing."[182] Critical realism encourages "cross-disciplinary integration, for the critical realist's configuration of truth has to remain open to further refinement by whatever tools are appropriate to the subject matter."[183]

178. Bock, *Studying the Historical Jesus*, 161.
179. Wright, *New Testament*, 35.
180. Wright, *New Testament*, 44.
181. Thiselton, *Concise Encyclopedia of Philosophy*, 253.
182. Wolfe, *Epistemology*, 72.
183. Moritz, "Critical Realism," 150.

Critical realism will be an important dimension of the epistemology adopted in this research.

CRITERIA OR INDICES FOR HISTORICAL METHOD

In this quest for evidence of historicity, Meyer's view is that it is necessary to have openness to "a scale of probability" in which "no method will be admitted to which caution, nuance, and the admission of doubt are alien."[184] However, his perspective is that the presence of these indices favors historicity, but their absence does not directly imply non-historicity. In developing his historiography, Meyer relies on some insights by Collingwood and Lonergan. Evans uses the term criterion, based on the Greek, as meaning judgment or a "basis for passing judgment."[185] Wright notes that there is currently significant debate among philosophers of science about the weight that should be attached to the various criteria used to establish verification or falsification of hypotheses in any field of study.[186] Also under discussion is the working out of what is considered adequate evidence for each index. These are important problems that need clarification. A balance is required to include the data but also to achieve verification by stating it with simplicity.

Blomberg calls into question a "major presupposition" that lies behind the pursuit of the criteria of authenticity. His issue is with the assumption that "the Gospel traditions are inherently suspect unless good reasons can be advanced for accepting them." He is convinced by the evidence that "excellent reasons" can be given to support the historical reliability of the Gospels, apart from presuppositions about the inspiration of Scripture. Blomberg's view is that instead of reverting to the criteria of authenticity, there should be an assumption of authenticity, and then one should "ask if there are good reasons for denying it (e.g., irreconcilably contradictory accounts)."[187] On this basis, problems in Gospel traditions are pursued critically and judgments given on an individual basis.

Bock does have a legitimate concern about naming such things "the criteria of authenticity,"[188] as this suggests a passing of tests to determine that historical events are authentic. Instead, these criteria should be seen

184. Meyer, *Aims of Jesus*, 84.
185. Evans, *Fabricating Jesus*, 47.
186. Wright, *New Testament*, 104.
187. Blomberg, "Form Criticism," 249.
188. Used by Evans, *Fabricating Jesus*, 46.

only as tests to help in arguing for a saying's authenticity, he contends, and not as "a necessary qualification to establish authenticity."[189] What are these indices of historicity? Here they will be prioritized and summarized.

PRIORITY OF INDICES

None of the following list of indices is given as a ranking estimate but as priorities given by some scholars.

- Kloppenborg lists his primary "criteria of authenticity" as: (1) dissimilarity, discontinuity, distinctiveness, or difference; (2) embarrassment; (3) multiple attestation; (4) coherence; and (5) historical plausibility.[190]
- Meier considers that the primary criteria for a disciplined historical method are: (1) embarrassment, (2) discontinuity, (3) multiple attestation, (4) coherence, and (5) rejection and execution.[191]
- Meyer states that the current indices of historicity include: (1) discontinuity, (2) originality, (3) personal idiom, (4) resistive form, (5) multiple attestation, (6) multiform attestation, and (7) Aramaic substratum.[192] Denton notes that Meyer in his publications "consistently prefers discontinuity, originality and multiple and multiform attestation" while maintaining the linguistic indices, especially the form of personal idiom.[193]
- Blomberg supports "four criteria of authenticity": (1) multiple attestation or forms, (2) Palestinian environment or language, (3) dissimilarity, and (4) coherence.[194]
- Evans considers the best criteria to be: (1) multiple attestation; (2) embarrassment; (3) dissimilarity; (4) Semitisms and Palestinian background; and (5) coherence or consistency, which he calls a "catch-all," because it relates to material that is consistent with data already judged as authentic.[195]

---

189. Bock, "Words of Jesus," 99n31.
190. Kloppenborg, "Sayings Gospel Q."
191. Meier, *Marginal Jew*, 1:168–77.
192. Meyer, *Aims of Jesus*, 87.
193. Denton, *Historiography and Hermeneutics*, 139.
194. Blomberg, *Historical Reliability of Gospels*, 247–48.
195. Evans, *Fabricating Jesus*, 48–51.

- For Bock, there are three "dominant criteria": (1) dissimilarity, (2) multiple attestation, and (3) coherence.[196]

Overall, the prominent indices of historicity are dissimilarity, multiple attestation, embarrassment, Semitisms and Palestinian environment, and coherence.

MAIN INDICES

Discontinuity or Dissimilarity

This means "historicity is inferred when a tradition about Jesus is discontinuous with the tendencies of the community which transmits it."[197] Meier defines discontinuity as a focus on Jesus's words or deeds "that either cannot be derived from the Judaism(s) of Jesus' time or from the early church."[198]

Wright prefers the term dissimilarity where historical Jesus data are similar to Judaism and the early Christian world but are also dissimilar. He states that the parable is an example of this criterion "as a retelling of Israel's story; but it also only makes sense as a profoundly subversive retelling of that story."[199]

The criterion of dissimilarity must be accompanied by the criterion of "double dissimilarity," according to Wright.[200] This occurs when something is credible within first-century Judaism, though "deeply subversive," and also credible "as the implied starting point (though not the exact replica) of something in later Christianity."[201] If there is not this kind of double dissimilarity, the historian cannot guarantee that the saying or deed originated with Jesus. The discontinuity with Judaism is called "the index of originality" by Meyer.[202]

---

196. Bock, "Words of Jesus," 90–94.

197. Meyer's assessment is that this differs from the index of the methodological skeptic in four ways: (1) it is not proposed as the only way to historicity, (2) it is an index and not a criterion, (3) it discerns between the contradictory and discontinuous, and (4) it desists in requiring that the data have a parallel in Judaism (*Aims of Jesus*, 86).

198. Meier, *Marginal Jew*, 1:5.

199. Wright, *Jesus*, 131–32.

200. Wright, *Jesus*, 132.

201. Evans claims that the criterion of dissimilarity is one of the most discussed today and is designed "to rule out sayings and deeds that may have originated in Jewish circles... or in early Christian circles" (*Fabricating Jesus*, 49–50).

202. Meyer, *Aims of Jesus*, 86. While the criterion of dissimilarity or discontinuity is supported by many historical Jesus scholars, there are some reasons to be somewhat skeptical of its use. Davids notes that for this criterion to support historical authenticity, two elements must be satisfied: (1) It must be dissimilar to Jewish tradition, including apocalyptic and rabbinic tradition, and (2) it should be discontinuous with

Theissen and Merz abandon the use of two criteria, as they are not convinced that dissimilarity and coherence (see below) are reliable criteria to separate the authentic from the inauthentic tradition of Jesus.[203]

Meyer considers that this index is evident with Jesus's use of Abba and amen.[204] He also discerns Gospel parables as a "royal road to authentic sayings-material"; they provide a foundation for assessing historicity of parallels.[205]

---

the post-Easter church's traditions. This includes the church's faith, practice, and life situation ("Tradition Criticism," 832). Theissen and Merz regard dissimilarity and its contrast with the Judaist background of Jesus as a means of undermining the Jewish features of Jesus's life (*Historical Jesus*, 115). Therefore, for them, an emphasis on dissimilarity will diminish the Jewish characteristics in Jesus's life.

203. Theissen and Merz, *Historical Jesus*, 115.

204. Meyer, *Aims of Jesus*, 86–87.

205. Examples would be:

(1) In the parable of the good Samaritan (Luke 10:25–37), Jesus chooses a person from a group that was regarded as unorthodox by the Jews. The parable was to demonstrate compassion from a person who unselfishly helped others. By choosing a Samaritan, Jesus is giving his audience an example that would be least likely to be attractive to them.

(2) In the parable of the mustard seed, Jesus uses an idiom or figure of speech of hyperbole. Jesus says, "It is like a grain of mustard seed, which, when sown on the ground, is the smallest of all the seeds on the earth" (Mark 4:31).

(3) In the parable of the prodigal son, Jesus uses an idiom that was common in everyday language for times of special occasions: "And bring the fattened calf and kill it, and let us eat and celebrate. For this my son was dead and is alive again; he was lost and is found. And they began to celebrate" (Luke 15:23–24).

(4) "He who has ears, let him hear" (Matt 13:9; Mark 4:9) at the conclusion of the parable of the sower was a characteristic personal idiom from Jesus (see also Matt 13:43 to conclude the parable of the weeds; also Mark 4:23; Luke 8:8; and 14:35).

(5) In the parable of the laborers in the vineyard (Matt 20:15), Jesus says, "Is it not lawful for me to do what I wish with my own things? Or is your eye evil because I am good?" (NKJV). The owner of the vineyard used the term "evil eye" when he questioned the workers about their complaints regarding his generosity. The idiom of the eye being evil is almost lost in Western society, but in the Hebrew language there was a relationship between the eyes and envy, covetousness and desire. The Hebrews used the phrase "your eye look grudgingly" (Deut 15:9); and in Prov 23:6 ("Do not eat the bread of a man who is stingy; do not desire his delicacies"), for "stingy," the ESV has the footnote "Hebrew: *whose eye is evil.*" Thus, the eye was seen as an avenue for envy, strife, and evil desires as a Hebrew idiom—also used by Jesus.

(6) Although it is not a parable, when Jesus is teaching on the cost of discipleship, he uses the idiom of exaggeration (hyperbole) when he states, "If anyone comes to me and does not hate father and mother, wife and children, brothers and sisters—yes, even their own life—such a person cannot be my disciple" (Luke 14:24).

MULTIPLE ATTESTATION

Evidence in multiple forms of data may indicate historicity, but it is not in itself a decisive index, because other indices such as originality or discontinuity may apply. For Meier, this criterion chooses Jesus's sayings or deeds that are located "in more than one independent literary source" and/or "more than one literary form or genre." Evans indicates that these independent sources could include the Synoptics and Q and that "a good amount of material that enjoys multiple attestation is itself a witness to the antiquity and unheard richness of our sources."[206]

The Jesus Seminar's fellows have a different view of the meaning of multiple attestations. They need to be "attested in two or more independent sources," and another is located in two different contexts independently circulated during an earlier period of early Christianity. With this limitation, each of the Gospels is not regarded as an independent source.[207]

EMBARRASSMENT

For Meier, this index "pinpoints Gospel material that would hardly have been invented by the early church, since such material created embarrassment or theological difficulty for the church even during the New Testament period."[208]

SEMITISMS AND PALESTINIAN ENVIRONMENT[209]

This is sometimes referred to as the Aramaic substratum.[210] Like multiple attestation, this is not a decisive indicator of historicity. The Semitisms refer to the observation of Aramaic or Semitic thought patterns and ancient tradition in the Gospels, particularly in Matthew and John.[211] A substratum refers to a different language that influences another language that replaces

---

206. Evans, *Fabricating Jesus*, 47–48.

207. Funk et al., *Five Gospels*, 26.

208. Meier, *Marginal Jew*, 1:5. Simply stated (Evans, *Fabricating Jesus*, 49), if it points to material that would have made the early church awkward or embarrassed, it is not what was created after the Easter event. An example could include the baptism of the sinless Jesus by John when John's baptism was for repentance of sins.

209. This phrase is my summary of Evans (*Fabricating Jesus*, 50). Semitic, of Semite, means "relating to, or constituting a subfamily of the Afro-Asiatic language family that includes Hebrew, Aramaic, Arabic, and Amharic" ("Semitic," in *M-WD*).

210. Meyer, *Aims of Jesus*, 87.

211. Evans, *Fabricating Jesus*, 50–51.

it. In the New Testament, this may be seen in Aramaic expressions in the Greek. Examples can be seen in:

- *Order of words.* Most Semitic languages tend to place the verb at the beginning of a sentence or clause. It can also be found in examples in New Testament Greek.[212]
- *Missing conjunctions.* When an expected conjunction is absent, known as *asyndeton* (Greek, "unconnected, loose"), many scholars indicate that this is divergent from the Greek language usage where Greek sentences are linked with a connecting particle.[213]
- *Coordination of clauses.* A sentence in classical Greek usually consisted of a main verb with other verbs in subordinate adverbial clauses of a variety of kinds. By contrast, the Hebrew language is disposed to place verbs alongside each other, joined by the Hebrew *waw* ("and"). Grammatically, this is called *parataxis* ("I set side by side").[214] This Hebrew pattern is found in Greek passages with καὶ ("and") joining verbs. See Mark 10:33–34 as an example.
- *Redundant pronouns.* The Hebrew relative pronoun does not have a gender and cannot be grammatically declined. Therefore, in the clause that follows, a personal pronoun is needed. There are a few New Testament passages that show this influence with an unnecessary pronoun after the relative pronoun. See Mark 7:25, which literally reads, "A woman *whose* little daughter *of her* was possessed by an unclean spirit." While such a structure can be found in Greek, it is native to Hebrew and Aramaic.

COHERENCE

Meier considers this criterion indicates historicity if Jesus's other sayings and deeds, discovered by use of the other criteria, fit in or cohere.[215] Crossan rejects this criterion, because, in his view, "it is subordinate to some or

---

212. These include the second part of the Magnificat (Luke 1:51–55), the place of imperative verbs in the Lord's Prayer (Matt 6:9–13), and the place of the verbs in 1 Tim 3:16 that has some qualities of a credal hymn.

213. This practice is seen especially in the Gospels and Acts. See examples in Matt 15:19, John 5:3, and Acts 20:17–35. This is explained as a Semitic influence.

214. For a fuller treatment of *parataxis*, see Marlowe's examples from J. B. Lightfoot's assessment of Semitisms in the New Testament (Marlowe, "J. B. Lightfoot"). Lightfoot's work was published in 1893 (see Lightfoot, *Biblical Essays*,144–46).

215. Meier, *Marginal Jew*, 1.5.

all of the others.[216] Evans sees a potential problem with this index because an assumption that something attributed to Jesus that is not supported by one or more of the above criteria does not necessarily make the statement inauthentic.[217]

OTHER INDICES

These include: (1) Resistive forms indicate traditions such as narrative, sayings, parable, and diverse strata in Mark, Luke, and John where historicity is indicated.[218] (2) Multiform attestation, which "is the recording of traditions in diverse forms" (e.g., narrative and sayings) and diverse strata.[219] Meyer does not find multiform attestation to be decisive by itself as seen in Aramaic substratum.[220] (3) Comprehensive plausibility combines different elements in Jesus's life that were a unique collection of Judaism and the origin of early Christianity.[221]

WARNINGS ABOUT AND OBJECTIONS TO THESE INDICES

Blomberg considers that the proper procedure for evaluating Gospel material is "to assume from the outset that its testimony is reliable" and then evaluate objections which may cause a change in assessment of the Gospels'

---

216. Crossan, *Birth of Christianity*, 144.

217. Evans, *Fabricating Jesus*, 51. Blomberg finds coherence to be "a very subjective concept." He presumes that in the minds of the evangelists, "all of the Gospel material cohered." He asks the legitimate question, "How is any modern scholar to say that apparent inconsistencies are sharp enough to call into question the truthfulness of accounts?" (Blomberg, "Form Criticism," 249).

218. Meyer, *Aims of Jesus*, 87.

219. Meyer, *Aims of Jesus*, 87.

220. This applies to "similar material attested in various forms" (Denton, *Historiography and Hermeneutics*, 139) such as the same material in saying, narrative, and parable. One of the Jesus Seminar's "rules of attestation" (Funk et al., *Five Gospels*, 26) is that "the same or similar content attested in two or more different forms has had a life of its own and therefore may stem from an old tradition." This is one of three criteria (e.g., multiple independent sources, multiple contexts, and multiple forms) used by the Jesus Seminar to isolate a body of sayings "on purely objective grounds." Examples include the parable of the sower in the Synoptics (Matt 13:1–9; Mark 4:1–12; Luke 8:4–10), which has another form in Gos. Thom. 9:1–5. The parable of the rich fool (Luke 12:12–21) is in a sayings form in Gos. Thom. 63:1–4. The parable of the great banquet (Luke 14:12–24) has another form in Gos. Thom. 64:1–12. There are multiforms between the parable of the wicked tenants and the vineyard (Luke 20:9–18 and Gos. Thom. 65:1–8).

221. Theissen and Winter, *Quest for Plausible Jesus*, 190.

contents. He objects to "much critical scholarship" for its inversion of this process "by assuming the Gospels to be unreliable unless powerful evidence can be brought forth in defence of specific passages or themes." This critical scholarship, by using these "stringent 'criteria of authenticity,'" leads to an acceptance of "a much smaller percentage of the Gospel material as authentic. Clearly much depends on one's starting point." Blomberg concludes that "critical scholarship is often *too* skeptical."[222]

Crossan acknowledges these criteria have been advocated for some time, but "their employment has not created any consensus on anything." This influences his questioning reaction: "Why have they not worked to create even the vestige of consensus so far?" He continues to ask whether any list of criteria represents a method: "Are criteria the *same* as method?" From this question, he asks of Meier's criteria:

1. "How are these criteria theoretically based?"

2. "How are these criteria operationally organized? Do you simply use now one, now the other; here this one, there that one?"

3. "Are these criteria publicly usable?" Crossan suggests that if a group of scholars applied these criteria to Gospel traditions, they would not come up with a common inventory as they had not up to the time of his publication, because "those criteria are too general, broad, or vague for common us." He does not consider *criteria*, no matter how good they are, to constitute *method* unless they can be included, based on some theoretical basis so that they can operate with application to everyone.[223]

Crossan sees the "weakness or vagueness" of these historical criteria "in Meier's interpretation of Jesus' eschatology," where Meier uses terms such as "in some way," "somehow," and, especially, "in some sense." Crossan asks: "Is it not part of an interpreter's job to define that 'somehow' as closely as possible and not simply to repeat, as if repetition were *somehow* explanation?"[224]

Evans considers that many skeptical scholars, with particular emphasis on prominent members of the Jesus Seminar, "go wrong" when they misapply a criterion such as dissimilarity and ignore or misunderstand other criteria such as Semitisms and Palestinian background. Part of Evans's critique of this skeptical view addresses the assumption that sayings and deeds of

---

222. Blomberg, *Historical Reliability of Gospels*, 246 (emphasis in original).
223. Crossan, *Birth of Christianity*, 144–45 (emphasis in original).
224. Crossan, *Birth of Christianity*, 145 (emphasis in original).

Jesus that are not endorsed by these criteria "must be judged as inauthentic." He finds that this "severe, sceptical method leads to limited results that can be badly skewed" if the starting points are "off-base and wrong-headed." He regards this as happening when the extracanonical and intracanonical Gospels are thrown into the same mix, resulting in a new level of distortion, as none of the five extracanonical Gospels "originated earlier than the middle of the second century."[225]

TWO DIVERGENT APPROACHES TO SOURCES FOR THE HISTORICAL JESUS

Mark Goodacre of Duke University (USA) acknowledges that the quest for the historical Jesus has been described as going in "phases" or "waves" that have become divisive and difficult in attempts to categorize them.[226] Elsewhere, Goodacre notes that this classification of the phases of the quest has become "a nightmare to teach" when he is trying to explain the nuances of "the third quest" to undergraduates. He particularly notes the progression in meaning that Wright has used since he coined the term third quest, the meaning of the term for others, and what Wright indicates when he currently uses the term. It is Goodacre's view that he would prefer the explanation "varieties" within contemporary Jesus scholarship, but he cannot go in that direction, because students will read Wright and hear of Wright's description of the third quest and another explanation from Meier who prefers to use the term third quest as referring "to all contemporary Jesus scholarship, without apology or reference to other usages of the term."[227] The phases of the quest, says Goodacre, are fascinating for research, but he finds it tough to teach with clarity.[228]

While Wright discusses historical phases of the quest, his view is that he does not believe the history of scholarship should be divided into "rigid 'periods' . . . except as heuristic aids to help us grasp currents of thought."[229]

---

225. Evans, *Fabricating Jesus*, 51–52.

226. Goodacre, "Quest to Digest Jesus." Biographical details for Dr. Mark Goodacre are available as of this writing at https://markgoodacre.org/bio.htm.

227. Goodacre seems to be referring to Meier's *Marginal Jew* (both vols).

228. Goodacre, "Jesus Seminar as Renewed."

229. Wright, *Jesus and the Victory*, 25. The *OED* gives the meaning of heuristic as "enabling someone to discover or learn something for themselves."

FROM THE OLD QUEST TO THE THIRD QUEST

For Wright, these heuristic historical aids for the quest are:

THE SIXTEENTH-CENTURY REFORMERS

He acknowledges that since the time of Schweitzer (*The Quest of the Historical Jesus*, first published 1906), it has been traditional to consider that the quest of the historical Jesus began with Reimarus (*Fragments*, first published posthumously from 1774 to 1778).[230] While affirming that "there is some truth in that," he considers that the "overall history of the subject" goes back much earlier to the Reformers.[231] Wright questions whether the Reformers' acceptance of the literal sense of the Gospels was able to help them to "worthwhile theological results" while they demonstrated "uncertainty about the value of the history of Jesus' life" in relation to their theology, including hermeneutics.[232]

THE OLD QUEST: REIMARUS TO SCHWEITZER[233]

Writing a biography of Jesus was a core reason for the research of members of the Old Quest of the historical Jesus. Schweitzer states that "before Reimarus, no one had attempted to form a historical conception of the life of Jesus."[234]

The intellectual environment that provided the impetus for the rise of the Old Quest was the Renaissance and the Enlightenment's age of reason.[235] This quest included Strauss, first published in 1835–1836, and his rationalistic, Hegelian philosophical emphases that discarded the miraculous in an a priori fashion. In addition, Ernest Renan offered the liberal life of Jesus in *La Vie de Jésus*, first published in 1863. While there were manifestations of the Old Quest in England, France, and the United States, "it was largely a German phenomenon," and its rise and demise can be attributed to German influence.[236]

---

230. Wright, *Jesus and the Victory*, 13–16. Reimarus's lifespan was AD 1694–1768 (Cairns, *Christianity through the Centuries*, 412).

231. Wright, *Jesus and the Victory*, 13.

232. Wright, *Jesus and the Victory*, 13, 16.

233. Wright's heading is "The Rise of the Critical Movement: From Reimarus to Schweitzer" (*Jesus and the Victory*, 16).

234. Schweitzer, *Quest of Historical Jesus*, 13.

235. Nelson, "Jesus Seminar's Search," 130–32.

236. Nelson notes that scholars have used Reimarus to mark "the beginning of the

Wrede's writing on the messianic secret in Mark's Gospel, first published in 1901, views Jesus as a Galilean teacher and prophet, while Mark's Gospel was theological fiction devised by the early church with an agenda divergent from Jesus' program.[237] Crossan acknowledges that this "First Quest lasted from Reimarus to Schweitzer, in round numbers from 1700 to 1900."[238]

No Quest to the New Quest: Schweitzer to Schillebeeckx

While Schweitzer's work was the turning point for the end of the Old Quest, Schweitzer provided an alternative that recoiled from history as a way to deal with Jesus. Wright states that Martin Kähler pointed in this direction with *The So-Called Historical Jesus* that was originally written in 1892. Kähler's criticism was against those who thought they could obtain "purely objective" history.[239]

During this period, 1906–1953, Bultmann discarded stories that affirmed Jesus as a historical figure and issued faith statements (appearing to be like stories of the historical Jesus) in an existential garb as he went in "quest for the kerygmatic church,"[240] thus making the Gospels to be "faith documents, not history-books.... History had nothing to do with faith."[241] Wright notes that during this era, Karl Barth's writings "ensured that little was done to advance genuine historical work on Jesus in the years between the wars."[242]

Old Quest even though they now recognize Reimarus' indebtedness to the writings of early English Deists, for example, John Toland, Matthew Tyndale, Peter Annet, Anthony Collins, and Thomas Woolston" ("Jesus Seminar's Search," 137–38n11).

237. Wright, *Jesus and the Victory*, 20. Beilby and Eddy also date the Old Quest from Reimarus to Schweitzer (AD 1778–1906) ("Quest for Historical Jesus," 11). The quest that ended with Schweitzer and included Strauss and Renan was labelled as the "so-called First (scholarly) Quest for the historical Jesus" by Witherington (*Jesus Quest*, 10).

238. Crossan, *Birth of Christianity*, 44. Nelson's research places the Jesus Seminar in parallel with the Old Quest: "Although the Jesus Seminar's quest is not identical to the Old Quest, the Old Quest clearly provides the closest analogy" (Nelson, "Jesus Seminar's Search," 137).

239. Wright, *Jesus and the Victory*, 21–25; Kähler, *So-Called Historical Jesus*.

240. *Kerygma* is from the Greek meaning "proclamation" or "preaching."

241. Wright, *Jesus and the Victory*, 22–23. Wright states that Bultmann's *Jesus and the Word* was originally published in 1926.

242. Wright, *Jesus and the Victory*, 22.

Schillebeeckx began his publications in the 1950s, but his major Christological works were the English writings of 1979 and 1980 in which Wright states that he builds on traditio-historical criticism in which the synoptics are regarded as providing evidence from the early Christian communities, and from this data, faith statements may emerge that provide glimpses of Jesus. Wright's view is that Schillebeeckx furnishes "the mirror-image of Bultmann's: the resurrection accounts are stories from Jesus' lifetime, brought forwards" and that Schillebeeckx makes the leap "from a purely historical Jesus to the incarnate Son of God," but this is not based on the main argument of my book.[243]

The New or Second Quest

While the Old Quest focussed on the biography of Jesus, the New or Second Quest concentrated on the words of Jesus. Meyer's language was that the New Quest "abandoned the quest for Jesus' biography," and its aim was "to define the continuity between Jesus and kerygma";[244] and Bornkamm's book was "to seek the history in the kerygma of the Gospels and the kerygma in this history."[245] Wright agrees that in the New Quest, attention was focussed on the "sayings of Jesus."[246]

He acknowledges Käsemann's lecture began a new phase, the New Quest, and that Bornkamm (*Jesus of Nazareth*, 1960) produced the "best known" of the books by the New Questers, which began with, "No one is any longer in the position to write a life of Jesus."[247]

Witherington[248] labels this the Second or New Quest and says that with the waning of existential philosophy and demise of Bultmann's influence,

---

243. Wright, *Jesus and the Victory*, 24. Beilby and Eddy chronicle "the (so-called) 'no quest' period," Schweitzer to Käsemann, from AD 1906–1953 ("Quest for Historical Jesus," 21). Witherington states, "The scholarly quest for the historical Jesus was assumed to be dead" until Käsemann's 1953 lecture to a gathering of Bultmann's former Marburg students, where Käsemann presented a view contrary to Bultmann's. He argued that the Gospel traditions were interpreted documents but "they could preserve authentic historical memories." Bultmann's skepticism was "too extreme" in Käsemann's view (Witherington, *Jesus Quest*, 11).

244. Meyer, *Aims of Historical Jesus*, 51.

245. Bornkamm, *Jesus of Nazareth*, 18.

246. Wright, *Jesus and the Victory*, 24.

247. Wright, *Jesus and the Victory*, 23–24.

248. Witherington, *Jesus Quest*, 11.

the Second Quest as a movement was "dead in the water by the early 1970s." However, Wright[249] regarded the New Quest as continuing in Germany with the collection of studies in Werner Kümmel (1985).[250] Crossan admitted that a Second or New Quest commenced with Käsemann as his reaction to Bultmann's historical Jesus' work.[251]

In this study, Crossan is understood as a dominant scholar in the Renewed New Quest (*The Historical Jesus*; *Jesus: A Revolutionary Biography*; *The Birth of Christianity*). Some have used another description for the New Quest—the Third Quest.

THE THIRD QUEST FOR THE HISTORICAL JESUS

Beilby and Eddy date the Third Quest from the 1980s to the present.[252] They acknowledge that the term Third Quest originated with an article by Wright, "Towards a Third Quest," and that the distinctions among various Quest designations are not always helpful and distinguishable.

Ben Witherington agrees with this chronology and contends that it was fuelled by new archaeological and manuscript data, methodological refinements, and renewed enthusiasm for historical research.[253] For him, the distinguishing features of the Third Quest include placing Jesus in his historical context (Galilee), a context that was illuminated by the Hellenized influence that included the social level of Jesus and his disciples, the absence or presence of synagogues and religious practices, taxation, and the shape of family structures, including the dominance of males. The Third Quest has been described by Sean Freyne as being "rapidly in danger of becoming the quest for the historical Galilee,"[254] because the assumption was that the more one could know about Galilee, the better one could understand the historical Jesus. The social, economic, and religious environments in

---

249. Wright, *Jesus and the Victory*, 25n53.

250. When Wright wrote in 1996, he maintained that the New Quest was not yet finished because "it would be silly to imagine that all scholars suddenly gave up on one kind of work and took up another," just as it was "silly" to gain the impression in Gospel scholarship in the twentieth century that suddenly "everyone" (i.e., every scholar) was doing form criticism, redaction criticism, or some other specialty (Wright, *Jesus of Nazareth*, 25). However, Wright affirmed that the main publications of the New Quest were "of little lasting value" (*Jesus of Nazareth*, 24). Beilby and Eddy place the New Quest in the period of 1953 to the 1970s ("Quest for Historical Jesus," 24).

251. Crossan, *Birth of Christianity*, 44.

252. Beilby and Eddy, "Quest for Historical Jesus," 28.

253. Witherington, *Jesus Quest*, 12–13.

254. Freyne, "Geography, Politics, and Economics," 76.

which Jesus lived are characteristics of the Third Quest and in some ways were a reaction to the Second Quest that was culturally distant in analyzing Jesus.[255] This means there is a strong emphasis on the Jewishness of Jesus in his first-century context, with a commitment to historical inquiry.[256]

Byrskog states that it is impossible to understand any social system without considering the "cultural heritage" of a given society.[257] Thus, historical investigation must include an examination of cultural relationships. For him, history is "an account of what people have done and said in the past," and he acknowledges this can involve "various kinds of biased, pragmatic and didactic features" in the writing of history. So, the "sense of history" is to be "defined as an interest in the past, seen as some sort of continuity, within a context of time."[258]

The "death of the author" is increasingly coming to center stage in biblical scholarship, and this issue raises the "problem of how to preserve and do justice to the authoritative textual witness," according to Vanhoozer.[259] Therefore, Vanhoozer opposes the postmodern, reader-response, deconstruction of the biblical text and wonders "what has happened to the 'about what' of discourse," which is the "question of reference to historical reality."[260] He pursued a similar emphasis in his earlier publication.[261]

While Crossan acknowledges Wright placed Crossan's scholarship in a "renewed 'New Quest,'" Crossan does not like the categorization of terms such as "search and quest," as they are "positivist delusions." He would prefer for Wright to put Crossan in a Third Quest and Wright and his group into a Fourth Quest that concludes that "the historical Jesus, like the Holy Grail, is to be found once and for all forever." Crossan's response is, "That is not how I see it."[262] As indicated above, Crossan has revealed his postmodern as-

---

255. Witherington, *Jesus Quest*, 14–15.

256. Witherington, *Jesus Quest*, 41. Bauckham acknowledges the serious problem of "naïve historical positivism" that the popular media present. His view is that "all history—meaning all that historians write, all historiography—is an inextricable combination of fact and interpretation, the empirically observable and the intuited or constructed meaning' and in the Gospels there is this unambiguous combination" (Bauckham, *Jesus and the Eyewitnesses*, 3).

257. Byrskog, *Story as History*, 43.

258. Byrskog, *Story as History*, 44.

259. Vanhoozer, *First Theology*, 258.

260. Vanhoozer, *First Theology*, 258.

261. Vanhoozer, *Is There a Meaning*.

262. Crossan, *Birth of Christianity*, 44.

sumptions that the historical Jesus of earliest Christianity is not "something you get once and for all forever."[263]

Crossan's point is valid regarding the Third and Fourth Quests. If this representation were followed, the quests would be:

- First Quest: Reimarus to Schweitzer
- No Quest: Schweitzer to Schillebeeckx
- Second Quest: Käsemann to 1970s
- Third Quest (Funk and the Jesus Seminar 1985—present, including Crossan)
- Fourth Quest (Wright and other scholars 1980s—present, emphasis on Jesus's Jewishness and historical inquiry)

The problem is complicated by Crossan's colleague Robert Funk who designates those in support of Crossan's Third Quest as "The ReNEWed Questers."[264] See *The Historical Jesus* and Gowler's assessment, *What Are They Saying about the Historical Jesus*. "The New Questers [of the Jesus Seminar] attempted to recover at least the message of Jesus in order to determine whether the intention of Jesus' words and the intention of early Christian preaching are coherent. Thus, Bultmann and the New Questers started with the sayings of Jesus, not the deeds, because their aim was to compare messages, not actions."[265]

Crossan's designation will not be pursued in this project, but his view will be that of the Renewed New Quest of the Third Quest. Thus, the Third Quest has two separate foci, those who follow Funk's model and those who pursue Wright's depiction.

Since Wright coined the term Third Quest, and he considers that he himself is a Third Quester,[266] what does he mean by the term? He emphasizes this is not a watertight compartment, but he uses it for heuristic value. Some Third Quest characteristics for Wright's model include:

A Real Attempt to Do History Seriously

Wright sees this as the pursuit of "historical truth" using a "serious historical method" instead of "the pseudo-historical use of home-made 'criteria.'" This

---

263. Crossan, *Birth of Christianity*, 45.
264. Funk, *Honest to Jesus*.
265. McGaughy, "Why Start with Sayings?"
266. Wright, *Jesus and the Victory*, 87.

means FC tools are being bypassed (rightly so, for Wright) and inquiry is proceeding by use of a clearly articulated method of hypothesis and verification. This is in opposition to the presupposition of FC that "the synoptic material could not be historical."[267]

Wright's stress on this historical method is stringent, as the Third Quest's design is not to reconstruct traditions about Jesus but to advance serious historical hypotheses and to examine "the *prima facie* relevant data to see how they fit."[268] For the Third Quest, Wright believes that new hypotheses must be proposed that are not based on "fixed point" assumptions from "the history of scholarship. All must be questioned." He admits the Renewed New Quest, and Crossan especially, "must be kept in mind throughout. But the essential argument must take place at a different level."[269]

The Gospels as Texts and Works of Literary Art

For Wright, scholars must move beyond what early redaction criticism conceived, and the Gospels must be seen as "works of literary art in their own right," but this does not denigrate their historical value.[270] The Gospel authors, especially among the Synoptics, "provide the bulk of the relevant source material," and they wrote about Jesus and not about their own church and theology. "They substantially succeeded in their intention."[271] This is in contrast to the Renewed New Quest where there needs to be "a large dose of skepticism about what can be learned from the gospels," according to Funk.[272]

In the Third Quest, Wright considers that "five major questions have emerged"[273] that need answering if progress is to be made in this quest and as the study of Jesus rejoins mainstream "historical work after drifting, for more years than was good for it," among methods and criteria.[274]

The Questions

These five questions are subdivisions of the major question:

267. Wright, *Jesus and the Victory*, 87.
268. Wright, *Jesus and the Victory*, 88.
269. Wright, "Christian Origins," 88.
270. Wright, *Jesus and the Victory*, 89.
271. Wright, *Jesus and the Victory*, 89.
272. Funk, *Honest to Jesus*, 300.
273. Wright, *Jesus and the Victory*, 89–113.
274. Wright, *Jesus and the Victory*, 89.

How do we account for the fact that by AD 110, there was a large and vigorous international movement, already showing considerable diversity whose founding myth (in a quite "neutral" sense) was a story about one Jesus of Nazareth, a figure of the recent past? How do we get . . . from the pluriform Judaism that existed within the Greco-Roman world of 10 BC to the pluriform Judaism and Christianity of AD 110—from (roughly) Herod the Great to Ignatius of Antioch?[275]

The five questions are:[276]

1. "How does Jesus fit into Judaism?"[277]
2. "What were Jesus' aims?"
3. "Why did Jesus die?"
4. "How and why did the early church begin?"
5. "Why are the Gospels what they are?"

These questions, when combined, form "a jigsaw of Jesus himself," which is a piece of "the larger jigsaw of the rise of Christianity as a whole." The five questions address Jesus's relation to Judaism and to the early church.[278]

Who are the scholars identified with the Third Quest?

IMPORTANT CONTRIBUTORS TO THE THIRD QUEST

By 1996, Wright had identified twenty writers whom he regards as "particularly important" contributors to the Third Quest, remembering that these are supporters of Wright's own view of Third Quest. These are, in chronological order: Caird (*Jesus and the Jewish Nation*, 1965), Brandon (*Jesus and the Zealots*, 1967), Betz (*What Do We Know about Jesus*, 1968), Hengel (*Was Jesus a Revolutionist*, 1971; *The Charismatic Leader*, 1981; *The Atonement*, 1981), Vermes (*Jesus, the Jew*, 1973; *Jesus and the World of Judaism*, 1983; *The Religion of Jesus the Jew*, 1993), Chilton ("Regnum Dei Deus Est," 1978; *The Galilean Rabbi and His Bible*, 1984; *The Temple of Jesus*, 1992), Meyer (*The Aims of Jesus*, 1979, 2002; *Christmas Father*, 1992; "Jesus Christ," 1992); Riches (*Jesus and the Transformation of Judaism*, 1980), Harvey (*Jesus*, 1982;

---

275. Wright, *Jesus and the Victory*, 90.
276. The following five questions appear in Wright, *Jesus and the Victory*, on pp. 91, 99, 106, 109, and 112, respectively.
277. Wright, *Jesus and the Victory*, 91.
278. Wright, *Jesus and the Victory*, 113.

Strenous Commands, 1990), Lohfink (*Jesus and Community*, 1984), Borg (*Holiness and Politics*, 1984; *Jesus: A New Vision*, 1987; *Meeting Jesus Again for the First Time*, 1994), Sanders (*Jesus and Judaism*, 1985; *The Historical Figure of Jesus*, 1993), Oakman (*Jesus and the Economic Questions of the Day*, 1986), Theissen (*The Shadow of a Galilean*, 1987), Horsley (*Jesus and the Spiral of Violence*, 1987), Freyne (*Galilee, Jesus and the Gospels*, 1988), Charlesworth (*Jesus within Judaism*, 1988), Witherington (*The Christology of Jesus*, 1990; *Jesus the Sage*, 1994; *The Jesus Quest*, 1995, 1997), Meier (*A Marginal Jew*, vols. 1 and 2, 1991 and 1994), and De Jonge (*The Servant-Messiah*, 1991). Wright acknowledges that these publications are very different from each other, but they are answering similar sets of questions to those pursued by the Third Quest.[279]

Thus, the two major emphases of the Third Quest are:

1. an investigation of the social and cultural milieu in which Jesus and the early church lived, and

2. historical method applied primarily to the New Testament Gospels and the rise of early Christianity.

The Renewed New Quest for the Historical Jesus

Coinciding with the Third Quest has been the emergence of another quest. This quest has been identified with the scholarship of the Jesus Seminar, a group of scholars called together in 1985. Hays notes in rather provocative language that it was "Funk's entrepreneurial venture, the Westar Institute," which involved a "self-selected group," some of whom are "fine scholars," but it "does not represent a balanced cross-section of scholarly opinion."[280] Hays's view was that the criteria for judgment that are employed in *The Five Gospels* by the Jesus Seminar "are highly questionable." The Jesus Seminar scholars use more restrained language: "At its inception in 1985, thirty scholars took up the challenge. Eventually more than two hundred professionally trained specialists, called fellows, joined the group" that met twice a year to debate technical papers and used colored beads "to indicate the degree of authenticity of Jesus' words."[281] Funk's language is that he "wrote to thirty colleagues" and asked them to join him "in collecting and analysing all the words and

---

279. Wright, *Jesus and the Victory*, 84.
280. Hays, "Corrected Jesus."
281. Funk et al., *Five Gospels*, 34.

deeds ascribed to Jesus in all the ancient sources up to about 300 C.E."²⁸²
These colleagues were asked to invite others to join the project.

How did it obtain the name of the Renewed New Quest? Funk is definite about how the labelling emerged. In the current quest, he says, there are "two categories of players." For one, he uses the sneering term of "pretend questers," and for the other, of which he is a member, "the 'reNEWed questers' (I capitalize NEW to indicate that the precursor of this quest was the new quest of the 1950s)."²⁸³ Scholars are assigned to either category by their answers to "three basic questions":

FIRST TEST: DO YOU DISTINGUISH BETWEEN THE HISTORICAL JESUS AND THE JESUS OF THE GOSPELS?

Funk's perspective was that if a quester did not want to make this distinction, then the scholar belonged to a rearguard action in "attempting to cover the retreat from orthodoxy." Renewed New Questers "seek to discriminate authentic from inauthentic material in the canonical gospels" relating to the sayings, parables, and deeds of Jesus.²⁸⁴ This material is categorized into:

1. that which stems from Jesus of Nazareth, and
2. material that belongs "to the overlay added by the gospel writers."

If a scholar is unwilling to acknowledge that there is material in the canonical Gospels that does not reflect the historical Jesus, that scholar is giving privilege to the Gospels because they are in the New Testament.²⁸⁵ Favoring the intracanonical Gospels is not one of the criteria for being a member of the Renewed Quest.

Crossan accepts that the fourfold Gospel record constitutes the literary problem of the Gospels, especially in light of the fact that over the last two hundred years of comparative work on the Gospels, Gospels have been found outside the New Testament, so that both the intra- and extracanonical sources must be considered in drawing a picture of the historical Jesus. His outlook means that the continuing presence of the risen Jesus and the experience of the Spirit "gave the transmitters of the Jesus tradition a creative

---

282. Funk, *Honest to Jesus*, 7.
283. Funk, *Honest to Jesus*, 64.
284. Funk, *Honest to Jesus*, 64.
285. Funk, *Honest to Jesus*, 64.

freedom" in writing Gospels that "are neither histories nor biographies" but are "good newses."[286]

This points to a presupposition that is underlying the Renewed Quest that will be examined in this book. Crossan admits there are presuppositions fundamental to this position and that some scholars have accused him of "fixing the evidence."[287] He refers to Luke Timothy Johnson who states that Crossan's inclusion of apocryphal and canonical writings on the same footing in the Jesus tradition "suggests that the game is fixed."[288] Johnson makes this allegation because of "Crossan's remarkably early dating for virtually all apocryphal materials," late dating of the canonical writings, and the assertion that the extracanonical are not affected by the canonical sources. Johnson's conclusion is that Crossan's assertions are "presumed, not proved." Johnson challenges Crossan's conclusions about the death of Christ, calling them "flawed," because Crossan tries to demonstrate that the Cross Gospel in the apocryphal Gospel of Peter is an early edition of the passion accounts. Johnson suspects that this is "textual prestidigitation" (sleight of hand, tricks).[289]

Funk requires that Renewed Quest scholars use a second criterion.[290]

The Second Test Concerns Sources

Which data are used? "If the quester is willing to employ sources other than the New Testament gospels, that scholar is engaged in the renewed quest" according to Funk.[291] If a scholar discredits extracanonical material, Funk believes that quester is "fighting a rearguard action" that is "probably clandestinely defending the canon," which was affirmed by a "decision of some ancient church body or council."[292]

---

286. Crossan, *Historical Jesus*, xxx.
287. Crossan, *Birth of Christianity*, 114.
288. Crossan, *Birth of Christianity*, 103.
289. Johnson, *Real Jesus*, 47.
290. Funk, *Honest to Jesus*, 64–65.
291. Funk, *Honest to Jesus*, 64.
292. Funk, *Honest to Jesus*, 64.

Final Test: Is Anything about Jesus at Risk in This Quest?

Are there any claims about Jesus at risk with these criteria, according to Funk? Nothing about Jesus is immune from this historical investigation. If the scholar thinks that nothing in the creed or church dogma is at risk, that person "is a pretend quester." Who belongs to the pretend group? "Fundamentalists and many evangelicals belong to the pretend group . . . . These questers collapse the historical Jesus into the creedal Christ and insist that the two are the same thing." These pretend questers defend the canonical Gospels as reliable while denying that the extracanonical texts "tell us anything significant about Jesus . . . . These questers are in fact apologists for traditional forms of Christianity." Funk brushes aside Third Questers such as Wright, because Wright does not authorize the distinction between the historical Jesus and the creedal Christ. Funk's view is that Wright and the "pretend" questers express no interest in "the Jesus of history beyond historical curiosity."[293]

Wright's analysis of the Third Quest is quite different: "Luke was precisely a *historian*, not too unlike Josephus,"[294] and Christianity is committed to history, answering Enlightenment questions, but it does not seek a "neutral" or "objective" history, which is "a positivist fantasy." Christianity appeals to "genuine historical reconstruction of actual events in the past" and includes the "inside" and "outside" of events. "Christianity has nothing to fear from the appeal to history. It makes the same appeal itself," says Wright.[295] Funk's retort is that New Questers include R. Brown (*The Birth of the Messiah*, 1993; *The Death of the Messiah*, 1994) and Meier (*A Marginal Jew*, vols. 1 and 2, 1991 and 1994) and "in their hands, orthodoxy is safe . . . . The third quest is an apologetic ploy" that Funk does not support.[296]

A characteristic feature of Renewed Questers is that they "distinguish the historical Jesus of the gospels and the Christ of the creeds." For Funk, these researchers are "aboveboard in identifying a database derived from sources for determining who Jesus was" (the inference is that other questers are underhand in their use of databases), critically using all surviving sources in their serious historical reconstruction (the inference is that others are not

---

293. Funk, *Honest to Jesus*, 65.
294. Wright, *New Testament*, 378 (emphasis in original).
295. Wright, *New Testament*, 137.
296. Funk, *Honest to Jesus*, 65.

serious in their kinds of sources used for historical reconstructions), and "everything is at stake. No Christian claim is immune to review and revision."[297]

IMPORTANT CONTRIBUTORS TO THE RENEWED NEW QUEST

Both Funk and the Jesus Seminar have suggested these authors for further reading in support of their Quest.[298] This is a sample of the authors in chronological order: Schweitzer (*The Quest of the Historical Jesus*, 1910), Bultmann (*Jesus and the Word*, 1934; *The History of the Synoptic Tradition*, 1963), Bornkamm (*Jesus of Nazareth*, 1960), Kuhn (*The Structure of Scientific Revolution*, 1970), Robinson (*A New Quest*, 1979), Pagels (*The Gnostic Gospels*, 1979), Vermes (*Jesus the Jew*, 1981; *The Dead Sea Scrolls in English*, 1987), Tatum (*In Quest of Jesus*, 1982; *John the Baptist and Jesus*, 1993), Crossan (*In Fragments*, 1983; *Four Other Gospels*, 1985; *The Cross That Spoke*, 1988; *The Dark Interval*, 1988; *The Historical Jesus*, 1991; *Jesus: A Revolutionary Biography*, 1994; *The Essential Jesus*, 1994; *Who Killed Jesus*, 1995; *The Birth of Christianity*, 1998), Sanders (*Jesus and Judaism*, 1985), Sheehan (*The First Coming*, 1986), Metzger (*The Canon of the New Testament*, 1987), Borg (*Jesus: A New Vision*, 1987; *Meeting Jesus Again for the First Time*, 1994; *Jesus in Contemporary Scholarship*, 1994), Kloppenborg (*The Formation of Q*, 1987), Mack (*A Myth of Innocence*, 1988; *The Lost Gospel*, 1993; *Who Wrote the New Testament*, 1995), Sanders and Davies (*Studying the Synoptic Gospels*, 1989), Kloppenborg et al. (*Q Thomas Reader*, 1990), Schaberg (*The Illegitimacy of Jesus*, 1990), Spong (*Rescuing the Bible from Fundamentalism*, 1990; *Born of a Woman*, 1992; *Resurrection: Myth or Reality*, 1994), Koester (*Ancient Christian Gospels*, 1990), Mitchell (*The Gospel According to Jesus*, 1991), Miller (*The Complete Gospels*, 1992), Patterson (*The Gospel of Thomas and Jesus*, 1993), R. Brown (*The Birth of the Messiah*, 1993; *The Death of the Messiah*, 1994), and Lüdemann (*The Resurrection of Jesus*, 1994).

How will these Renewed New Quest emphases impact Crossan's presuppositions for stratification methodology and outcomes for the resurrection data? As a fellow and co-director of the Jesus Seminar,[299] how can Crossan's presuppositions be exempt from those articulated by Funk,[300] which Funk made as a requirement for joining the Jesus Seminar? Funk calls for "a wholly secular account of the Christian faith" with the aim to liberate Jesus from scriptural, creedal, and experiential prisons that have

---

297. Funk, *Honest to Jesus*, 66.
298. Funk, *Honest to Jesus*, 322–25; Funk et al., *Five Gospels*, 538–41.
299. Crossan, *Long Way from Tipperary*, 174.
300. Funk, *Honest to Jesus*, 296–304.

"incarcerated" Jesus.[301] This will be assessed in chapter 5 as it applies to Crossan. Crossan admits that his reconstruction of the historical Jesus is "a way of doing necessary open-heart surgery on Christianity itself."[302] Is this an admission that his presuppositions are in conflict with orthodox Christianity? These presuppositions were identified and assessed in chapter 3.

Before we move to the next chapter, there is an important consideration in the analysis of Crossan: how do we discern the historicity of Crossan's position? Most of this chapter has expounded on indices to be used for testing Crossan's position on history in the next chapter.

SUMMARY OF CHAPTER 4

Methodology for the project was described. In defining the limits of the project, the nature of the Gospels as historical or noncritical documents was examined, including an assessment of whether they include mythology. Since Crossan's works show signs of postmodern influences, reader-response theories of interpretation were critically scrutinized.

The specific methodological task was to see history as inferential knowledge, using the hypothesis verification/falsification model within a critical realist epistemology.

The various indices used to assist with establishing historicity were explained, along with objections to the indices. These indices were discontinuity or dissimilarity, multiple and multiform attestations, Semiticisms and Palestinian background, embarrassment, and coherence. The priority of indices was outlined.

The history of the quests for the historical Jesus was identified.

---

301. Funk, *Honest to Jesus*, 298, 300.
302. Crossan, *Long Way from Tipperary*, 175.

FIVE

Fourth Crossan Lesson

That never happened, of course, but it was true nonetheless.[1]

TESTING HYPOTHESIS 1: THE RESURRECTION NARRATIVES IN THE NEW TESTAMENT ARE NOT HISTORICAL[2]

By way of review, hypothesis testing in this and the next chapter involves these five steps:

1. State your research hypothesis as a null hypothesis (H_O), based on the data from the subject (i.e., Crossan) I am investigating and an alternate (H_A) hypothesis, which is developed by the researcher.
2. Collect data in a way designed to test the hypothesis.
3. Perform an appropriate statistical test with an alternate (H_A) hypothesis.
4. Decide whether the null hypothesis is supported or refuted.

---

1. This is based on Crossan's unusual postmodern interpretation of Matt 27:19: "Pilate's wife had troubled dreams the previous night. That never happened, of course, but it was true nonetheless. It was a most propitious time for the Roman Empire to start having nightmares" (Crossan, *Historical Jesus*, 394).

2. This is a scaled-back statement of an enlarged hypothesis to facilitate its testing. In addition, the post-resurrection apparitional appearances (Crossan's language) are examined in this presupposition: the empty tomb of Jesus was not a historical fact but involved apparitions that were historically factual in their entirety.

5. Present the findings in your results along with a discussion section.

In this chapter, the null hypothesis (H_0) is "The resurrection narratives in the New Testament are not historical." Much of this chapter involves collecting data to test the hypothesis. The appropriate statistical test will involve testing whether the Crossan data supports or rejects the null hypothesis (H_0), with care taken to weigh the validity of Crossan's use of extracanonical books.

There are glaring issues raised in Crossan's scholarship that indicate Crossan does not support the New Testament narratives on Christ's resurrection as recording the resurrection as a historical event. According to Crossan, something did not happen factually, but it was true, because of the postmodern reconstruction (seen as a metaphor) of the resurrection accounts' referring to the nightmares happening in the Roman Empire. This is relativism in free fall.[3]

This hypothesis pursues some of these issues and is based on two presuppositions:

Presupposition Number 1: Crossan's Redefinition of Miracles That Affects His Definition of Jesus's Resurrection

Crossan was asked in a letter, "Do you yourself believe in miracles?" His response was: "'Yes, but not as periodic intrusions in some closed natural order. I leave absolutely open what God *could* do, but I have very definite thoughts about what God *does* do. The supernatural or divine is not something that periodically or temporarily breaks through the normal surface of the natural or human world. The supernatural is more like the permanently hidden but perpetually beating heart of the natural."[4]

In his debate with William Lane Craig, Crossan explains the content of his presupposition concerning the nature of the supernatural:

> The supernatural *always* (at least till this is disproved for me) operates through the screen of the natural. The supernatural is like the beating heart of the natural . . . . Miracles are acts of faith, which say, "Here the supernatural, which is permanently present, is made, as it were, visible to us." That is how I understand miracles. That is not naturalism. It is a belief that the supernatural never forces faith.[5]

3. Crossan, *Historical Jesus*, 394.
4. Crossan and Watts, *Who Is Jesus*, 96 (emphasis in original).
5. Crossan, as cited in Copan, *Will the Real Jesus*, 45–46 (emphasis in original).

However, in this same debate, in a discussion on miracles where a doctor might announce at Lourdes that God had intervened, Crossan states that "it's a theological presupposition of mine that God does not operate that way."[6] As an a priori principle, Crossan's premise is that God does not perform supernatural interventions in the physical world. He defines away the supernatural God and supernatural acts.

Nature miracles are symbolic of authority and are not to be taken literally, as Crossan states with the examples of Jesus's walking on the water and the unusual catch of fish:

> Those miracles are not for ordinary people, but for the official followers of Jesus . . . . Consider those twin stories to be clearly symbolic: without Jesus nothing, with Jesus everything. In the boat of the Church it is Jesus who counts and Jesus who is in charge. The disciples even as leaders are totally dependent on Jesus . . . . It is the ancients who know how to tell a good metaphorical story (a parable, if you prefer) and we moderns who are silly enough to take them factually . . . . The nature miracles are authority parables. They are not about Jesus' power over nature, but about the disciples' authority in the Church.[7]

He associates miracles with social changes: "I believe that miracles are not changes in the physical world so much as changes in the social world. It would, of course, be nice to have certain miracles available to change the physical world if we could, but it seems to me much more desirable to make certain changes which lie within our power in the social world."[8] Also, "the so-called *nature* miracles are not about Jesus' physical power over the world but about the apostles' spiritual power over the community."[9]

He gives further examples of miracles interpreted as metaphor. These are plurally attested miracles: the Beelzebul controversy,[10] the leper cured,[11] sickness and sin,[12] and the blind man healed.[13] "None of those plurally at-

---

6. Crossan, as cited in Copan, *Will the Real Jesus*, 61.
7. Crossan and Watts, *Who Is Jesus*, 79–80.
8. Crossan and Watts, *Who is Jesus*, 88.
9. Crossan, *Jesus*, 170 (emphasis in original).
10. Luke 11:14–15, 17–18; Matt 12:22–26; also Matt 9:32–34; Mark 3:22–26, identified as no. 121 (Crossan, *Historical Jesus*, 441).
11. *Egerton Gospel* 3b (35–47); Mark 1:40–45; Matt 8:1–4; Luke 5:12–16; Luke 17:11–19, identified as no. 110 (Crossan, *Historical Jesus*, 440).
12. John 5:1–9a, 12; Mark 2:1–12; Matt 9:1–8; Luke 5:17–26, identified as no. 127 (Crossan, *Historical Jesus*, 441).
13. John 9:1–7; Mark 8:22–26, identified as no. 129 (Crossan, *Historical Jesus*, 441).

tested miracles makes a connection between Kingdom and cure," but the framework makes the "programmatic social function very clear."[14] In terms of his methodology, the only exorcism considered, as "a very powerful case," is the Beelzebul controversy.[15] He states that the multiple attestation of Q[16] and Mark 3:22 means that it "must, therefore, be taken very seriously."[17] Regarding this information—"He casts out demons by Beelzebul, the prince of demons"[18]—Crossan makes "one very tentative suggestion." He asks, *"Did Jesus sometimes, or always, heal while he himself was in a state of trance?"*[19] He wants "to leave the question open for the future," admitting that "there is not much evidence for Jesus as an *entranced* healer using contagious trance as a therapeutic technique."[20] Why is he pursuing the topic if he admits "there is not much evidence" for it? Also, as already covered in chapter 4, he does not believe in demon possession, but with multiple attestations, he is prepared to grant it is "a very powerful case," not literally but with a social interpretation.

More examples of his interpretation of miracles and the symbolic are provided. "Revelations to *specific leaders* and/or *leadership groups* come to overpower and suppress revelations to the *general community* . . . . These are dramatizations of power and visualizations of authority."[21] Two examples are (1) Emmaus and Jerusalem[22] and (2) community and leadership.[23] For the latter, Crossan uses the example of the miracle of loaves and fish (feeding the five thousand), which appears in two different settings (his language is "as told independently") in Mark 6:35-44 and John 6:5-13. There is another account in Mark 8:1-10 (feeding the four thousand), but he believes that it "is best seen not as separate tradition but as a deliberate doubling of the story by Mark himself. He thereby obtains a miracle on the lake's western shore in a Jewish context and on its eastern shore in a Gentile context."[24] In Crossan, his language is, "I would argue exactly the opposite process" to Robert Fowler. Here Crossan describes Mark 8:1-10 "as a Markan

14. Crossan, *Historical Jesus*, 332.
15. Crossan, *Historical Jesus*, 318.
16. Luke 11:14-15;
17. Crossan, *Jesus*, 91.
18. Luke 11:15.
19. Crossan, *Jesus*, 91-92 (emphasis in original).
20. Crossan, *Jesus*, 93 (emphasis in original).
21. Crossan, *Jesus*, 170 (emphasis in original).
22. Luke 24:13-36.
23. Crossan, *Jesus*, 174.
24. Crossan, *Jesus*, 174.

development," and the concern is the movement from Jesus to disciples and then to the crowds, "from Jesus to *leadership group* to *general community*."[25] So, he does not want to affirm literal miraculous intervention but symbolism instead.

Of the story of the Gerasene demoniac and Jesus,[26] he writes that "an individual is, of course, being cured, but the symbolism is also hard to miss or ignore. The demon is both one and many; is named Legion, that fact and sign of Roman power; is consigned to swine; and is cast into the sea.... *Legion, I think*, is to colonial Roman Palestine as *bindele* was to colonial European Rhodesia."[27] With the language "the symbolism is also hard to miss or ignore," Crossan provides further evidence for his factive presupposition.[28]

Crossan has another metaphorical understanding of miracles when he cites and agrees with David Aune that "most of the nature miracles are 'creations out of whole cloth by the early church.'"[29] However, he adds that two processes are at work in the miracles of the Beelzebul controversy, bread and fish, walking on water, and fishing for humans. Of this group of miracles, he states: "I am concerned with two processes at work within that corpus, one moving from event to process and the other in the opposite direction from process by event. By *event* I mean the actual and historical cure of an afflicted individual at a moment in time. By *process* I mean some wider socioreligious phenomenon that is symbolized in and by such an individual happening."[30]

Another redefinition of miracles is Crossan's view that "the 'nature' miracles of Jesus are 'actually credal statements about ecclesiastical authority, although they all have as their background Jesus' resurrectional victory over death, which is, of course, the supreme 'nature' miracle."[31] This is a paradox of Crossan's method that he can make the resurrection "the supreme 'nature' miracle," but it's a phantom—an apparition.

He emphasizes "that *is* the resurrection, the continuing presence in a continuing community of the past Jesus in a radically new and

---

25. Crossan, *Historical Jesus*, 401 (emphasis in original).

26. Mark 5:1–17.

27. Crossan, *Historical Jesus*, 314–15 ("*I think*" emphasis added). "Sufferers from *bindele*, which is the Luvale word for 'European,' are believed to be possessed by the spirit of a European" (Barrie Reynolds, in Crossan, *Historical Jesus*, 315). The Lunda-Luvale tribes were in what was formerly Northern Rhodesia.

28. This is a revised version of "I know" for a factive.

29. Crossan, *Historical Jesus*, 320.

30. Crossan, *Historical Jesus*, 320 (emphasis in original).

31. Crossan, *Historical Jesus*, 404.

transcendental mode of present and future existence. But how to *express* that phenomenon" is his question.³²

Another of Crossan's symbolic understandings comes with the example of the two stories of the centurion's servant and the Syrophoenician woman's daughter, examples of people who were cured at a distance by Jesus—sick and near death and demon-possessed.³³ They were the only two miracles preformed for gentiles and were at a distance. Of course, he would reject the casting out of demons, because he excludes this supernatural ministry from his worldview. To encounter reality, Crossan needs to be let loose with the witch doctors (shamans) of northern Peru and there proclaim his disbelief in demon possession.³⁴

Walter Martin tells of an incident in Newport Beach, California, involving five persons, including Martin. There was a girl, five feet, four inches in height, weighing 120 pounds who attacked a 180-pound man and flung him 5–6 feet with one hand. It took four people to hold her body down "while we prayed in the name of Jesus Christ for the exorcism of the demon within her." During one of the exorcisms it was discovered she had worshipped Satan. During that worship, she came under Satan's control. She had been a "tare among the wheat" before returning to the Lord God. Then she and her husband served on the mission field.³⁵

The country was Mozambique, Africa, bordering on the Indian Ocean. Southern Baptist missionaries Brian and Becky Harrell attempted to reach witches: 'The persuasive power of the Gospel finally convinced a witch to abandon her animist ways and turn to Christ—even though it took a year for her to do that . . . . "I need you to help me to do something," she [the former witch] said. "I know that what I have been doing is wrong and I want to get rid of my witchcraft."'³⁶

Crossan claims of examples such as these, "It is quite likely, it seems to me, that those cases are not at all a movement from event to process but actually from process to event. Early Christian communities symbolically retrojected their own activities back into the life of Jesus."³⁷ "It seems to me" is his presuppositional projection—his opinion. Instead, they are events that happen in the supernatural world.

---

32. Crossan, *Historical Jesus*, 404 (emphasis in original).
33. See Luke 7:1–10; Mark 7:24–30.
34. Santos, "Witch Doctors."
35. Martin, *Exorcism*, 17–18.
36. Torres, "Witch Finally Turns."
37. Crossan, *Historical Jesus*, 328.

He admits, "I presume that Jesus, who did not and could not cure that disease or any other one, healed the poor man's illness by refusing to accept the disease's ritual uncleanness and social ostracization."[38] This is avoiding the reality of what is stated in the biblical text.

There is another understanding of his view of the supernatural: "I myself, for example, do not believe that there are personal supernatural spirits who invade our bodies from outside and, for either good or evil, replace or jostle for place with our own personality. But the vast, vast majority of the world's people have always so believed."[39] To claim a miracle, he asserted, was "to make an interpretation of faith, not just a statement of fact."[40] It is time for Crossan to encounter a witchdoctor and cast out the demon, instead of denying this supernatural power.

His response to the raising of Lazarus from the dead is, "I do not think that anyone, anywhere, at any time, including Jesus, brings dead people back to life. (I am not, of course, talking about near-death experiences or about resuscitating apparent corpses. Death means you don't come back. If you come back, it was not death. Death, like pregnancy, is either/or, not more or less)."[41]

Crossan's view is "that the healings or exorcisms of Jesus are miracles does not mean for me that only Jesus could do such things but that in such events I see God at work in Jesus." Thus, there were no supernatural healings or exorcisms within history, but they were metaphorical manifestations of God's being. His words are "I see that same God at work—in the healing and in the eating as nonviolent resistance to systematic evil."[42]

Presuppositional operators for this redefinition of miracles topic include as articulated above, include:

1. *Presuppositions admitted*: "It's a theological presupposition of mine that God does not operate that way" by performing supernatural miracles; "I presume that Jesus, who did not and could not cure that disease or any other one, healed the poor man's illness by refusing to accept the disease's ritual uncleanness and social ostracization"; "I myself, for example, do not believe that there are personal supernatural spirits who invade our bodies from outside and, for either good or evil, replace or jostle for a place with our own personality"; "I do not

---

38. Crossan, *Jesus*, 82.
39. Crossan, *Jesus*, 85.
40. Crossan, *Birth of Christianity*, 304.
41. Crossan and Watts, *Who Is Jesus*, 98.
42. Crossan, *Birth of Christianity*, 304.

think that anyone, anywhere, at any time, including Jesus, brings dead people back to life"

2. *Factives*: "the supernatural always operates"; "miracles are acts of faith"; the nature miracles "are actually credal statements";

3. *Quantifiers*: the "vast, vast majority of the world's people," "two processes at work"; "the supreme 'nature miracle'"

4. *Names*: Emmaus, Jerusalem, Gerasene, Legion, Roman Palestine, European Rhodesia, Syrophoenician, Gentiles

5. *Intonation*: "supernatural . . . natural . . . permanently present"; "miracles are acts of faith"; "miracles . . . clearly symbolic"; "ordinary people . . . official followers"; "without Jesus nothing, with Jesus everything"; "metaphorical story (a parable) . . . factually"; "nature miracles are authority parables"; "Jesus' power over nature . . . disciples' authority in the Church"; "miracles are not changes in the physical world so much as changes in the social world"; "nature miracles . . . apostles' spiritual power over the community"; "kingdom and cure"; "cure . . . social function"; "tentative suggestion . . . Did Jesus sometimes, or always, heal while he himself was in a state of trance?"; "there is not much evidence for Jesus as an entranced healer"; "specific leaders; leadership groups"; "dramatizations of power and visualizations of authority"; "leadership group to general community"; "being cured, but the symbolism"; "Jewish context . . . Gentile context"; "*bindele*"; "process . . . event"; "actual and historical cure . . . wider socioreligious phenomenon that is symbolized"; "bodily miracle . . . social signification"; "nature miracles . . . credal statements"; Jesus's "resurrection, the continuing presence in a continuing community"; "present and future existence"; "past . . . present . . . future"; "resurrectional victory over death"; "early Christian communities symbolically retrojected their own activities back"; "the healing and in the eating as nonviolent resistance to systematic evil"

6. *Projection*: "Yes, but not as periodic intrusions"; "I have very definite thoughts about"; "the supernatural or divine is not something that periodically or temporarily breaks" in; "supernatural is more like the permanently hidden but perpetually beating heart of the natural"; "it is a belief that the supernatural never forces faith"; "those miracles are not for ordinary people but for the official followers"; "the so-called *nature* miracles are not," "none of those plurally attested miracles makes a connection"; "must, therefore, be taken very seriously"; "I would argue exactly the opposite process"; "he thereby obtains a miracle"; "I would argue"; "*Legion*, I think"; "nature miracles are creations

... by the early church"; "death means you don't come back. If you come back, it was not death"

7. *Cancellability*: "That is not naturalism."

Thus, presuppositional aspects include:

- God does not perform supernatural miracles.
- Jesus's healing of illness was a symbolic example of refusing to accept ritual uncleanness and social ostracism.
- There are no personal, supernatural spirits who invade people from the outside.
- Nobody, including Jesus, brings people back to life.
- Miracles are acts of faith, credal statements.
- Nature miracles were created by the early church.
- Healing was symbolic of nonviolent resistance to systematic evil.

If Crossan's rejection of an interventionist God is not support for naturalism, what does the interpretation of symbolism indicate about his theistic worldview?

Crossan's Presupposition Deals with Factuality and the Empty Tomb

According to Crossan, the empty tomb of Jesus was not a historical fact but involved apparitions that were historically factual in their entirety. Crossan's statement rules out the possibility of the miraculous resurrection a priori by his non-miraculous presupposition:

> I do not think that anyone, anywhere, at any time, including Jesus, brings dead people back to life. (I am not, of course, talking about near-death experiences or about resuscitating apparent corpses. Death means you don't come back. If you come back, it was not death. Death, like pregnancy, is either/or, not more or less).[43]

---

43. Crossan and Watts, *Who Is Jesus*, 98.

HISTORY, MYTH, AND FICTION

Does Crossan regard Jesus's empty tomb as reliable history? He asks, "Is the story of the empty tomb historical? No . . . I doubt there was any tomb for Jesus in the first place. I don't think any of Jesus' followers even knew where he was buried—if he was buried at all." Instead of stating some more objective data, he moves to this personal opinion that "the gospel writers don't come close to agreeing with each other on what they report," so this is his assessment: "My conviction is that motives other than just history writing are clearly at work here. By the way, Paul is the earliest writer we have on resurrection—his letters are much earlier than the gospels—and he nowhere shows awareness of having heard an empty tomb story."[44]

He uses the language of Easter stories to describe the passion-resurrection events. What happened by the Sunday following the crucifixion? "On Easter Sunday evening Jesus himself had appeared to his closest followers and all was well once again. Friday was hard, Saturday was long, but by Sunday all was resolved. Is this fact or fiction, history or mythology? Do fiction and mythology crowd closely around the end of the story just as they did around its beginning? And if there is fiction or mythology, on what is it based?"[45]

He argues that

> Jesus' burial by his friends was totally fictional and unhistorical . . . . We can still glimpse what happened before, behind, and despite those fictional overlays precisely by imagining what they were created to hide. What happened on Easter Sunday? Is that the story of one day? Or of several years? Is that the story of *all* Christians gathered together as a single group in Jerusalem? Or is that the story of but one group among several, maybe of one group who claimed to be the whole?[46]

His answers are:

- "First of all, *resurrection* is but one way, not the only way, of expressing Christian faith."

- "Second, *apparition*—which involves trance, that altered state of consciousness . . . is but one way, not the only way, of expressing Christian experience."

---

44. Crossan and Watts, *Who Is Jesus*, 154.
45. Crossan, *Jesus*, 160.
46. Crossan, *Jesus*, 160 (emphasis in original).

- "Third, Christian faith experiences the *continuation* of divine empowerment through Jesus, but that continuation began only after his death and burial."[47]

His added emphasis is that "it is precisely that continued experience of the Kingdom of God as strengthened rather than weakened by Jesus' death that is Christian or Easter faith. And that was not the work of one afternoon. Or one year. Since the Easter story at the end is, like the Nativity story at the beginning, so engraved on your imagination as factual history rather than fictional mythology."[48] Crossan's free play continues. They are out of the mind of a creative writer and researcher. I have not seen evidence by Crossan that supports his view that Jesus's resurrection was an apparition.

His conclusion is that he can harmonize the resurrection accounts and that fiction was involved. He asks, "With the Easter stories, are we standing on the solid rock of historical fact?" His answer is "I raise these questions also because the New Testament record forces me to raise them. Matthew, Mark, and John tell the Easter story quite differently—so differently, in fact, that we simply cannot harmonize their version."[49]

So how does he deal with this alleged conflict? He is convinced that he has "to ask questions of intention and meaning" rather than seek harmonization of the Gospel resurrection accounts.[50]

The presuppositional triggers that emerge include:

- *Factives*: "Jesus' burial by his friends was totally fictional and unhistorical"; "first of all, *resurrection* is but one way, not the only way, of expressing Christian faith. Second, *apparition*—which involves trance, that altered state of consciousness . . . is but one way, not the only way, of expressing Christian experience. Third, Christian faith experiences the continuation of divine empowerment through Jesus, but that *continuation* began only after his death and burial"; "It is precisely that *continued* experience of the Kingdom of God as strengthened rather than weakened by Jesus' death that is Christian or Easter faith. And that was not the work of one afternoon. Or one year"; "Since the Easter story at the end is, like the Nativity story at the beginning, so engraved on your imagination as factual history rather than fictional mythology"

- *Intonation*: Again he uses questions to focus the tone. "What happened on Easter Sunday? Is that the story of one day? Or of several years? Is

---

47. Crossan, *Jesus*, 160–61 (emphasis in original).
48. Crossan, *Jesus*, 160.
49. Crossan and Watts, *Who Is Jesus*, 153.
50. Crossan and Watts, *Who Is Jesus*, 153.

that the story of all Christians gathered together as a single group in Jerusalem? Or is that the story of but one group among several, maybe of one group who claimed to be the whole?" "With the Easter stories, are we standing on the solid rock of historical fact?"

- *Projection*: "Is the story of the empty tomb historical? No . . . I doubt here was any tomb for Jesus in the first place"; "I don't think any of Jesus' followers even knew where he was buried—if he was buried at all. And the gospel writers don't come close to agreeing with each other on what they report"; "My conviction is that motives other than just history writing are clearly at work here. By the way, Paul is the earliest writer we have on resurrection—his letters are much earlier than the gospels—and he nowhere shows awareness of having heard an empty tomb story"; "On Easter Sunday evening Jesus himself had appeared to his closest followers and all was well once again. Friday was hard, Saturday was long, but by Sunday all was resolved. Is this fact or fiction, history or mythology? Do fiction and mythology crowd closely around the end of the story just as they did around its beginning? And if there is fiction or mythology, on what is it based?"; "We can still glimpse what happened before, behind, and despite those fictional overlays [of Jesus's burial and resurrection] precisely by imagining what they were created to hide"; "I raise these questions [about the historicity of the resurrection stories] also because the New Testament record forces me to raise them. Matthew, Mark, and John tell the Easter story quite differently—so differently, in fact, that we simply cannot harmonize their versions"; "to ask questions of intention and meaning rather than seek harmonization of the Gospel resurrection accounts"

Which presuppositional projections are found in those triggers?

- Jesus's burial by friends was unhistorical and fictional.
- Resurrection is only one way of expressing Christian faith and experience. Another way is through apparition, which includes trance and an altered state of consciousness.
- Christian faith includes the continuation of divine empowerment, but this could happen only after Jesus's death and burial. This is the continued experience of the kingdom of God.
- Jesus's death and resurrection were not the work of one afternoon or of one year.
- The Easter story, like that of the nativity, is engraved in the Christian imagination as factual history, when it should be fictional mythology.

- Fiction and mythology crowd around the end of Jesus's life as they did at the beginning (the nativity).
- What happened on Easter Sunday is not dealing with factual history and is not the story of one day or several years but could be the story of one group representing the whole.
- The Easter stories are not built on the foundation of historical fact.
- There is doubt that there was an empty tomb in which to place Jesus.
- It is doubtful that Jesus's followers knew where he was buried.
- The Gospel writers cannot agree with each other on what they report about Jesus's burial.
- The motive for the writing of the Easter stories was not to deliver history.
- Paul, the earliest writer on the resurrection, nowhere shows an awareness of an empty tomb story.
- There are fictional overlays in writing Jesus's burial and resurrection, and they were created to hide information.
- The Easter story in the four Gospels cannot be harmonized.
- It is more important to ask questions about intention and meaning of the Easter accounts than to seek harmonization.

Miracles Are Not Supernatural Interventions

According to Crossan, there were no New Testament miracles by God's supernatural interventions in the natural world, but there were symbolic, credal statements of benefit for Christians and the church. This is not a perspective of naturalism, in Crossan's view.

Presupposition Number 2: Jesus's Resurrection Is Not Fact, So We Focus on Meaning and Intention

Crossan also states Jesus's body was not resuscitated and the empty tomb was not a historical fact. For him, the Emmaus story was not factually true, and Jesus's other post-resurrection appearances were reflections of the beliefs of his followers.

THE GENERAL RESURRECTION HAS BEGUN

Crossan links Jesus's resurrection with the general resurrection: "Those who proclaimed Jesus's resurrection were not simply proclaiming his *exaltation* to the right hand of God. That would have been a stunning enough climax to Jesus's destiny as Messiah, Son of God, and Lord, based, for example on Psalm 110."[51] However, the climax was even better: "Going much further than that, however, *they proclaimed that the general bodily resurrection had already begun with Jesus's bodily resurrection*, and that of course was why 'resurrection' was the only proper and adequate word for what had happened to Jesus." This meaning was "not assumption, nor exaltation, but precisely resurrection that meant Jesus's resurrection was not just an individual privilege but a communal process—and a communal process from past, present, and future, with Jesus's resurrection as the heart of that process."[52] In similar fashion, "the general bodily resurrection was not a future and instantaneous flash of divine time, but an event with a past beginning, a present continuation, and a future consummation in human time. Of course, they thought that future conclusion was still rather imminent" and that "the present was an in-between period in which Christian believers were called to a resurrected life with, in, and through the resurrected Jesus. It was not as if there is a start (the Christ resurrection), a yawning gap, and then an end (the general resurrection)—like two bookends but with no books in between. We Christians *are* the books in between."[53]

Crossan considers "there is one final and even more basic question whose answer may serve as a summary not only of 1 Corinthians 15, but of Paul's transmutation of both general Jewish apocalyptic eschatology and specific Pharisaic resurrection theology." That question is "Why did Paul not agree with his 'wise' Corinthian converts by accepting Platonic theology and insisting that Christ's soul, as purer even than Socrates's, resided now with God in a state of such eternal holiness that it judged positively or negatively all other souls before or after it?" This Platonic questioning continues: "Plato, after all, had insisted (against Homer's Hades) that the soul's immortality was necessary for divine justice, so that virtuous souls could be rewarded and evil souls punished after this life. Why not, at least, leave two options for Christian faith: The resurrection of the body or the immortality of the soul?" Crossan and Reed's answer is "quite simply, *the general resurrection was, first of all, about the justice of God amid the goodness of*

---

51. Crossan, *God and Empire*, 186.
52. Crossan, *God and Empire*, 186–87 (emphasis in original).
53. Crossan, *God and Empire*, 187.

creation here below upon a transformed earth, and, second, within that, it was about the martyrs who had died for justice and from injustice with their bodies tortured, brutalized, and murdered." So, instead of resurrection being only "'about us and survival,' it was about God and this earth. It was not about the heavenly evacuation, but the earthly transfiguration of this bodily world. The soul's immortality, even with all due post-mortem sanctions, did not restore a world disfigured by human evil, injustice, and violence. For the Jewish and Pharisaic Paul, divine justice was necessarily about transfigured bodies upon a transfigured earth."[54]

Presuppositional triggers from Crossan include:

- *Factives*: "Quite simply, the general resurrection was, first of all, about the justice of God amid the goodness of creation here below upon a transformed earth, and, second, within that, it was about the martyrs who had died for justice and from injustice with their bodies tortured, brutalized, and murdered"; the resurrection was "about God and this earth. It was not about the heavenly evacuation, but the earthly transfiguration of this bodily world."

- *Aspectual verbs*: "Plato, after all, had insisted (against Homer's Hades) that the soul's immortality was necessary for divine justice, so that virtuous souls could be rewarded and evil souls punished after this life. Why not, at least, leave two options for Christian faith: The resurrection of the body or the immortality of the soul?" "The soul's immortality, even with all due post-mortem sanctions, did not restore a world disfigured by human evil, injustice, and violence"; "For the Jewish and Pharisaic Paul, divine justice was necessarily about transfigured bodies upon a transfigured earth."

- *Quantifiers*: "there is one final and even more basic question"; "like two bookends but with no books in between. We Christians *are* the books in between."

- *Names*: Paul, Plato, Socrates, and Homer.

- *Intonation*: "That would have been a stunning enough climax to Jesus's destiny"; "There is one final and even more basic question whose answer may serve as a summary not only of 1 Corinthians 15, but of Paul's transmutation of both general Jewish apocalyptic eschatology and specific Pharisaic resurrection theology"; "*first of all, about the justice of God amid the goodness of creation here below upon a transformed earth*"; "*second, within that, it was about the martyrs who had*

---

54. Crossan and Reed, *In Search of Paul*, 344–45 (emphasis in original).

died for justice and from injustice with their bodies tortured, brutalized, and murdered."

- *Projection*: "Those who proclaimed Jesus's resurrection were not simply proclaiming his exaltation to the right hand of God. That would have been a stunning enough climax to Jesus's destiny as Messiah, Son of God, and Lord, based, for example on Psalm 110"; "Going much further than that, however, *they proclaimed that the general bodily resurrection had already begun with Jesus's bodily resurrection*, and that of course was why 'resurrection' was the only proper and adequate word for what had happened to Jesus"; "not assumption, nor exaltation, but precisely resurrection"; "that meant that Jesus's resurrection was not just an individual privilege but a communal process—and a communal process from past, present, and future, with Jesus's resurrection as the heart of that process"; "the general bodily resurrection was not a future and instantaneous flash of divine time, but an event with a past beginning, a present continuation, and a future consummation in human time. Of course, they thought that future conclusion was still rather imminent"; "the present was an in-between period in which Christian believers were called to a resurrected life with, in, and through the resurrected Jesus. It was not as if there is a start (the Christ resurrection), a yawning gap, and then an end (the general resurrection)—like two bookends but with no books in between. We Christians are the books in between"; "Why did Paul not agree with his 'wise' Corinthian converts by accepting Platonic theology and insisting that Christ's soul, as purer even than Socrates's, resided now with God in a state of such eternal holiness that it judged positively or negatively all other souls before or after it?"

Presuppositional understandings arising from these triggers embrace:

- The general resurrection was about God's justice and the goodness of creation on a transformed earth, but it also is about the martyrs who died for justice.
- The resurrection is about transfigured bodies on a transfigured earth and not about a heavenly evacuation.
- The resurrection of the body and the immortality of the soul belong to Platonic theology, and Paul did not follow this perspective.
- The immortality of the soul will not restore a world disfigured by evil.

- Those who proclaimed Jesus's resurrection were not promoting only his exaltation but that the general resurrection had begun with Jesus's resurrection.
- Resurrection as interpreted by Crossan is the only proper word for Jesus's resurrection.
- Jesus's resurrection was not just an individual, unique privilege for one person but was a communal process—from past, present, and future—with Jesus's resurrection at the heart of that process in human time.
- The general bodily resurrection is not a future, divine event.
- The resurrection does not involve a start (Jesus's resurrection), a long gap, and then an end with the general resurrection. Instead, Christians are involved in the continuing process of the resurrection.

WHAT ARE CROSSAN'S SPECIFICS THAT CHALLENGE THE NEW TESTAMENT RESURRECTION NARRATIVES AS HISTORY?

These Crossan particulars are summarized according to five main topics:

- Nature of history
- Hermeneutics of reconstruction
- Non-supernatural God and Jesus's resurrection
- Nature of Jesus's resurrection
- Post-resurrection events

NATURE OF HISTORY

See chapter 2 for a discussion of the nature of history and how it applies to Crossan's and other historians' views of history. Crossan's conclusion is radically different from that of many historians. His working definition of history is "*History is the past reconstructed interactively by the present through argued evidence in public discourse.*"[55]

What is the nature of history and how is historiography determined? The definition of historiography used for this project is that of Robert Kraft, professor of religious studies, focusing on the history and philosophy of

---

55. Crossan, "Historical Jesus as Risen Lord," 3 (emphasis in original).

religion (Christian origins). History is "the study of how those who attempted to record information about the past went about their tasks."[56]

One of the issues pursued in this analysis of Crossan's approach to history is, since it is granted that interpretation is needed in an association with the bare facts of history, where do interpretation and deconstruction part ways? The isolation of Crossan's presuppositions regarding the historical or nonhistorical nature of Christ's resurrection is based on Crossan's data regarding history, myth, and fiction.

I could include other historians and the core elements of their historiography to try to demonstrate Crossan's view does not harmonize with these perspectives. I could examine the views from the father of history, Herodotus of Hilcaranassus (ca. 484–425 BC)[57] down to a contemporary historian such as Paul W. Barnett,[58] including a plethora of other historians.

There is a problem with that approach. It only adjudicates the opinion and evaluation of certain other historians, comparing one with another. It does not consider the data of canonical, extracanonical, myth, and fiction. Therefore, the approach used here is to examine the data to consider its most appropriate outcome. Should it be included in the data of historical substance?

Hermeneutics of Reconstruction

Crossan explains what he considers is a core understanding—the meaning of the resurrection:

> The resurrection of Jesus means for me that the human empowerment that some people experienced in Lower Galilee at the start of the first century in and through Jesus is now available to any person in any place at any time who finds God in and through that same Jesus. Empty tomb stories and physical appearance stories are perfectly valid parables expressing that faith, akin in their own way to the Good Samaritan story. They are, for me, parables of resurrection not the resurrection itself. Resurrection as the continuing experience of God's presence in and through Jesus is the heart of Christian faith.[59]

---

56. Kraft, "History and Historiography."
57. Lifespan dates for Herodotus are from Herodotus himself, *History of Herodotus*.
58. Barnett, *Is the New Testament History?*
59. Crossan, *Who Killed Jesus*, 216.

Crossan is specific in labelling his kind of unique interpretation of the historical Jesus:

> Christianity is historical reconstruction interpreted as divine manifestation. It is not (*in a postmodern world*) that we find once and for all who the historical Jesus was way back then. It is that each generation and century must redo that historical work and establish its best reconstruction, a reconstruction that will be and must be in some creative interaction with its own particular needs, visions, and programs . . . . It is that Jesus reconstructed in the dialogues, debates, controversies, and conclusions of contemporary scholarship that challenges faith to see and say how that is for now the Christ, the Lord, the Son of God . . . . The gospels are, for me, even more normative as process than as product . . . . You cannot believe in a fact, only in an interpretation.[60]

Crossan's methodology of postmodern deconstruction outlines his strategy. He does not prefer to speak of the search or quest for the historical Jesus or Christian origins. Rather, "I speak instead of *reconstruction*, and that is something that is done over and over again in different times and different places, by different groups and different communities, and by every generation again and again and again." Concerning this method, he states, "I insist that Jesus-reconstruction, like all such reconstruction, is always a creative interaction of past and present." He declares that this is his "method, method, and, once again, method. It will not guarantee us the truth because nothing can do that. But method, as self-conscious and self-critical as we can make it, is our only discipline. It cannot take us out of our present skins and bodies, minds and hearts, societies and cultures. But it is our one best hope of honesty. It is the due process of history."[61] So, in the methodology of postmodern deconstruction that must be repeated in every generation, does Crossan have another subjective index for discerning the authenticity of Gospel content?

Is this reasoned deconstruction of the past through creative interaction associated with deconstructed, but idiosyncratic, interpretation, or is it driven by another agenda? The following are but a few examples of how the deconstructionist methodology works for Crossan in relation to the resurrection accounts:

---

60. Crossan, *Who Killed Jesus*, 217 (emphasis added).
61. Crossan, "Historical Jesus as Risen Lord," 5 (emphasis in original).

1. "Within three days [after Jesus was officially tortured and legally executed by Roman imperial power], however, his tomb was found empty and he appeared to his former companions as risen from the dead. Those resurrectional visions explain the miracle of Christianity's birth and growth, spread and triumph, across the Roman empire."[62] Is the resurrection of Jesus a vision to be regarded as Crossan's individualistic understanding, or can this be justified by exegetical, contextual, and historical interpretations?

2. Of Jesus's "resurrectional visions," "I use vision and apparition interchangeably, and I understand them within the psychosocial and cross-cultural anthropology of comparative religion."[63]

3. "Mark created the empty tomb story just as he created the sleeping disciples in Gethsemane . . . . The empty tomb is neither an early historical event nor a late legendary narrative but a deliberate Markan creation . . . . Mark created the empty tomb narrative to replace any risen apparition story as the conclusion of the gospel."[64]

4. There are "two very early Christians who believed absolutely in the resurrection of Jesus," but for one (Paul's received tradition in 1 Corinthians 15) "risen apparitions were . . . fully emphasized." The second, where "risen apparitions were . . . completely avoided," is "Mark 15–16 which, in my view, created both the honorable burial and empty tomb precisely to avoid such resurrectional visions."[65]

5. "There are not two Jesuses, one pre-Easter and another post-Easter, one earthly and another heavenly, one with a physical and another with a spiritual body. There is only one Jesus, the *historical* Jesus who incarnated, for believers, the Jewish God of justice in a community of such life back then and continued to do so ever afterwards."[66]

In a presentation at the Westar Institute's Jesus Seminar in October 1999, Crossan's "main proposal was that, since the Age of Enlightenment had been replaced by the Age of Entertainment, the future clash would not be between science and religion but between both of them and fantasy." He said, "What I am trying to imagine is what Christianity must do clearly

---

62. Crossan, "Historical Jesus as Risen Lord," 6.
63. Here he refers to "works such as those by Ioan Lewis, Erika Bourguignon, Felicitas Goodman, or Raymond Prince" (Crossan, "Historical Jesus as Risen Lord," 6n5).
64. Crossan, "Historical Jesus as Risen Lord," 11–12, 16. There is a similar statement in Crossan, *Birth of Christianity*, 558–59.
65. Crossan, "Historical Jesus as Risen Lord," 26.
66. Crossan, "Historical Jesus as Risen Lord," 45 (mphasis in original).

and honestly to distinguish itself from fantasy. If it does not do that, it will certainly survive but as an important and even lucrative sub-division of world-wide entertainment and global illusion."[67] He assessed in 2007 that "in 1999 I never imagined, even as prophetic nightmare, the speed with which faith-based thinking would morph into fantasy-based dreaming to infiltrate medicine, education, domestic program, foreign policy, and even news reporting."[68]

When Crossan conducted a seminar in Portland, Oregon, at Marcus Borg's church, Trinity Episcopal Cathedral, a person who purchased one of his books said to him, "My pastor told me not to come here tonight because you are even to the left of Borg." Crossan's response was, "Give your pastor my best regards . . . and tell him that is the good news. The bad news is that both Borg and Crossan are to the right of Jesus. And worse still, if he will recall Psalm 110, Jesus is to the right of God."[69] Those were the last words of his autobiography.

So, the historical reconstruction of the historical Jesus that he uses to interpret the divine manifestation is designed to satisfy the requirements of a postmodern world.

Triggers identified in his conclusions include:

- *Factives*: "Christianity is historical reconstruction interpreted as divine manifestation. It is not (*in a postmodern world*) that we find once and for all who the historical Jesus was way back then. It is that each generation and century must redo that historical work and establish its best reconstruction, a reconstruction that will be and must be in some creative interaction with its own particular needs, visions, and program"; "it is that Jesus reconstructed in the dialogues, debates, controversies, and conclusions of contemporary scholarship that challenges faith to see and say how that is for now the Christ, the Lord, the Son of God"; "I speak instead of reconstruction, and that is something that is done over and over again in different times and different places, by different groups and different communities, and by every generation again and again and again"; "Mark created the empty tomb story just as he created the sleeping disciples in Gethsemane"; "The empty tomb story is neither an early historical event nor a late legendary narrative but a

---

67. Crossan, *God and Empire*, 197.

68. Crossan, *God and Empire*, 197. What is the significance of 1999? Crossan states that "in late October 1999, I discussed 'A Future for Christian Faith?' at the Westar Institute's Jesus Seminar in Santa Rosa, California, and it was published the following year in a book entitled, like the conference itself, *The Once and Future Jesus*."

69. Crossan, *Long Way from Tipperary*, 204.

deliberate Markan creation"; Mark created the empty tomb narrative to replace any risen apparition story as the conclusion of the gospel"; "There are not two Jesuses, one pre-Easter and another post-Easter, one earthly and another heavenly, one with a physical and another with a spiritual body. There is only one Jesus, the historical Jesus who incarnated, for believers, the Jewish God of justice in a community of such life back then and continued to do so ever afterwards"; "Give your pastor my best regards . . . and tell him that is the good news [that Crossan is to the left of Borg]. The bad news is that both Borg and Crossan are to the right of Jesus. And worse still, if he will recall Psalm 110, Jesus is to the right of God."

- *Intonation*: "method, method, and, once again, method. It will not guarantee us the truth because nothing can do that. But method, as self-conscious and self-critical as we can make it, is our only discipline. It cannot take us out of our present skins and bodies, minds and hearts, societies and cultures. But it is our one best hope of honesty. It is the due process of history"; "What I am trying to imagine is what Christianity must do clearly and honestly to distinguish itself from fantasy. If it does not do that, it will certainly survive but as an important and even lucrative sub-division of world-wide entertainment and global illusion"; "in 1999 I never imagined, even as prophetic nightmare, the speed with which faith-based thinking would morph into fantasy-based dreaming to infiltrate medicine, education, domestic program, foreign policy, and even news reporting."

- *Projection*: "I insist that Jesus-reconstruction, like all such reconstruction, is always a creative interaction of past and present"; "the resurrection of Jesus means for me that the human empowerment that some people experienced in Lower Galilee at the start of the first century in and through Jesus is now available to any person in any place at any time who finds God in and through that same Jesus"; "empty tomb stories and physical appearance stories are perfectly valid parables expressing that faith, akin in their own way to the Good Samaritan story. They are, for me, parables of resurrection not the resurrection itself. Resurrection as the continuing experience of God's presence in and through Jesus is the heart of Christian faith"; "the gospels are, for me, even more normative as process than as product"; "You cannot believe in a fact, only in an interpretation"; "those resurrectional visions explain the miracle of Christianity's birth and growth, spread and triumph, across the Roman empire"; Jesus's "resurrectional visions"; "I use *vision* and *apparition* interchangeably, and I understand them within the psychosocial and cross-cultural anthropology of comparative religion"; "two very early Christians who believed absolutely in the resurrection of Jesus," but for one (Paul's received tradition in 1 Corinthians 15) "risen apparitions were . . . fully emphasized." The second, where "risen apparitions were . . . completely avoided," is "Mark 15–16 which, in my view, created both the honourable burial and empty tomb precisely to avoid such resurrectional visions"; "since the Age of Enlightenment had been replaced by the Age of Entertainment, the future clash would not be between science and religion but between both of them and fantasy."

Presuppositional indicators from these triggers include:

- The divine manifestation of Christianity is a historical reconstruction, interpreted for a postmodern world.
- The postmodern historical Jesus is not found once and for all from the first century (way back then) but has to be reinterpreted (redone) in each generation and century.
- The reconstructed, postmodern Jesus is redone in creative interaction with particular needs, visions, programs, debates, and controversies—including conclusions from contemporary scholarship.
- Jesus reconstruction, like all other reconstruction, is always a creative interaction of past and present.
- Jesus's resurrection means Jesus's human empowerment, which can be experienced by any person throughout Christian history and today.
- Mark deliberately created the empty tomb story, which is not a historical event or legendary narrative.
- The empty tomb and appearance stories are valid parabolic expressions of faith.
- The Gospels are not a normative product but a process that involves not belief in facts but only in interpretations.
- Self-conscious and self-critical use of method will not guarantee truth or take us out of ourselves or our cultures. However, it is the one best hope of honesty in the due process of history.
- Christianity must distinguish itself from fantasy.
- Jesus's resurrection is described as a vision or an apparition (terms used interchangeably) within the framework of psychosocial and

cross-cultural anthropology of comparative religion. It is not unique to Christianity.

Presuppositional indicators pointing to the resurrection as divine empowerment of human beings were covered above. The empty tomb and resurrection appearances as parable are not dealt with in this assessment.

NON-SUPERNATURAL GOD AND JESUS'S RESURRECTION

Mark 15:33 states, "When the sixth hour [that is, noon] had come, there was darkness over the whole land until the ninth hour [that is, 3 p.m]." Borg and Crossan's comment, "That it was a 'supernatural' darkness is also exceedingly unlikely. Not only would this require an interventionist understanding of God's relation to nature, but an inexplicable darkness of this duration most likely would have been remarked upon by non-Christian authors, and we have no such reports." Instead, their interpretation is that "the darkness is the product of Mark's use of religious symbolism. . . . The darkness from noon to 3 PM is best understood as literary symbolism."[70]

In other words, there was no supernatural intervention by God, and the writing of this information was not of factual intent but was to be "understood as literary symbolism" or from a metaphorical perspective.

Crossan's statement is that "in my view the supernatural always (at least till this is disproved for me) operates through the screen of the natural. The supernatural is like the beating heart of the natural. It does not come seeping through cracks every now and then, so we can see it. It is always there—but we seldom see it." What then are miracles? They are "acts of faith which say, 'Here the supernatural, which is permanently present, is made, as it were, visible to us.; That is how I understand miracles. That is not naturalism. It is the belief that the supernatural never forces faith. Maybe that's the blunt way to put it."[71]

Elsewhere, in his debate with William Lane Craig, Crossan states in a discussion on miracles that a doctor might announce at Lourdes that God had intervened. However, Crossan states that "it's a theological presupposition of mine that God does not operate that way [by performing supernatural miracles]."[72]

---

70. Borg and Crossan, *Last Week*, 148.
71. Crossan, as cited in Copan, *Will the Real Jesus*, 45–46.
72. Crossan, as cited in Copan, *Will the Real Jesus*, 61.

Therefore, any supernatural, factual event of darkness at noon on crucifixion day at Golgotha (Mark 15:33) could not happen. Meaning here is not related to what actually happened according to the Gospels but is based on Crossan's presupposition. Crossan is imposing his subjective, presuppositional bias (an anti-supernatural interpretation) on the text by not allowing the text to speak for itself.

What are the biblical indicators that Jesus's resurrection involved supernatural interventions?

The Scriptures indicate that there was a great earthquake. An angel of the Lord descended from heaven and intervened in rolling back the stone covering the entrance to the tomb. The appearance of the angels was like lightning and their clothing was as white as snow; this caused the guards of the tomb to tremble and become like dead men (Matt 28:2–4).

There appeared two angels in white to Mary inside Jesus's empty tomb, and they spoke to Mary (John 20:11–13). Jesus, the formerly dead and buried one, stood before Mary and spoke to her (John 20:14–17).

To this point, the evidence is pointing to a bodily resurrection of Jesus through supernatural intervention. However, Crossan's call "When all else fails, read the text"[73] is automatically excluded for Crossan's own reading of the biblical text because of his apriori anti-supernaturalist worldview.

Crossan was asked about the events of Easter and his own Easter faith. His response began, "Easter means for me the divine empowerment which was present in Jesus." It was once available for a limited time to people in Galilee and Judea who had contact with him. However, that "is now available to anyone, anywhere in the world, who finds God in Jesus." Crossan's own meaning "has nothing to do, literally, with a body coming out of a tomb, or a tomb being found empty, or visions, or anything else. All those are dramatic ways of expressing the faith. The heart of resurrection for me is that the power of God is now available through Jesus, unconfined by time or space, to anyone who believes and experiences it."[74] From where does Crossan obtain such a meaning?

NATURE OF JESUS'S RESURRECTION

When the Bruce Highway at North Lakes, north of Brisbane, was closed after a crash in which a semitrailer became jammed under an overpass, does that mean that the truck was too tall to travel under the overpass?[75] Or does

---

73. White and Crossan, *Is Orthodox Biblical Account*.
74. Crossan and Watts, *Who Is Jesus*, 161.
75. "Trailer Vertical."

it mean through postmodern reconstruction that this refers to the hierarchy of the Queensland government being jammed with legislation that is preventing the progress of the state?

How is one to understand Crossan's statement that "anyone who wants to dramatize the death of Jesus in play or film should first read the text and get the story right"?[76] Is it based on the plain reading of the text that understands the semantic, etymological meanings of "anyone," "dramatize," "death of Jesus," "play or film," "first read the text," and "get the story right"? Or does Crossan want the reader to put his or her own creative, multivalent, free play meaning on the text? Is this Crossan statement meant to indicate what "it means to me"? The answers to these types of questions occupy much of the assessment of this hypothesis.

For Crossan and Watts, Easter "has nothing to do, literally, with a body coming out of the tomb, or a tomb being found empty, or visions, or anything else." Instead, all of those "are dramatic ways of expressing the faith," thus making an empty tomb independent of meaning. Crosssan states that "the heart of resurrection for me is that the power of God is now available through Jesus, unconfined by time or space, to anyone who believes and experiences it."[77]

However, there is a challenge: does Crossan want his readers to understand all of the words and the syntax of his own writings according to their conventional (and so determinate) meaning, or does he want the readers to create meaning according to the readers' own indeterminate desires and subjective imposition on the text? Can such a view of Jesus's resurrection be verified from the biblical and supporting evidence, or is it promoting another worldview, where meaning is independent of the crucified body of Christ being placed in Joseph of Arimathea's tomb and the tomb being empty on resurrection morning? Is it possible to separate the meaning of Jesus's resurrection from the fact of an empty tomb? That is the primary task to be examined in testing this hypothesis.

When asked by White about Crossan's presupposition of divine consistency and "what kind of evidence could possibly exist in antiquity" that would prove to Crossan that "miraculous events such as the virgin birth or the resurrection of Christ from the dead, actually took place in historical context," Crossan's response is: "The only way I can accept the claims of any one of them is what it means. Therefore when I read these claims about Jesus, for example, what is important for me?" He places the miraculous in a pre-Enlightenment world in which "what's important to me about the

---

76. Crossan, *God and Empire*, 137.
77. Crossan and Watts, *Who Is Jesus*, 161.

miracles of Jesus," including healing, is that "in the ancient world . . . I make no difference between Asclepius and Jesus in terms of reality."[78]

POST-RESURRECTION EVENTS

N. T. Wright explains that "when the early Christians said 'resurrection' they meant it in the sense it bore both in paganism (which denied it) and in Judaism (an influential part of which affirmed it). 'Resurrection' did not mean that someone possessed 'a heavenly and exalted status.' When predicated of Jesus, it did not mean his 'perceived presence' in the ongoing church. Nor, if we are thinking historically, could it have meant 'the passage of the human Jesus into the power of God.' It meant bodily resurrection; and that is what the early Christians affirmed."[79]

That is what the Scriptures affirmed to the disciples. Jesus's resurrection was not a mere resuscitation. Unlike what happened to Lazarus (John 11:1–44), Jesus rose from the dead with a new kind of life. For instance, Jesus was not immediately recognized by his disciples on the road to Emmaus (LUKE 24:13–22). And Mary Magdalene failed to recognize Jesus at first at the tomb on Sunday morning (John 20:1).

On the other hand, there was continuity between Jesus's resurrected body and his previous body. Though people may have been initially startled at meeting Jesus again, they were convinced he had risen from the dead (Luke 24:33, 37). Paul writes to the Corinthians that Christ "appeared to Peter, and then to the Twelve. After that, he appeared to more than five hundred of the brothers at the same time, most of whom are still living, though some have fallen asleep. Then he appeared to James, then to all the apostles, and last of all he appeared to me [Paul] also, as to one abnormally born" (1 Cor 15:5–8).

There are some important aspects of Jesus's resurrected body:

- It was a physical body (Matt 28:9).
- Jesus ate food (John 20:15; Acts 10:41).
- Jesus said he was not a spirit but flesh and bones (Luke 24:39).
- Jesus gave them "greetings" and said he would meet his disciples in Galilee (Matt 28:9–10).
- Some "took hold of his feet," and Jesus spoke to them (Matt 28:9).
- "They saw him" and "worshiped him" (Matt 28:17).

78. White and Crossan, *Is Orthodox Biblical Account*.
79 Wright, *Resurrection of the Son*, 209 (emphasis added).

- Two people going to the village of Emmaus urged Jesus to stay with them. "He took bread and blessed and broke it and gave it to them," and their eyes were opened concerning who he was (Luke 24:28–35).
- Jesus stood among his disciples and said, "See my hands and my feet, that it is I myself. Touch me and see. For a spirit does not have flesh and bones as you see that I have" (Luke 24:39).
- "He showed them [the disciples] his hands and his feet." While they still disbelieved, Jesus asked: "Have you anything here to eat?" They gave him a piece of broiled fish, and he took it and ate before them (Luke 24:42–43).
- Jesus "opened their minds to understand the Scriptures" and told them that "you are witnesses of these things"—of Jesus suffering and rising from the dead on the third day (Luke 24:45–48).
- Jesus said to Mary [Magdalene], "Do not cling to me, for I have not yet ascended to the Father, but go to my brothers and say to them, 'I am ascending to my Father and your Father, to my God and your God'" (John 20:17).
- Jesus stood among his disciples (the doors were locked) and said to them, "'Peace be with you.' When he had said this he showed them his hands and his side. Then the disciples were glad when they saw the Lord" (John 20:19–20). Then Jesus breathed on them and told them to receive the Holy Spirit (John 20:22).
- Doubting Thomas was told by the other disciples that "we have seen the Lord," but he said, "Unless I see in his hands the mark of the nails and place my finger into the mark of the nails, and place my hand into his side, I will never believe" (John 20:25). Eight days later, Thomas was with the disciples again, and Jesus stood among them and said to Thomas, "Put your finger here, and see my hands; and put out your hand and place it in my side. Do not disbelieve, but believe." Thomas answered him, "My Lord and my God!" Jesus said to him, "Have you believed because you have seen me? Blessed are those who have not seen and yet have believed" (John 20:27–29).

Crossan's metaphorical, postmodern resurrection is an extra added to the biblical texts.

Crossan's View of Historiography

This is a recap of Crossan's statement on the definition of history in chapter 2. Crossan was specific in labelling his approach to history and hermeneutics of the historical Jesus:

> Christianity is *historical reconstruction* interpreted as divine manifestation. It is not (*in a postmodern world*) that we find *once and for all* who the historical Jesus was way back then. It is that each generation and century must redo that historical work and establish its best reconstruction, a reconstruction that will be and must be in some creative interaction with its own particular needs, visions, and programs . . . . The historical Jesus (fact) is the manifestation of God for us here and now (interpretation). *You cannot believe in a fact, only in an interpretation.*[80]

His position is unadorned, unorthodox, and he cannot consistently apply it: "This is my working definition of history: *History is the past reconstructed interactively by the present through argued evidence in public discourse.* . . . History as argued public reconstruction is necessary to reconstruct our past in order to project *our* future."[81] This is a question-begging view of historiography, especially in light of the consensus of other historians examined in this book. Crossan's statement affirms a worldview of postmodern deconstruction that places another spin on the historical data that so skews the agenda to accommodate Crossan's reader-response philosophy. Imagine using Crossan's view of history for the September 11, 2001, terrorist attacks in the USA. It turns history into nonsense. Am I being too harsh on this eminent historical Jesus scholar? I don't think so. He did not use his approach to history in his own autobiography.[82] He is selective with his application of deconstruction.

Crossan writes that "by *historical study* I mean an analysis whose theories and methods, evidence and arguments, results and conclusions are open, in principle and practice, to any human observer, any disciplined investigator, any self-conscious and self-critical student . . . . The historical Jesus is always an interpretive construct of its own time and place but open to all of that time and place."[83] He is pointed in his challenge that historians should say, "This, in my best professional reconstruction, is what happened; that did not."[84]

---

80. Crossan, *Who Killed Jesus*, 217 (emphasis added).
81. Crossan, *Birth of Christianity*, 20 (emphasis in original).
82. See Crossan, *Long Way from Tipperary*.
83. Crossan, *Jesus*, 199 (emphasis in original).
84. Crossan, *Who Killed Jesus*, 37. For an assessment of postmodern reconstruction/

He does not use that approach for his life in Ireland and then in the USA as a university professor. Postmodern deconstruction falls flat when it meets Columbus's voyages to the Americas and the Taliban suicide bombers in Afghanistan: "And so it ends like this for America and its patient allies: in terrorism, sorrow and regret. After twenty years, the mission in Afghanistan is over, finished in a bloodied disastrous mess that threatens to spawn a nastier strain of global jihadism," according to *ABC News*.[85] Crossan cannot consistently apply a postmodern deconstructionist interpretation to the specifics of suicide bombers, Columbus's voyages, and the Afghanistan war. History requires an admission of specifics of historical investigation.

Resurrection and the Cross Gospel

Crossan places so much emphasis on the role of the Cross Gospel from the Gospel of Peter as the foundation of the passion accounts in the New Testament that he states, "The signal achievement of the Cross Gospel to move from the *prophetic passion* to the *narrative passion*" was "to create from discrete prophetic allusions and composite prophetic fulfillments a coherent and sequential story."[86]

How does this prominence influence the resurrection accounts in the Gospels? Crossan promotes the view that "the first writer to use and develop the Cross Gospel composition was, in my judgment on the extant texts, the evangelist Mark himself. I see no convincing evidence that Mark has any other basis for his passion narrative than that source and his own theological creativity." How does that apply to the resurrection? Mark "made three profound changes" to the Cross Gospel in the Gospel of Peter. "The first and most basic one was to change the overarching model from *innocence rescued to martyrdom vindicated*. No salvific miracle *here below* would save Jesus before, during, or after death. Only at the parousia would the resurrectional victory become visible, according to Mark 13:26 and 14:62." Therefore, "Mark had . . . to negate completely both the visible resurrection and the subsequent Roman confession from the Cross Gospel. He did it by retrojecting both back into preceding sections of his Gospel." These were in Mark 9:2–8 and Mark 15:39.[87]

Presuppositional triggers include:

---

deconstruction, see the next chapter in testing postmodern deconstruction.

85. Probyn, "Afghanistan Mission."
86. Crossan, *Historical Jesus*, 389 (emphasis in original).
87. Crossan, *Historical Jesus*, 389 (emphasis in original).

- *Names*: Mark, Roman
- *Intonation*: "The signal achievement of the Cross Gospel to move from the *prophetic passion* to the *narrative passion*" was "to create from discrete prophetic allusions and composite prophetic fulfillments a coherent and sequential story"; Mark "made three profound changes" to the Cross Gospel; "the first and most basic one was to change the overarching model from *innocence rescued to martyrdom vindicate*"
- *Projection*: "the first writer to use and develop the Cross Gospel composition was, in my judgment on the extant texts, the evangelist Mark himself. I see no convincing evidence that Mark has any other basis for his passion narrative than that source and his own theological creativity"; "no salvific miracle here below would save Jesus before, during, or after death. Only at the parousia would the resurrectional victory become visible, according to Mark 13:26 and 14:62"; "Mark had . . . to negate completely both the visible resurrection and the subsequent Roman confession from the Cross Gospel. He did it by retrojecting into preceding sections of his Gospel."

Suggested presuppositional understandings from these triggers include:

- The first New Testament Gospel writer to use the Cross Gospel in his passion-resurrection narrative was Mark.
- The Cross Gospel moved the passion story from prophetic to narrative passion.
- The passion accounts were created from prophetic allusions.
- Mark changed the overarching passion model from innocence rescued to martyrdom vindicated.
- There was no salvation miracle that would save Jesus before, during, or after his death.
- Mark negated the visible resurrection and Roman confession from the Cross Gospel by retrojecting other sections from his Gospel.

Abduction: Crossan and the Philosophical Crusher

As indicated in chapter 3, methodological abduction refers to a procedure that is central to the scientific process of an "inferential step from some initial puzzling fact to some theoretical hypothesis which can explain it."[88] The initial puzzling fact that was observed by me as a researcher is related to what Ben Meyer calls "the philosophical crusher"[89] as it applies to Crossan's definition of history and its application to his historical understanding and examples.

What is a philosophical crusher? Meyer learned it from Alex Tourigny, his teacher in philosophical psychology, whose "version of the crusher was a deadly 'reduction to first principles.'"[90] Meyer expounds on one example of a philosophical crusher as referring to "the reduction of implicit to explicit self-contradiction." The nature of this reduction is that it "takes place by making explicit, not the content of an affirmation, but the performance of affirming (or denying)." The self-contradiction of this crusher is that "the actuality of performance belies the all-comprehensive explanation."

I hope you notice how Crossan's promotion of deconstruction cannot be maintained in all historical examples without contradiction. For example, Crossan has not told us to interpret all of his writings as a postmodern deconstructionist. The crusher of contradiction is evident when Crossan does not apply his foundation postmodern principles to, say, his autobiography, *A Long Way from Tipperary*. He uses standard historiography when he states, "Both Tacitus and Josephus were aristocratic historians, one from the consular nobility, the other from the Jewish priestly elite."[91] As a further example, when Crossan does not interpret the Afghani suicide bombings in a postmodern way (his method), he is promoting a contradiction that is a crusher.

Practitioners can be demonstrated as inconsistent in the application of their own theories of knowing in appropriating them to their own works, and scholars can be shown as contradictory in not practicing in their publications what they preach in their own theories! This book demonstrates the self-contradiction that is evident in Crossan's own writings where Crossan affirms deconstruction as a method but practices traditional historiography in his autobiography and elsewhere.[92]

As for Crossan, does the philosophical crusher expose the practice of his theories of

---

88. Svennevig, "Abduction," 1.
89. Meyer, "Philosophical Crusher."
90. Meyer, "Philosophical Crusher."
91. Crossan, *Birth of Christianity*, 10.
92. Compare Crossan's *Long Way from Tipperary* (his autobiography) with the promotion of reconstruction in his other publications. The philosophical crusher has crushed Crossan's philosophy of history.

1. the nature of history, and

2. postmodern hermeneutics that are found to be wanting?

Is there self-contradiction in how Crossan applies these theories in his own writings? Thomas W. Manson writes, "It may be said of all the theological schools of thought: By their lives of Jesus ye shall know them."[93] Crossan objects to this perspective, "'You are not reconstructing history,' I am told . . . . 'You are only seeing your face at the bottom of a deep well.' It is usually a cheap crack, not so much in theory as in practice."[94] He calls it "an oft-repeated and rather cheap gibe that historical Jesus researchers are simply looking down a deep well and seeing their own reflections from below."[95] Is it a genuine challenge that Crossan is reconstructing history and hermeneutics according to his own definitions and then inconsistently applying such definitions in his own works? Does the philosophical crusher expose his approach to history? I am convinced it does.

THE DEFINITION OF HISTORY REVISITED

As indicated previously, Crossan's "working definition of history is that *'history is the past reconstructed interactively by the present through argued evidence in public discourse* . . . . History as argued public construction is possible because it is necessary. We reconstruct our past to project our future. And it is, unfortunately, *not* possible *not* to do it.'"[96]

What does Crossan mean when he speaks of history involving the reconstruction of the past "interactively"? He explains in an article that "I will call it *interactivism* or *historical dialectic*. The past and the present must interact with one another, each changing and challenging the other. The ideal is an absolutely fair and equal reaction between one another."[97] Later in this article, he explains how this applies to Jesus's resurrection:

> It is the same Jesus, the one and only historical Jesus of the late 20s [of the first century] in his Jewish homeland, but now untrammeled by time and place, language and proximity. It is the one and only Jesus absolutely the same, absolutely different. He is trammeled, of course, then, now, and always, by faith. Bodily

---

93. Manson, "Failure of Liberalism," 92.
94. Crossan, *Long Way from Tipperary*, 150.
95. Crossan, "Historical Jesus as Risen Lord," 2.
96. Crossan, "Historical Jesus as Risen Lord," 3 (emphasis in original). See also Crossan, *Birth of Christianity*, 20.
97. Crossan, "Historical Jesus as Risen Lord," 3 (emphasis in original).

resurrection has nothing to do with a resuscitated body coming out of its tomb. And neither is it just another word for Christian faith itself. Bodily resurrection means that the embodied life and death of the historical Jesus continues to be experienced, by believers, as powerfully efficacious and salvifically present in this world. That life continues, as it always has, to form communities of like lives.[98]

Robert Stewart makes the critical and decisive assessment that "Crossan's commitment to understanding history, like texts, as polyvalent leads him to stress that the historical Jesus must be meaningful for today. The result is that for Crossan historical truth is fluid and relative in nature. This leads him to reject authoritative interpretations of who Jesus as the word of God is and what it means to be one of his disciples."[99]

Method and Truth

What is the meaning of truth in assessing Crossan's philosophical crusher? Here, "truth" is used as Meyer explains it: it is a "bleak spectacle of theories shattering on the rock of fact, the fact in question is special. It has to do with how the human subject functions. What if we were to come into possession of truth on fundamental aspects of human functioning?" He explains that such would be a "powerful instrument for discriminating, methodically and productively, among a vast range of significant truths and errors." Crossan's statement is: "The test of the answer is the field of human performance. Once the pattern of human operations has been brought to light in radically unrevisable fashion, new possibilities heave into view: in particular, the new possibility of systematically confronting theories of knowing with facts of knowing."[100]

Here, the truth of Crossan's theoretical system of historiography—a theory of postmodern reconstruction—is tested by his practice in determining the facts of his knowing. What's the truth about Crossan's system of knowing history and its implementation in the practice of history in his publications? Is Crossan a consistent reconstructionist in his applications? The philosophical crusher will find him to be truthful or inconsistent in his application, in the postmodern reconstruction of history in his writings, particularly those since he articulated his reconstructionist definition

---

98. Crossan, "Historical Jesus as Risen Lord," 46.
99. Stewart, *Quest of Hermeneutical Jesus*, 126.
100. Meyer, "Philosophical Crusher."

of history.[101] There is evidence that demonstrates he reveals a contradiction in the application of his own definition of history as reconstructed interactivism.

As early as the epilogue of Crossan's 1991 *The Historical Jesus*, Crossan was articulating his postmodern, reconstructive approach to history with the statement that his book "challenges the reader on the level of formal method, material investment, and historical interpretation. It presumes that there will always be divergent historical Jesuses, that there will always be divergent Christs built upon them, but above all, it argues that the structure of a Christianity will always be: *this is how we see Jesus-then as Christ-now.*"[102]

His 1991 view of reconstruction is also found and applied in the abridged version.[103] One application of his postmodern reconstructive methodology is in his three understandings of Jesus's resurrection:

1. It is one way but not the only way of expressing Christian faith.
2. It is "*apparition*—which involves trance, that altered state of consciousness."
3. "Christian faith experiences the *continuation* of divine empowerment through Jesus, but that continuation began only after his death and burial."[104]

An examination of Crossan's use of the philosophical crusher can be incorporated for all publications from and including *The Historical Jesus* (1991).

Note Crossan's claim that "in quoting *secondary* literature I spend no time citing other scholars to show how wrong they are. Those who are cited represent my intellectual debts."[105] However, within seven pages of making that statement, he violates his own claim by criticizing John Davis for Davis's castigating his anthropological peer, Julian Pitt-Rivers.[106] Crossan has a conflict with Luke Timothy Johnson when Johnson writes that

> *the game is fixed*. Crossan's remarkably early dating for virtually all apocryphal materials, and his correspondingly late dating for virtually all canonical materials, together with his frequent assertion that the extracanonical sources are unaffected by the canonical sources and therefore have independent evidentiary

---

101. This was articulated in Crossan, *Birth of Christianity*, 20, and Crossan, "Historical Jesus as Risen Lord," 3.
102. Crossan, *Historical Jesus*, 423 (emphasis in original).
103. Crossan, *Jesus*, xiv.
104. Crossan, *Jesus*, 160–61 (emphasis in original).
105. Crossan, *Historical Jesus*, xxxiv (emphasis in original).
106. Crossan, *Historical Jesus*, 7.

value *rests on little more than his assertions and those of the likeminded colleagues he cites.*[107]

Crossan takes offence over this comment, admitting "the use of *both* intracanonical and extracanonical (apocryphal) gospels is rather controversial. The charge of having 'fixed' the evidence is the most serious accusation one scholar can make against another.... I repeat, once again, that you must decide your presuppositions about gospel traditions before reconstruction [of] either the historical Jesus or earliest Christianity. Everyone must. Everyone does."[108] Crossan needs to get over the fact—yes, the fact—he *does not* seek to show how wrong a scholar is in his or her position. That is a false statement, as I've just shown.

What are some examples of Crossan's methodology being exposed by the philosophical crusher? What demonstrates contradictions between his stated postmodern, reconstructive definition of history and his practice of historical statements and authentication? Crossan does this in two ways: firstly, through his acceptance of the narratives of other authors without a postmodern, reconstructive interpretation and, secondly, through acceptance of traditional historiography.

An examination of Crossan's practice reveals an inconsistent application of his stated historical method. Crossan advocates postmodern reconstruction, but in many examples (see evidence below) he uses traditional historiography throughout his publications.

The following abduction analysis will provide limited samples from Crossan's major publications, beginning in 1991 with *The Historical Jesus*, as a comprehensive examination of examples is beyond the scope of this project. This researcher has identified at least five hundred examples in Crossan's publications of the use of the philosophical crusher. In what follows, this evidence will be in abbreviated form.

Crossan's Self-Contradiction: Acceptance of Traditional History

It is observed from details in his autobiography and other evidence supplied in this book, including the historiography of other historians (above): Crossan's reconstruction is in contrast to the dominant view of secular and sacred historians who regard the study of history as involving an examination of recorded facts (oral and written) from the past and interpretations—based

---

107. Johnson, *Real Jesus*, 47 (emphases added).
108. Crossan, *Birth of Christianity*, 103.

on those facts—but the facts cannot be discounted through a postmodern reconstruction. Samples of abduction from Crossan deal with the topics of

1. his acceptance of the results of traditional historiography, without reconstruction; and
2. his acceptance of the narrative of other authors, without reconstruction.

(A) Crossan's Autobiographical Details

One of the key examples of the philosophical crusher's impact on Crossan's writings can be found throughout his autobiographical publication where he provided personal details of his life from the past that affirmed the traditional model of history, with his writing of his life in his home country of Ireland and then in the United States.[109]

He writes of being ten years of age in 1944, going to boarding school, attending primary school in the late 1930s and early 1940s, and becoming a Roman Catholic priest and monk in Ireland.[110] Elsewhere, he notes, "I have never been unwillingly hungry in all my life. I was five when the Second World War broke out in Europe, but politically neutral and minimally rationed Ireland had enough food so that hunger was not a wartime reality."[111]

He was one of a dozen scholars in the spring of 1998 who appeared on the American public television program "From Jesus to Christ: The First Christians." His father died at age sixty-seven, when Crossan was thirty-seven. From 1965 to 1967, he was engaged in "postdoctoral specialization at the French Biblical and Archeological School in Jerusalem," a school that "was founded in 1890 by Father Marie-Joseph Lagrange."[112]

He requested a dispensation from the priesthood to become married to Margaret in a Catholic Church in 1969. He was contracted as an associate professor and went on to become a full professor in biblical studies and comparative religion for twenty-six years at DePaul University, a Roman Catholic institution in Chicago, until his retirement in 1995.[113] Margaret's heart attack and death occurred in 1983. He married Sarah, an older student, in 1986, moving to Florida in 1995.[114] There is no hint of reconstruc-

---

109. Crossan, *Long Way from Tipperary*.
110. Crossan, *Long Way from Tipperary*, 1, 3.
111. Crossan, *Birth of Christianity*, 421.
112. Crossan, *Long Way from Tipperary*, 3, 31, 65.
113. Crossan, *Long Way from Tipperary*, 90, 95, 106; Crossan and Watts, *Who Is Jesus*, xiv, 179.
114. Crossan, *Long Way from Tipperary*, 121–23, 127, 178–79, 181.

tion in his autobiography. Why not, when he considers history involves reconstruction?

> This is my working definition of history: *History is the past reconstructed interactively by the present through argued evidence in public discourse.* There are times we can get only alternative perspectives on the same event. (There are *always* alternative perspectives, even when we do not hear them.) But history as argued public reconstruction is necessary to reconstruct *our* past in order to project *our* future.[115]

He writes of many interviews in which he was involved for newspapers and magazines, as well as on radio and television, regarding the life, death, and resurrection of Jesus.[116] He participated in the Jesus Seminar in the 1980s.[117]

In all of these autobiographical historical examples from his life, he uses a traditional model of historical understanding and not a reconstructive, interactive perspective. He presents events as fixed and happenings from his past as unchanged, as historical events.

In the midst of his recording personal, traditional, historical events from his life, he mentions a cover story about him in the magazine section of the *Chicago Tribune*, Sunday, 17 July 1994, in which the writer summarizes Crossan as saying that "Jesus was a mortal man in the fullest sense of the term. He was conceived and born in the conventional way (no Virgin Birth), did not perform miracles (no Lazarus, no loaves and fishes, no lepers), did not undergo resurrection (no Easter) and after his execution, was probably eaten by wild dogs (no joke)."[118]

Crossan's response to this content is "No mistake in that, but no sense of parable either." In the interview with the journalist for the story, he conveys that it is not enough to say that "a story is not history," as one also has to ask "if it was intended as fact or fiction and, if as fiction, what its purpose was." His viewpoint is that one needs to ask if the "nonhistorical, that is, the fictional story was intended as pedagogical challenge."[119] Since he regards the virgin birth, miracles, the body of Jesus being eaten by wild dogs, and no resuscitation at Easter as being parables, what does he mean by parable?

---

115. Crossan, *Birth of Christianity*, 20 (emphasis in original).
116. Crossan, *Who Killed Jesus*, 189.
117. Crossan, *Long Way from Tipperary*, 173–74.
118. Crossan, *Long Way from Tipperary*, 133.
119. Crossan, *Long Way from Tipperary*, 133.

His definition is that a parable is "a fictional story with a theological punch, a made-up tale that kicked you in the rear when you weren't looking."[120]

By 2012, Crossan had widened his understanding of parable to include these two dimensions:

1. The parables *by* Jesus invented both characters and stories about them—for example, the good Samaritan and the prodigal son—but

2. "Parables *about* Jesus presumed historical characters—for example, John and Jesus, Annas and Caiaphas, Antipas and Pilate—but invented stories about what they said and did."[121]

His personal new understanding of parable was that he understood each of the four Gospels was "a book-length *megaparable* about the life, death, and resurrection of the historical character Jesus of Nazareth."[122]

Later in my assessment, it will be investigated whether Crossan's interpretation of the meaning of parable is fundamentally different from or in contrast to that defined in the Gospels.

Questions emerge for this researcher. If events from the past in Crossan's personal life are taken literally in a traditional, historical understanding and are not given a postmodern, interactive reconstruction or presented as parables, why can the events of Jesus's life from the past not be taken literally in a traditional, historical understanding? Why must the Gospels be megaparables of Jesus's life?

(B) TRADITIONAL HISTORICAL EXAMPLES

In these listed examples, Crossan agrees with, endorses, and/or uses traditional historical examples. These include:

The Church Fathers

Crossan writes of the martyrdom of St. Cyprian, of there existing no early Christian Roman writings with a knowledge of Mark, of Justin Martyr's writing *The First Apology* in mid second-century, and of Celsus's anti-Christian attacks.[123]

---

120. Crossan, *Long Way from Tipperary*, 133.
121. Crossan, *Power of Parable*, 3–5 (emphasis in original).
122. Crossan, *Power of Parable*, 5–6 (emphasis in original).
123. Crossan, *Historical Jesus*, 69; Crossan, *Who Killed Jesus*, 17; Crossan, "Historical

FOURTH CROSSAN LESSON 169

Contemporary Examples

Crossan writes there was anti-Semitism that led to the death of six million Jews on Hitler's list, while twelve hundred on Schindler's list were saved. Archbishop Oscar Romero, Archbishop of San Salvador, was murdered in 1980.[124] Crossan states that his first visit to the Oberammergau Passion Play was in 1960, which was the version Hitler saw before his 1930 election. Crossan went to the healing shrines at Lourdes in France, Fatima in Portugal, Epidaurus in Greece, and Pergamum in Turkey, and "at both the Catholic and pagan shrines the miracles were remarkably the same." Dresden was bombed by British and American planes in February 1945.[125]

Crucifixion and Cultural Issues

Crossan writes of the June 1968 finding of "the only skeleton of a crucified person ever uncovered" in a Jerusalem tomb and dating to the first century.[126]

Mortality rates in pre-industrial society were that about 60 percent of live births were dead by age sixteen and 90 percent by age forty-six. He writes of the Jewish revolt against Rome "of 66 to 73 C.E."[127] There is no deconstructionist interpretation here.

Extracanonical Material

Crossan writes of the Gospel of Thomas that was found at Nag Hammadi, Upper Egypt, in 1945, and of papyri found in the excavated rubbish dumps of ancient Oxyrhynchus, the modern El Bahnasa.[128] The ancient city of Panopolis, modern Akhimim, on the Nile River, Egypt, was excavated in 1886–1887 by a French archeological mission that found in the cemetery of Panopolis a small papyrus of fragmentary texts, one presumed to be a fragment of the long-lost Gospel of Peter, dating from the seventh to ninth centuries.[129]

Jesus as Risen Lord," 30.

124. Crossan, *Who Killed Jesus*, IX, 35; Crossan and Watts, *Who Is Jesus*, 173, 175.

125. Crossan, *God and Empire*, 2, 74, 129. Crossan, as cited in Copan, *Will the Real Jesus*, 45.

126. Crossan and Watts, *Who Is Jesus*, 124; Crossan, *Jesus*, 124.

127. Crossan, *Historical Jesus*, 4, 210; Crossan, *Who Killed Jesus*, 52.

128. Crossan, *Jesus*, xi, 63; Crossan, *Who Killed Jesus*, 26; Crossan, *Birth of Christianity*, 124.

129. Crossan, *Who Killed Jesus*, 23.

The First Century AD

"Pontius Pilate governed for ten years from 26 to 36 C.E., and Joseph Caiaphas remained as High Priest from 18 to 36 C.E."[130] Crossan identifies a peasant Jesus, not the Son of God, who "was the son of Ananias, and the year was 62 C.E., under Albinus, Roman governor between then and 64 C.E."[131] He writes of "unarmed Jews gathered before the governor Petronius" of Syria who planned to place a statue of the emperor Caligula in Jerusalem's temple.[132]

Historians and Historicity

Does Crossan want to present a traditional understanding of history or reconstructive interactivism? In his writings, he has produced an assortment that mixes both of these perspectives, even though his favored definition of history is postmodern reconstruction. Lack of consistency is being uncovered in this abduction. The philosophical crusher has found him out.

In seeking to provide a refutation of a decree from Emperor Augustus, based on Luke 2:1, Crossan states that "there was no such worldwide census under Octavius Augustus."[133] He writes of historical events surrounding Octavius, soon to become Augustus, and his military defeats.[134] "Augustus expanded Rome's territorial control eastward to Armenia."[135]

Crossan writes of Uragit, immediately north of Israel-to-be in the fourteenth century BCE.[136] He states the Shepherd of Hermas is "dated from Rome around the year 100." A copy of "the Didache was hidden in a manuscript codex, along with six other early Christian texts" in an ancient library in a Jerusalem monastery, and "the scribe who copied those seven texts signed the last leaf as 'Leon, notary and sinner,' and dated that completion to June 11, 1056."[137]

He writes of the Babylonian Empire destroying Jerusalem and its Temple in 587 BCE.[138] Beginning in 1977, archaeologist Bargil Pixner super-

---

130. Crossan, *Jesus*, 136.
131. Crossan, *Who Killed Jesus*, 56.
132. Crossan, *Birth of Christianity*, 284–85; Crossan, *Who Killed Jesus*, 92.
133. Crossan, *Jesus*, 20.
134. Crossan and Reed, *In Search of Paul*, 21, 25, 231.
135. Crossan and Reed, *In Search of Paul*, 84.
136. Crossan, *Birth of Christianity*, 185.
137. Crossan, *Birth of Christianity*, 363–64, 394.
138. Crossan, *Birth of Christianity*, 439.

vised excavations at what he called the Gate of the Essenes in the Protestant Cemetery, southern slope of Mount Zion.[139] Crossan writes of Eusebius, bishop of Caesarea, who "lived between 263 and 339 and saw Christianity pass from persecuted cult to imperial religion."[140]

There is an overabundance of information provided as traditional historiography in the two co-authored books by Crossan and archaeologist Jonathan L Reed.[141] These demonstrate the self-contradiction and incoherence in comparing Crossan's stated theory of historiography and his practice of it in his writings. A couple more examples will suffice: "In 1962 Italian archaeologists, clearing sand and overgrowth from the ruined theater at Caesarea Maritima, longtime seat of Roman power on the eastern Mediterranean shore, uncovered an inscription bearing the name of Pontius Pilate." It was "reused from the ruined theater's renovation in the fourth century" and was a "Latin inscription" and "settled scholarly quibbles over Pilate's exact title and ruling authority by naming him a prefect rather than an inferior procurator, but was more celebrated as the first physical witness to such a prominent New Testament figure."[142] There was an archaeologically "spectacular discovery" at Pompeii in 1909 when "Italian archaeologists uncovered perhaps the world's most famous frescoes in a house outside the city that they later called the Villa of the Mysteries."[143]

Crossan's view is that he clarified "the situation on historical origin" of the "general bodily resurrection," and he "presumes, summarizes, and reorganizes earlier responses to Tom's book[144] . . . at the Annual Meetings of the Evangelical Philosophical Society, Atlanta, Saturday, November 11, 2003, and the Evangelical Theological Society, San Antonio, TX, Friday, November 19, 2004."[145] Crossan writes of "Greece, having invented democratic rule" and "Rome, having invented republican rule."[146] He takes a traditional historical line that St Augustine's Confessions were written in 397–398, and "Jesus lived, most likely, from about 4 BCE to about 30 CE."[147]

---

139. Crossan, *Birth of Christianity*, 435.
140. Crossan, *Birth of Christianity*, 467.
141. Crossan and Reed, *Excavating Jesus*; *In Search of Paul*.
142. Crossan and Reed, *Excavating Jesus*, 2.
143. Crossan and Reed, *In Search of Paul*, 312.
144. He refers to Wright, *Resurrection of the Son*.
145. Wright and Crossan, "Resurrection," 174, 216n4.
146. Crossan, *God and Empire*, 7.
147. Crossan, *Power of Parable*, 62, 128.

Historical Jesus Studies

Crossan writes of the problem of reconstruction becoming obvious when Robert Funk of the Westar Institute convened the Jesus Seminar to try to establish some scholarly consensus on the historical Jesus, scholars meeting twice a year for five years at seminaries or universities, working on an inventory of what they considered was originally from Jesus.[148]

Crossan states that there is a similar story to Jesus's virginal conception in Suetonius, the Roman historian "who tells us that the night Augustus (the emperor at the time of Jesus' birth) was conceived, his mother Atia was in the temple of Apollo, and Apollo impregnated her so that Atia bore a divine child. 'Augustus is the Son of God and divine,' says the pagan Roman. 'Jesus is Son of God and divine,' the Christian believes."[149] Crossan states that "before Jesus was born, Caesar Augustus was proclaimed as Divine, Son of God, God, and God from God, as Lord, Redeemer, Liberator, and Savior of the world. Those claims of Roman imperial theology were found everywhere through texts, images, inscriptions, and structures."[150]

In discussing bodily-resurrection faith, Crossan notes he was already thinking along similar lines as Wright on general bodily resurrection within Jewish tradition, when he spoke on "The Resurrection of Jesus in Its Jewish Context" at the annual meeting of the New Testament Society of South Africa at Potchefstroom, on Tuesday, April 9, 2002.[151]

Ireland, Judaism, and Religious Movements

Crossan writes of NASA's weather satellites finding a clear day over Ireland.[152] Of different historical eras, he articulates details of martyrs at the time of the Maccabean revolt and persecution, the Bar-Kochba revolt, the Celts, and "the problem of martyrdom during the Seleucid persecution in the 160s B.C.E."[153] As for the Jewish people, they gained their independence from the Hellenistic empire of Antiochus Epiphanes around 164 BCE.[154]

---

148. Funk et al, *Gospel of Mark*, 424; Crossan and Watts, *Who Is Jesus*, xv.
149. Crossan, as cited in Copan, *Will the Real Jesus*, 38.
150. Wright and Crossan, "Resurrection," 182.
151. Wright and Crossan, "Resurrection," 216n3.
152. Crossan, *God and Empire*, 40.
153. Wright and Crossan, "Resurrection," 25, 41, 175.
154. Borg and Crossan, *Last Week*, 12.

Diogenes of Sinope (400–320 BCE), born on the southern coast of the Black Sea, founded the Greek philosophical movement of Cynicism.[155] The Essenes arose in the first half of the second century BCE, and their Qumran library is that of the Dead Sea Scrolls.[156]

In Crossan's discussion of Ireland, Judaism, and other religious movements there is not a hint of his deconstruction. The philosophical crusher has exposed the contradictions in his stated version of the nature of history and his own practice of history.

The Roman Empire

Crossan writes of the assassination of Julius Caesar on March 15, 44 BCE, and conveys recorded details of Augustus becoming emperor, the death of Herod Agrippa I in 44 CE, and all of Palestine reunited under direct Roman administration.[157]

In Judea, "the war had not yet started there, and when Gallus [governor of the Roman province of Syria], marching southward in the fall of 66 C.E., sent forces into Galilee, only one battle against 'rebels and brigands' is recorded . . . according to [Josephus,] Jewish War 2.511–513."[158] The dates for Octavius are all well known.[159] Julius Caesar's nineteen-year-old "adopted son and legal heir, deified Caesar in January of 42, defeated Antony and Cleopatra in September of 31, and was declared Augustus in January of 27 B.C.E."[160] Crossan provides other historical details for Octavian,[161] Julius Caesar, and Augustus.[162]

He mentions these historical personages; Herod the Great's three sons, who assumed "different portions of their father's domains after his death in 4 B.C.E"; Cato as one of Rome's official censors; in 184 BCE, Lucius Quinctius Flaminius being expelled from the senate; the orator Cicero, who died in 43 BCE; the historian Livy, who died in 17 CE; and "the aristocratic Roman historian Tacitus" wrote "a biography of his father-in-law, Gnaeus Julius

---

155. Crossan, *Jesus*, 114; Crossan, *Birth of Christianity*, 333.

156. Crossan, *Jesus*, 180; Crossan, *Birth of Christianity*, 180.

157. Crossan, *Historical Jesus*, 34, 57, 178; Crossan, *Who Killed Jesus*, 3; Crossan, *Birth of Christianity*, 27.

158. Crossan, *Historical Jesus*, 193; Crossan, *Jesus*, 137–44, 180; Borg and Crossan, *Last Week*, 15.

159. Crossan, *Jesus*, 26.

160. Crossan, *Birth of Christianity*, xv, 413–14.

161. Crossan, *God and Empire*, 10, 147.

162. Crossan, *Power of Parable*, 7, 158.

Agricola, governor of Britain between 77 and 84 C.E."[163] There is more on Herod the Great in Crossan's writings: "In the 1960s, the famous Israeli archaeologist and statesman Yigael Yadin excavated Herod the Great's palace on Masada's northern edge."[164]

A traditional approach to history continues. The Roman poet, "Juvenal, who lived around 60 to 127 C.E., was banished from Rome by the emperor Domitian."[165] The Syrian governor, Publics Quinctilius Varus, needed three legions as well as auxiliary troops to quell revolts after Herod the Great's death in 4 BCE.[166] This traditional historiography includes a statement that on 28 October 312 CE, the Roman emperor Constantine, following his victory at Rome's Milvian Bridge, converted to Christianity.[167]

Secular Evidence

Crossan uses the traditional historical method in citing Publius Cornelius Tacitus—senator, consul, provincial governor, orator, and historian—whom he claimed was prudent and always the aristocrat. Tacitus wrote in the early years of the second century CE, and one should "read Tacitus for history as aristocratic politics, dynastic intrigues, and imperial wars. Do not read him for anything about socioeconomic realities, about the lower classes.... His dislike for Judaism was matched, of course, by that for Christianity. He called it 'a class of men, loathed for their vices.'"[168]

Crossan writes of the first incident of Archelaus (son of Herod the Great) at Passover in 4 BCE. There was a second incident at Passover in 44 CE; Ventidius Cumanus was governor between 48 and 52 CE. He states Christianity was possibly in Rome by the late 40s and certainly by the mid-50s. This "possibility stems from the emperor Claudius's decree expelling Jews from Rome in 49 because of disturbances 'at the instigation of Chrestus [= Christus? = Christ?],' as Suetonius recorded in *The Lives of the Caesars: The Deified Claudius* 25.4."[169]

---

163. Crossan, *Jesus*, 33, 36, 39.

164. Crossan and Reed, *Excavating Jesus*, 104; see also Borg and Crossan, *Last Week*, 13–14,

165. Crossan, *Jesus*, 97.

166. Crossan, *Jesus*, 125.

167. Crossan, *Jesus*, 201.

168. Crossan, *Historical Jesus*, 91; Crossan, *Who Killed Jesus*, 15.

169. Crossan, *Who Killed Jesus*, 54–55; Crossan, *Birth of Christianity*, 416 (emphasis in original).

The above examples are statements of Crossan's inconsistency over which model of historiography he follows. He articulates his view of history is that of postmodern, reconstructive interactivism, but these examples show he is caught out by the philosophical crusher in using a traditional historical method despite his approved model being postmodern deconstruction.

(C) NARRATIVES OF OTHER AUTHORS AS TRADITIONAL HISTORY

The following samples are from Crossan's use of other authors where Crossan reads the material as narrative and accepts their information as traditional history, whether recent or distant, and not that of reconstructive interactivism, whether metaphorically or in some other semiotic form. They are organized according to broad subject areas.

The Church Fathers

Crossan, citing de Ste. Croix, describes the term *patrocinium*,[170] stating it was used by the late fourth century and was "applied to the activity of the apostles and martyrs on behalf of the faithful." It was found in the writings of St. Ambrose, Prudentius, St. Augustine, St. Paulinus of Nola, and others. Crossan's claim is that "the martyrs are the most powerful of *patroni*." Also, there is a description of the death of Judas in two texts outside the New Testament by Papias of Hierapolis from the mid-second century.[171]

Contemporary Examples

"The Easter issues of *Newsweek*, *Time* and *U.S. News & World Report*, April 8, 1996, all had cover stories on the historical Jesus."[172] Crossan writes of Margaret Alexiou's classical study of the Greek ritual lament and Bruce Metzger's reports for the United Bible Societies' Greek New Testament.[173] In a paper presented to the 1995 spring meeting of the Jesus Seminar,

---

170. Patrocinium means "protection, defence patronage, legal defence" ("Patrocinium," Latin Dictionary, https://www.online-latin-dictionary.com/latin-english-dictionary.php?parola=patrocinium).

171. Crossan, *Historical Jesus*, 69 (emphasis in original); Crossan, *Who Killed Jesus*, 74 (emphasis in original).

172. Crossan, *Birth of Christianity*, 39; Crossan, "Historical Jesus as Risen Lord," 46.

173. Crossan, *Birth of Christianity*, 530; Crossan, "Historical Jesus as Risen Lord," 14.

"Stacy Davids summarized recent psychiatric literature on grief and bereavement."[174] Again, he regards this as narrative history that does not need a deconstuctionist application.

Jonathan Schell writes about Gandhi's goals of "ending untouchability, cleaning latrines, improving the diet of Indian villagers, improving the lot of Indian women, making peace between Muslims and Hindus—through all of which he believed he would find God." Crossan and Reed's comment is "that is why Gandhi was assassinated not by a British imperialist, but by a Hindu fundamentalist."[175]

"I had read and been persuaded by Mann's fourfold analysis of social and imperial power before the terrorist attacks against our country on September 11, 2001, but that day confirmed it for me."[176]

There is no postmodern, reconstructive, interactive methodology in "the most obscenely egregious invocation of God as Divine Punisher" that occurred in his conversation on the Christian Broadcasting Network's show *The 700 Club* between Jerry Falwell and Pat Robertson immediately after 9/11. Crossan writes of John F. Harris who reported in the *Washington Post*, September 14, 2001, a citation of "Falwell's claim that the 9/11 tragedy was simply God's punishment on America" for the actions of pagans, abortionists, feminists, gays, and lesbians who have "tried to secularize America—I point the finger in their face and say, 'You helped this happen.'"[177]

Another recent historical example is Mel Gibson's movie *The Passion of the Christ*, which made the death of Jesus "big news" in the United States and elsewhere. There were cover stories in national news magazines, features on prime-time television shows, and major stories in newspapers across the country, dealing with this movie.[178] Crossan writes of Paul Boyer citing Hal Lindsey's claim that "when he spoke at the American Air War College 'virtually the entire school turned out, including many officers accompanied by their wives, and that, at the Pentagon, hundreds . . . [jammed] the room' with more crowding outside."[179]

---

174. Crossan, "Historical Jesus as Risen Lord," 31.

175. Crossan and Reed, *In Search of Paul*, 410; Crossan and Reed, *Fabricating Jesus*, 192.

176. Crossan, *God and Empire*, 13.

177. Crossan, *God and Empire*, 71.

178. Borg and Crossan, *Last Week*, vii; Crossan, *God and Empire*, 130.

179. Crossan, *God and Empire*, 199.

A citation of Augustine of Hippo "was magnificently misquoted by Desmond Tutu of Cape Town in 1999: 'St Augustine says, God, without us, will not: as we, without God, cannot.'"[180]

Crucifixion and Other Means of Death

"We know from Josephus that thousands of Jewish victims were crucified outside the walls of Jerusalem in the first common era century. This includes two thousand by Varus in 4 BCE., according to Josephus *Antiquities* 2.75 to five hundred or more a day by Titus in 70 CE according to *Jewish War* 5.450 but 'only one crucified skeleton has so far been found in that area for that or any other period.'"[181] He continues with traditional historiography: "The Jewish historian Josephus and the pagan historian Tacitus both agree that Jesus was executed by order of the Roman governor of Judea."[182]

"In June 1968, a complex of four tombs was excavated at Giv'at ha-Mivtar in northern Jerusalem. Three tombs held fifteen ossuaries[183] containing the bones of thirty-five different individuals. . . . Professor Haas of the Hebrew University/Hadassah Medical School's Department of Anatomy has observed that 'evidence of death by violence was found in five cases.'"[184] The crucified skeleton of Jesus's contemporary Jehochanan from this tomb "still bears an iron nail about four and a half inches long in his right heel bone but he was honorably interred in ossuary and tomb."[185] Crossan accepts the narrative giving a traditional understanding of history provided by Martin Hengel, when Hengel states that "crucifixion was aggravated further by the fact that quite often its victims were never buried. It was a stereotyped picture that the crucified victim served as food for wild beasts and birds of prey. In this way his humiliation was made complete. What it meant for a man in antiquity to be refused burial, and the dishonour which went with it, can hardly be appreciated by modern man."[186] Hengel's further language was that, in crucifixion, the body was "fastened [and] nailed . . . [as] evil food for birds of prey and grim pickings for dogs," was used to "feed the crows on the cross," and was "hung . . . alive for the wild beasts and birds of

---

180. Crossan, *Power of Parable*, 135.
181. Crossan, *Historical Jesus*, 391.
182. Crossan, and Watts, *Who Is Jesus*, 122.
183. An ossuary is "a place where the bones of dead people are kept" ("Ossuary," in *CD*).
184. Crossan, *Birth of Christianity*, 544.
185. Crossan, "Historical Jesus as Risen Lord," 17; Crossan, *Jesus*, 124.
186. Hengel, *Crucifixion in Ancient World*, 87–88; Crossan, "Historical Jesus as Risen Lord," 17; Crossan, *Who Killed Jesus*, 162.

prey."[187] What is Crossan's application of this research by Hengel to Jesus's crucifixion? There is no reconstructive interactivism here:

> In normal circumstances the soldiers guarded the body until death and thereafter it was left for carrion crow, scavenger dog, or other wild beasts to finish the brutal job. . . . His body [was] left on the cross or in a shallow grave barely covered with dirt and stones, the dogs were waiting . . . . What happened after the death and burial of Jesus is told in the last chapters of the four New Testament gospels . . . . Jesus' burial by his friends was totally fictional and unhistorical. He was buried, if buried at all, by his enemies and the necessarily shallow grave would have been easy prey for scavenging animals.[188]

How does this compare with the accounts in the Gospels? It will be shown in the following assessment that this kind of information is in contrast to that gleaned through an inductive study of Christ's death and burial in the biblical material.

> The Judeo-Roman history of crucifixion can be summarized over four stages. The first stage is biblical crucifixion—the traditional Jewish method, which is quite different from the later Roman system. Jewish crucifixion was *dead* crucifixion. An executed and already-dead criminal was hung upon a cross . . . . The second stage is Roman crucifixion. Contrary to the biblical tradition, this was live crucifixion . . . . The third state is Hasmonean crucifixion. The biblical and Roman traditions were clearly contradictory. The fourth stage is Essene crucifixion.[189]

Note Crossan's language: "The Judeo-Christian *history* of crucifixion . . ." There is no mention of deconstructionist history.[190]

"Josephus mentions three major incidents of corporate crucifixion in the decades before and after Jesus. The Roman governor Varus crucified 'about two thousand' in 4 B.C.E. . . . . The Roman procurator Florus crucified 'about three thousand six hundred' in 66 C.E. . . . . The Roman general Titus crucified 'five hundred or sometimes more . . . daily' in 70 C.E. . . . . Yet only a single crucified skeleton has been found so far from that terrible first century in the Jewish homeland."[191]

187. Hengel, *Crucifixion in Ancient World*, 9, 58, 76. This is emphasized in Crossan, *Jesus*, 127.
188. Crossan, *Jesus*, 153, 154, 160.
189. Crossan, *Birth of Christianity*, 541-42.
190. Emphasis added.
191. Crossan, *Birth of Christianity*, 543.

"Jesus' contemporary Philo, the Jewish philosopher from Alexandria in Egypt, observed in his Flaccus 83 that decent governors sometimes had crucified criminals 'taken down and given up to their relations, in order to receive the honours of sepulture' at the time of the emperor's birthday since 'the sacred character of the festival ought to be guarded.'"[192]

In the Mishnah, a Jewish code from around 200 3.C.E., Sanhedrin 6:5–6 notes that "'they used not' to bury executed criminals in their ancestral tombs but kept two burial places in readiness, one for those 'beheaded and strangled,' the other for those 'stoned or burnt.'"[193]

The above statements from Crossan indicate he is using the traditional historical method and not postmodern, reconstructive interpretations of historiography.

Cultural Issues

"Agrarian societies have, according to Lenski's view, nine classes but with an abysmal gulf separating the five upper from the four lower ones." Crossan finds David Gilmore's anthropological studies to include an "extremely useful 1982 survey of Mediterranean anthropology."[194]

Crossan reads Lenski and Wolf in a straightforward historical narrative manner.[195] He cites information on illiteracy, observing that "peasants, almost by definition, are illiterate. William Harris estimated that 'the likely overall illiteracy level of the Roman Empire under the principate is almost certain to have been above 90%.'" As for other countries in the world, he uses statistics from Meir Bara-Ilnan, noting "data for illiteracy gathered from different societies in the first half of the 20th century," including Turkey, Egypt, South Africa, India, Afghanistan, Iran, Iraq, and Saudi Arabia. He asks, rhetorically, but in agreement with Harris, "Can't a tentative conclusion be drawn that in ancient 'traditional' societies the rate of literacy was less than 10%?"[196]

The First Century AD

Crossan writes of Koester's older and later works (*Introduction to the New Testament*, 1982; *Ancient Christian Gospels*, 1990), in which Koester

192. Crossan, "Historical Jesus as Risen Lord," 17.
193. Crossan, "Historical Jesus as Risen Lord," 20.
194. Crossan, *Historical Jesus*, 45, 66.
195. Crossan, *Historical Jesus*, 126.
196. Crossan, *Birth of Christianity*, 234.

presumes a single written source behind the three independent passion accounts in Mark, John, and the Gospel of Peter. While Koester doesn't use the terminology of "written source" in 1990, he presumes it. Koester states that "Crossan's reconstruction of one single source for all passion narratives seems justified. However, it is doubtful whether this account was as comprehensive and as fixed a literary document as Crossan assumes."[197] This is not Crossan's reconstructive understanding of Koester but Koester's reading of Crossan's material as a recent historical narrative.

Crossan writes of the biographies of Jesus's contemporary, the Roman governor Tiberius, and of "Josephus, a priestly Jewish historian, who published his twenty-volume Jewish Antiquities, a history of his people, around 93 or 94 C.E." Josephus "died probably around the end of the first century. So, at least for the First Roman-Jewish War, he was a participant and eyewitness on both the Jewish and Roman sides. Josephan accuracy, however, cannot always be taken for granted."[198]

Josephus records these historical details that are not reconstructed by Crossan: the execution of James and the existence of the high priest Ananus the Younger; James, the brother of Jesus; and certain others.[199] In 38, Agrippa returned from Rome to the Jewish homeland;[200] "Herod the Great died in 4 B.C.E., Caesar Augustus in 14 C.E., and Jesus was crucified around 30 C.E."; Eusebius, the bishop of Caesarea and later biographer of Constantine, described the work carried out under imperial Constantinian decree: "as layer after layer of the subsoil came into view, the venerable and most holy memorial of the Savior's resurrection, beyond all our hopes came into view."[201] There is no intimation of reconstruction in these historical details.

Historians and Historicity

Crossan's epigraph cites Edward Gibbon (1837) on the decline and fall of the Roman Empire, one of the duties of the historian being to discover the inevitable mixture of error and corruption and the reasons for the successful spread of Christianity in the Roman world.[202] Crossan takes a couple elements "as probably historical" for James, the Lord's brother. These are his

---

197. Koester, *Ancient Christian Gospels*, 220n1; also cited in Crossan, *Birth of Christianity*, 563.

198. Crossan, *Birth of Christianity*, 99; Crossan, *Jesus*, 11, 30, 40.

199. Josephus, *Antiquities*, 20.197–203; Crossan, *Jesus*, 134.

200. Crossan, *Birth of Christianity*, 507.

201. Crossan and Reed, *Fabricating Christianity*, 248.

202. Gibbon, *Decline and Fall*, as cited in Crossan, *Birth of Christianity*, 1–2.

asceticism and that he was possibly a Nazarite (a Nazarite vow is a voluntary dedication to the Lord, according to Numbers 6:1–21). He refers to James's death by execution, based on Eusebius's citing of the lost Outlines of Clement of Alexandria (AD 150–215). Note his language: "*I take* one element *as probably historical*," where historical refers to traditional history and not postmodern reconstruction.[203]

Crossan cites Gerald O'Collins and Daniel Kendall, who quote Rudolf Bultmann, and Joseph Fitzmyer.[204] Crossan's perspective on O'Collins, Kendall, Bultmann, and Fitzmyer was gained from reading these authors as narrative, traditional history, without interpreting them as postmodern reconstruction, including Fitzmyer's support for the historicity of Joseph of Arimathea. Crossan accepts "Tobit, a fourth- or third-century B.C.E. novel" and not as reconstructive interactivism.[205]

Crossan refers to Sebastian Junger's nonfiction book *The Perfect Storm* as a "powerful elegy" that was deservedly high on the *New York Times* bestseller list.[206] In that publication, Junger "centers on the *Andrea Gail*, a 72-foot steel swordfisher out of Gloucester which disappeared with all hands off Sable Island east of Nova Scotia, October 28, 1991, in waves 100 feet high." Crossan accepts these facts as traditional history and then adds: "Dale Murphy, who disappeared on the Andrea Gail, left a three-year-old son, Dale, an ex-wife, Debra, and a mother behind him. His son 'wakes up screaming in the middle of the night' because 'Daddy's in the room.'"[207]

What is Crossan's application? He does not refer to the traditional history of the disappearance of *Andrea Gail*, a swordfisher boat. He immediately applies the dreams and visions: "Remember the statement about Christianity's birth that I suggested . . .: it is the resurrectional apparition of a dead man that explains the power of Christianity's birth and growth, spread and triumph, across the Roman Empire."[208] Why this selection of vision, dream, and application to Jesus's resurrection as apparition rather than a bodily, historical resurrection? As will be seen in what follows, there are other factors (a priori premises, imposed personal interpretation, and/or speculation and idiosyncratic judgment) that seem to be influencing

---

203. Crossan, *Birth of Christianity*, 468 (emphasis added).

204. O'Collins and Kendall, "Did Joseph of Arimathea," 235–41, as cited in Crossan, "Historical Jesus as Risen Lord," 18–19. Crossan further disagrees with O'Collins and Kendall in Crossan, *Birth of Christianity*, 553.

205. Crossan, "Historical Jesus as Risen Lord," 20.

206. An elegy is "(in modern literature) a poem of serious reflection, typically a lament for the dead" ("Elegy," in *OED*).

207. Crossan, "Historical Jesus as Risen Lord," 32.

208. Crossan, "Historical Jesus as Risen Lord," 32.

Crossan's choice of a view that is in contrast to the resurrection as happening in traditional history.

Historical Jesus Studies

While Crossan disagrees with some of Schweitzer's emphases, he accepts the plain reading of Schweitzer's text where "Albert Schweitzer insisted that John and Jesus were both apocalyptic preachers, each attempting in his own way to force the advent of the avenging God."[209] Crossan endorses the plain meaning of the last words of Schweitzer:[210]

> He comes to us as One unknown, without a name, as of old, by the lake-side, He came to those men who knew Him not. He speaks to us the same word: "Follow thou me!" and sets us to the tasks which He has to fulfil for our time. He commands. And to those who obey Him, whether they be wise or simple, He will reveal Himself in the toils, the conflicts, the sufferings which they shall pass through in His fellowship, and, as an ineffable mystery, they shall learn in their own experience Who He is.[211]

Crossan notes that Schweitzer divides historical Jesus researchers "into *haters* and *lovers*," and the haters include Hermann Reimarus (1694–1768) and David Strauss (1808–1874).[212] At this point, Crossan tries his reconstructionist methodology but concludes: "If historical reconstruction is often a minefield, historical *Jesus* reconstruction is all mine, no field."[213] That's it! It belongs to Crossan and is all his.

Ireland, Judaism, and Life after Death

In his history class in Ireland and courses on Greek and Roman classics, with texts chosen by British education, Crossan learned from Caesar's *Gallic Wars* to admire the syntax and ignore the slaughter—even of our ancient Celtic ancestors.[214] He writes of Charles Morris's recent summary description of Ireland's Great Famine (1845–1849).[215] "About one million people

---

209. Crossan, *Jesus*, 51.
210. Schweitzer, *Quest of Historical Jesus*, 401.
211. Schweitzer, *Quest of Historical Jesus*, 409.
212. Crossan, *Birth of Christianity*, 23.
213. Crossan, *Birth of Christianity*, 23 (emphasis in original).
214. Crossan, *Who Killed Jesus*, 213.
215. These dates are from Mokyr et al., "Great Famine."

died from starvation or from typhus and other famine-related diseases.[216] The number of Irish who emigrated during the famine may have reached two million."[217] Crossan also makes statements about Ireland, a legally constituted part of Great Britain in the early nineteenth century, and the British commissions assigned to solve the terrorism and violent resistance—without a hint of reconstruction.[218]

He relies on Geza Vermes's research to promote a strong case for a "holy man" of Hasid tradition within charismatic Judaism that was a Galilean tradition stemming from Elijah and Elisha, Honi and Hanina, and also Jesus of Nazareth, which he considers to be "a profoundly correct framework for discussion."[219]

Crossan and Reed have no difficulty in recording details of "the Flavian dynasty of Vespasian and Titus, surving even that dynasty's disastrous Domitian"[220] reign, while "in November of 333 B.C.E., Alexander the Great defeated and humiliated Darius of Persia at Issus in northwestern Syria, as we saw . . . on that bronze monument at Thessaloniki's seafront."[221] They discuss "the great revolt of 66–74 C.E." in Jerusalem and how "after the terrible war Rome could only see Judaism as a rebel religion."[222] Traditional historiography is used in these examples, with no taste of reconstruction. The philosophical crusher has found them to be inconsistent practitioners of Crossan's proclaimed method of deconstruction.

A common understanding of life-after-death in the Greco-Roman world (not dismissed by pagans or Jews) was that "the dead could return and interact with the living." This "was a commonplace of the Greco-Roman world and neither pagans nor Jews would assert that it could not happen."[223] Crossan rejects that teaching, as "it never occurs to Paul that Jesus' resurrection might be a special or unique privilege given to him because he [Jesus] is Messiah, Lord, and Son of God. It never occurs to Paul that Jesus' case

---

216. "Typhus is a disease caused by rickettsia [unusual type of bacteria that can live only inside the cells of another organism] or orientia bacteria. You can get it from infected mites, fleas, or lice. Modern hygiene has mostly stopped typhus, but it can still happen in places where basic sanitation is bad or if it gets passed on by an infected animal" (Svoboda, "Typhus").

217. Mokyr et al., "Great Famine."

218. Crossan, *Birth of Christianity*, 156, 168.

219. Vermes, *Jesus the Jew*, 58–82. See Vermes citation in Crossan, *Historical Jesus*, 156–57.

220. Crossan and Reed, *In Search of Paul*, 160.

221. Crossan and Reed, *In Search of Paul*, 167.

222. Crossan and Reed, *In Search of Paul*, 353.

223. Crossan, "Historical Jesus as Risen Lord," 28.

might be like Elijah, taken up individually to live with God but without any wider, communal, or cosmic effects."[224] When testing this hypothesis, Crossan's emphasis and conclusion will be challenged from the biblical data.

In these examples, Crossan does not advocate a deconstructionist historiography. The philosophical crusher has found him out to be contradictory in his interpretation of history.

The New Testament Gospels

Crossan affirms disagreement rather than agreement among the four Gospel records, noting that there were pagan opponents such as Celsus by the middle of the second century, and Christian apologists like Justin, Tatian, and Marcion were aware of those discrepancies, even if only between Matthew and Luke.[225] Ramsay MacMullen's research notes social pedigree would have been easily known in the Greco-Roman world, and referring to Jesus as a "carpenter" indicated lower-class status.[226]

Crossan cites an epigraph from Wright in which Crossan indicates "Wright does not accept the existence of what other scholars call the Q *Gospel* as the best explanation for the twin but divergent versions of the three 'units' . . . found in Matthew 22:1–10 = Luke 14:16–24 (the parable of the great supper), Matthew 25:14–30 = Luke 19:12–27 (the parable of the talents/pounds), and Matthew 5:3–4, 6, 11–12 = Luke 6:20b–26 (the beatitudes)."[227] Wright clearly states that Crossan's statement that "Wright does not accept the existence of . . . the Q *Gospel*" is false. However, Wright does have some doubts about certain dimensions of Q. He states that "if this Q-and-*Thomas* hypothesis creates so many difficulties, *does this mean that we should abandon the Q hypothesis altogether? By no means.*"[228] Crossan quotes Ronald Piper's 1989 publication and its "very persuasive analysis of smaller sayings-clusters in the earlier, sapiential, or Q1 layer of the Q *Gospel*," and he concludes "quite correctly, that *these are not haphazard collections of aphoristic sayings; they display a design and argument unique in the synoptic tradition.*"[229] The important emphasis for this abduction is that Crossan does

---

224. Crossan, "Historical Jesus as Risen Lord," 10.
225. Crossan, *Historical Jesus*, xxx.
226. Crossan, *Jesus*, 24.
227. Crossan, *Birth of Christianity*, 103–4, referring to Wright, *Jesus*, 170.
228. Wright, *New Testament*, 441 (emphasis added).
229. Crossan, *Birth of Christianity*, 392 (emphasis in original). Sapiential means "relating to wisdom" ("Sapiential," in *OED*). An aphorism is "a pithy observation which contains a general truth" ("Aphorism," in *OED*).

not interpret Wright or Piper as a postmodern reconstructionist but as an interpreter of recent, historical, narrative writers.

Roman Empire

Crossan uses a traditional historical method in his analysis of Roman governor Gaius (Caligula), who reigned 39–41 CE, and in the infamous story of Caligula's statue as told twice by Josephus. Crossan mentions Philo, a Jewish philosopher from Alexandria (20 BCE–45 CE) and Emperor Felix (52–60 CE).[230]

There is further use of the traditional historical model and not reconstruction with statements concerning Herod the Great's temple being burned and dismantled, although Tacitus records that "even some battle-hardened officers were reluctant to carry out Titus's demolition order."[231] Crossan makes statements concerning Octavian before he became Augustus, two thousand years ago, who said, "'Aphrodisias is the one city from all of Asia I have selected to be my own,' and the citizens carved that accolade on the archive wall of their theater."[232] He cites Koester, who claimed Julius Caesar and Jesus of Nazareth had two things in common: both were murdered, and both received divine worship after their deaths.[233]

Secular Evidence

Pagan philosopher Celsus, "writing in the last quarter of the second century," declared that Judaism and paganism covered up "bastardy" as the real reason behind the claim of the virginal conception and divine generation for Jesus. The father of Jesus, Celsus claimed, was a Roman soldier named Panthera.[234] Crossan cites this example as traditional history and not as reconstruction.

Crossan refers to the pagan Roman witness Cornelius Tacitus (*Annals*, 15.44), who alluded to a rumor blaming the dynasty's last emperor, Nero, for the disastrous fire that swept through Rome in 64 CE. Nero scotched the rumor by blaming Christians whose founder, Christus, "had undergone the death penalty in the reign of Tiberius, by sentence of the procurator Pontius

---

230. Crossan, *Who Killed Jesus*, 45, 50; Crossan, *Jesus*, 41.
231. Crossan and Reed, *Fabricating Jesus*, 186.
232. Crossan and Reed, *In Search of Paul*, 14.
233. Crossan, *Birth of Christianity*, 413.
234. Crossan, *Jesus*, 18.

Pilatus."²³⁵ In his 1995 publication, Crossan summarizes the view that Jesus's execution under Pontius Pilate was "as sure as anything historical can ever be. For, if no follower of Jesus had written anything for one hundred years after his crucifixion, we would still know about him from two authors not among his supporters." They are Josephus and Tacitus.

Thus, there are "not just Christian witnesses but one major Jewish [Josephus] and one major pagan [Tacitus] historian who both agree on three points concerning Jesus." Those points are: "There was a *movement*, there was an *execution* because of that movement, but, despite that execution, there was a *continuation* of the movement."²³⁶ Note especially how Crossan uses this language: Jesus's death under Pontius Pilate "is as sure as *anything historical* can be."²³⁷ Crossan is referring to anything traditionally historical and not anything reconstructed interactively for a postmodern world.

An examination of this abduction data reveals that Crossan has committed the philosophical crusher. The coherence of his methodology has floundered with explicit self-contradiction in his demonstration of historicity in some of his writings being a contrast to his stated theory of reconstruction of interactivity. The rock of fact—his use of some traditional historiography—reveals the crusher of self-contradiction in the inconsistent application of his own theory of postmodern, reconstructive interactivism.

Further evidence will be gathered in chapter 6 to test hypothesis 1. To this point, it does not look promising for Crossan, when these indices are applied to his data:

1. He is self-contradicting in not being consistent in his application of his own definition of history.

2. He imposes a priori premises on some of the data, including his presuppositions.

3. Often, he does not inductively accept the plain meaning of the text but engages in deconstructionist free play with concepts and meaning.

4. He imposes his opinionated reason on some of the biblical texts associated with the historical Jesus and Jesus's resurrection.

See chapter 6 for more data to challenge Crossan's material and test his data.

---

235. Tacitus, as cited in Crossan, *Jesus*, 162.
236. Crossan, *Who Killed Jesus*, 5 (emphasis in original).
237. Crossan, *Who Killed Jesus*, 5 (emphasis added).

WHAT ABOUT THE BIBLICAL DATA?

As indicated at the beginning of this chapter, Crossan states that "it's a theological presupposition of mine that God does not operate that way" (with supernatural miracles).[238] As an a priori principle, Crossan's premise is that God does not perform supernatural interventions in the physical world. Crossan defines the actions of the supernatural God in an a priori fashion. Therefore, God's supernaturally raising Jesus bodily from the dead is impossible, for Crossan has dismissed it by an a priori presumption against miracles: "God does not operate that way." So the human being, John Dominic Crossan, decides what God does and does not do. God does not perform miracles as supernatural acts.

Crossan's Own Free Play Formulations of the Resurrection Data

Crossan's interpretations of Jesus's resurrection are based on his own reconstructions of the data and do not use a literal-factual reading of the text. His resurrectional conclusions are:[239]

1. There was no literal, historical, or supernatural bodily resurrection of Jesus.

2. The appearances of Jesus after his resurrection were apparitions, visions, or trances, with parallels in spiritistic literature.

3. Notice how Crossan's presuppositions of the resurrection shout at him and us. Crossan uses the example from John 20 of "the race to the empty tomb between Peter and the Beloved Disciple." Observe his assessment: "*I do not think* that story was ever intended as a historical event, intended to describe something that first Easter morning. It *always looked to me like a calculated and deliberate parable* intended to exalt the authority of the Beloved Disciple over that of Peter."[240] This is not a researcher's authoritative approach: "*I do not think*" and "*it always looked to me.*" What does it matter what Crossan subjectively

---

238. Crossan, as cited in Copan, *Will the Real Jesus*, 61.

239. See details for this list in Crossan, *Historical Jesus*, ch. 15, "Resurrection and Authority," 395–416; Crossan, *Jesus*, ch. 7, "Biography," 159–92; Crossan, *Who Killed Jesus*, ch. 7, 189–210; Crossan, *Birth of Christianity*, 481–525; Crossan, "Historical Jesus as Risen Lord," 1–47; Crossan, *Long Way from Tipperary*, 164–66, 194; Borg and Crossan, *Last Week*, 189–216; Crossan and Reed, *In Search of Paul*, 133–35, 168–70, 173–77, 296, 241–45; and Crossan, *God and Empire*, 183–86.

240. Crossan, *Long Way from Tipperary*, 164–65 (emphasis added).

"thinks" and "looked to me"? A personal opinion goes down the gurgler when pursuing research. Notice what an inductive approach to the biblical text does (see below).

4. The writings about Jesus's resurrection were not factual history but were literary fiction, metaphor and parable, some of it being created by the Gospel authors. There was no resuscitated body.

5. The passion-resurrection events were not unique to Jesus, in order to grant a special privilege to Christianity.

6. In the description of Jesus's resurrection, metaphors were used to express Jesus's continuing presence of empowerment for the first Christians.

7. The primary emphasis was to assign meaning to Jesus's resurrection, which was that the general resurrection had begun. Jesus's resurrection does not deal with the afterlife, but Jesus's post-Easter appearances were literary fiction to tell of the struggles over power and authority in the early church. They deal with personal and political transformations that are not exclusivist but are pluralist in application.

8. The appearance stories after the resurrection are reflections of Jesus's followers after his death.

9. Historical reconstruction, interpreted for a postmodern world, is how to present the divine manifestation of Christianity, including the resurrection. It is not done, once for all, but has to be redone for the different needs to be reinterpreted in each generation, based on the issues of that era.

Crossan can't be consistent in his application of his own deconstructionist approach to his data. Too often he reverts to traditional historiography and casts aside his deconstructionist promise.

WHAT IS THE INTRABIBLICAL EVIDENCE?

This is an inductive summary of the post-resurrection biblical appearances. Crossan is one among many who refuse to accept Jesus's resurrection as a bodily resurrection. This is Jesus's assertion of what his post-resurrection body is: "'Look at my hands and my feet. It is I myself! Touch me and see; a ghost does not have flesh and bones, as you see I have.' When he had said this, he showed them his hands and feet" (Luke 24:39–40 NIV). These are not the features of a ghost.

Nothing could be clearer, when one allows the Scriptures to speak for themselves. These verses unmistakably refute Crossan's view that the resurrection was an apparition. But there is more evidence:[241]

- What did the women do on resurrection morning? "Suddenly Jesus met them. 'Greetings,' he said. They came to him, clasped his feet and worshiped him" (Matt 28:9). Prophetically, David had seen this day of resurrection: "Because you will not abandon me to the realm of the dead, nor will you let your faithful one see decay" (Ps 16:10).[242]

- Both Mark and John announced the empty tomb with the graveclothes (Mark 16:6; John 20:5–7). Mary Magdalene, Mary the mother of James, and Salome took spices to the tomb to anoint Jesus's body. "Don't be alarmed," a young man dressed in white said. "You are looking for Jesus the Nazarene, who was crucified. He has risen! He is not here. See the place where they laid him" (Mark 16:6).

- "Look at my hands and my feet. It is I myself! Touch me and see; a ghost does not have flesh and bones, as you see I have" (Luke 24:39). So Jesus revealed his hands and feet to those in his presence and invited them to "touch me and see; a ghost does not have flesh and bones, as you see I have." With application to Crossan, we could say, "Touch me and see; an apparition does not have flesh and bones as you see Jesus has." An inductive study of these biblical texts refutes Crossan's view.

- Jesus appeared to his disciples, but Thomas, one of the Twelve, was not with other disciples. He was told by them: "We have seen the Lord!" Thomas's response was, "Unless I see the nail marks in his hands and put my finger where the nails were, and put my hand into his side, I will not believe" (John 20:24–25).

- A week later, Thomas and the disciples were together in a house. "Though the doors were locked, Jesus came and stood among them and said, 'Peace be with you!' Then he said to Thomas, 'Put your finger here; see my hands. Reach out your hand and put it into my side. Stop doubting and believe.' Thomas said to him, 'My Lord and my God!'" (John 20:26–30).

- This raises the issue of Jesus's post-resurrection body being more than physical as Jesus stood among the disciples in spite of the doors being closed. Wright describes this as a "transphysical" body "that was robustly physical but also significantly different from the present

---

241. With prompts from Thiessen, *Introductory Lectures*, 335.
242. Acts 2:31 confirms the psalmist referred to the resurrection of the Messiah.

one.... We might say the new body will not be corruptible—we might say not that it will be *less* physical, as though it were some kind of ghost or apparition, but more."[243]

- It is hard to imagine any biblical scholar wanting to turn this verse into support of the resurrected Jesus coming from an apparition: "Then the disciple whom Jesus loved said to Peter, 'It is the Lord!; As soon as Simon Peter heard him say, 'It is the Lord,; he wrapped his outer garment around him (for he had taken it off) and jumped into the water" (John 21:7).

- Luke 24:30–31 confirms Jesus post-resurrection body was not an apparition: "When he [Jesus] was at the table with them, he took bread, gave thanks, broke it and began to give it to them. Then their eyes were opened and they recognized him, and he disappeared from their sight." These words confirm the nature of Jesus's body as physical. He could eat, give thanks, break the bread with them, and then enter into his transphysical dimension—not an apparition.

- The post-resurrection Jesus asked for a piece of fish to eat. "And while they still did not believe it because of joy and amazement, he asked them, 'Do you have anything here to eat?' They gave him a piece of broiled fish, and he took it and ate it in their presence" (Luke 24:41–43).

In addition to the above, some other Scriptures make no sense if Jesus's resurrection was an apparition:

- "Do not be amazed at this, for a time is coming when all who are in their graves will hear his voice and come out—those who have done what is good will rise to live, and those who have done what is evil will rise to be condemned" (John 5:28–29).

- "But in fact, Christ has been raised from the dead. He is the first of a great harvest of all who have died" (1 Cor 15:20 NET).

- "And his incomparably great power for us who believe. That power is the same as the mighty strength he exerted when he raised Christ from the dead and seated him at his right hand in the heavenly realms (Eph 1:19–20 NIV).

---

243. Wright, *Resurrection of the Son*, 477–78.

The Nature of the Resurrection

The New Testament has a distinctive way (in Greek) to define carefully the nature of Jesus's resurrection and believers' future resurrection. Philippians 3:20-22 states the Jewish (and Pauline) view: "But our citizenship is in heaven. And we eagerly await a Savior from there, the Lord Jesus Christ, who, by the power that enables him to bring everything under his control, will transform our lowly bodies so that they will be like his glorious body." The word for body is *sōma*. "For one who had been a Pharisee such phraseology could carry only one meaning—physical resurrection." So, "in this light, the failure of Paul to mention an empty tomb is insignificant. He would feel no need to mention it, for it would follow as a matter of course. The only question is that which has to do with the kind of physical body in which the dead will rise."[244]

Paul does not provide a list of those who were witnesses to Christ's resurrection, as that would provide weak evidence from one who is a Jew. To discard the "glorious body" would contradict Jewish belief in the physical, bodily resurrection. So, Crossan's apparitional resurrection contradicts the Jewish and Christian view of the nature of the resurrection. "Except for the Sadducees and those who insisted on a final disembodied state, resurrection had been woven into the very fabric of first-century Jewish praying, living, hoping and acting."[245]

The Greek text uses *sarx* (flesh) and *sōma* (body) alternatively in 1 Corinthians 15:35-40 to indicate the body of flesh sown and the body raised. *Sōma* is used in verses 35, 37, and 38. However, *sarx* and *sōma* are both used in verses 39-40. With what kind of body do the dead come (v. 35)? Paul writes of "the *sōma* of grain, human *sarx*, animal *sarx*, fishy *sarx*, celestial *sōmata*, and terrestrial *sōmata*. The interchange shows that Paul does not here use *sōma* in the sense of 'form'; the alternate term 'flesh' would contradict such a meaning."[246] So here we have the interchangeability of *sarx* and *sōma*, clearly indicating that the Jewish Jesus's resurrection and believers' future resurrection will be bodily and not an apparition. Gundry could not be more specific: "'The unfalteringly physical meaning of *sōma* resists' a resurrection that is not material."[247]

---

244. Gundry, *Sōma in Biblical Theology*, 177.
245. Wright, *Resurrection of the Son*, 204.
246. Gundry, *Sōma in Biblical Theology*, 166.
247. Gundry, *Sōma in Biblical Theology*, 172,

Summary: It Cannot Be a Supernatural, Bodily Resurrection

The emphases of this chapter point to Crossan's presuppositions of what God does not do with the resurrection. Crossan was asked, "Do you yourself believe in miracles?" His response was: "Yes, but not as periodic intrusions in some closed natural order. I leave absolutely open what God *could* do, but I have very definite thoughts about what God *does* do. The supernatural or divine is not something that periodically or temporarily breaks through the normal surface of the natural or human world. The supernatural is more like the permanently hidden but perpetually beating heart of the natural."[248]

He explains, "It is the ancients who know how to tell a good metaphorical story (a parable, if you prefer) and we moderns who are silly enough to take them factually."[249] He emphasizes "that *is* the resurrection, the continuing presence in a continuing community of the past Jesus in a radically new and transcendental mode of present and future existence. But how to *express* that phenomenon" is his question.[250] Crossan has a presuppositional bias against the supernatural and, hence, against Jesus's resurrection: "I do not think that anyone, anywhere, at any time, including Jesus, brings dead people back to life. (I am not, of course, talking about near-death experiences or about resuscitating apparent corpses. Death means you don't come back. If you come back, it was not death. Death, like pregnancy, is either/or, not more or less)."[251]

Further evidence for testing hypothesis 1 is in chapter 6.

---

248. Crossan and Watts, *Who Is Jesus*, 96 (emphasis in original).
249. Crossan and Watts, *Who Is Jesus*, 79–80.
250. Crossan, *Historical Jesus*, 404 (emphasis in original).
251. Crossan and Watts, *Who Is Jesus*, 98.

SIX

Fifth & Final Crossan Lesson

First, read the text.[1]

This chapter is a continuation of testing hypothesis 1: "The resurrection narratives in the New Testament are not historical." I'm collecting further data from Crossan's publications, and these reveal some of . . .

CROSSAN'S SELF-CONTRADICTIONS

Crossan objects to the way Barabbas was portrayed in a prominent film, stating that Barabbas, "by the way, was not the loutish buffoon portrayed in *The Passion of the Christ* but simply the Jewish version of the Scottish anti-imperialist *Braveheart* or the American anti-imperialist *The Patriot*. Anyone who wants to dramatize the death of Jesus in play or film *should first read the text and get the story right*."[2]

In an earlier publication, he writes that "no amount of anthropological modeling can obscure the fact that any study of the historical Jesus stands or falls on *how one handles the literary level of the text itself*," and he states that even with his triadic emphases on three levels—anthropological, historical, and literary—he accepts the "necessity" of "*focusing directly on the textual level.*"[3] However, what does he mean by historical? Is it traditional history or reconstructive, interactive history?

---

1. Crossan, *God and Empire*, 138.
2. Crossan, *God and Empire*, 138 (emphasis added).
3. Crossan, *Historical Jesus*, xxix (emphasis added).

Crossan's protest was raised briefly in "read the story to get the correct story" when it was asked whether Crossan's objection to the theology of substitutionary atonement in Mel Gibson's film *The Passion of the Christ*, "in two hours of unspeakable suffering as Jesus bears punishment for all the sins against God since the dawn of creation,"[4] was a violation of one of the fundamentals of hermeneutics. Is Crossan contravening one of the foundational understandings of "responsible interpretation"? One of these fundamentals is that "the meaning of a biblical statement is the ordinary, or normal, meaning of the statement (usually literal with some figures of speech) in terms of its context and the author's purpose." A second fundamental building block of interpretation is that "the meaning of a biblical statement fits the historical and cultural setting of the writer and the first readers."[5]

These two fundamentals of hermeneutics not only apply to the biblical material but also to the reading of any text, whether poetry, fiction, or narrative. They relate to the ordinary or normal reading of this researcher's local newspaper, the Brisbane *Courier-Mail*, with the story of 2 August 2021, whose headline was, "State on High Alert as Delta Outbreak Sparks Strict Lockdown," while the narrative read, "More schools have been dragged into a fast-moving southeast Queensland Covid-19 outbreak that has plunged millions into lockdown."[6] Fundamentals apply to work in education; reading the Bible or poetry; listening to the content of radio and television news; or reading of historians such as Josephus, Tacitus, Eusebius, Toynbee, Hengel, Judge, Barnett, Wright, and Crossan. That news item of 2 August 2021 dealt with "thousands [who] are now in isolation, millions in lockdown, schools have been closed, and several of Brisbane's biggest hospitals were on high alert. After six new local cases of the Delta strain of the virus were announced on Saturday morning, it is understood new cases will be announced on Sunday but the number was unknown last night."[7]

The literal meaning of the text was that millions of people in southeast Queensland, Australia, were in lockdown because of the possible spread of coronavirus, the Delta strain. That's the plain meaning of the text, which is obtained from the online newspaper's text and is what one should understand when told to "first read the text and get the story right." The principle that applies to the story line of Mel Gibson's movie also applies to the reading and hearing of all literature and other media: the first thing one should do is to read the text and listen to the content to get the meaning out of what is stated.

---

4. Crossan, *God and Empire*, 138.
5. Lewis and Demarest, *Integrative Theology*, 1:30.
6. Sinnerton and Rosel, "State on High Alert."
7. Sinnerton and Rosel, "State on High Alert."

This basic principle of interpretation applies to the reading of all of Crossan's publications to obtain Crossan's intended plain meaning of words and semantics. The following is a deliberate lengthy citation to demonstrate how Crossan wants readers to understand the regular meaning of words and concepts:

> In discussing the crucifixion, I argued that the story of Jesus' burial by his friends was totally unhistorical. If he was buried at all, he was buried not by his friends but by his enemies. And not in a tomb hewed out of stone, but in a shallow grave that would have made his body easy prey for scavenging animals. Those are grim conclusions, but I cannot escape them.... In a nutshell, these are my conclusions: First, the Easter story is not about events of a single day, but reflects the struggle of Jesus' followers over a period of months and years to make sense of both his death and their continuing experience of empowerment by him. Second, stories of the resurrected Jesus appearing to various people are not really about "visions" at all, but are literary fiction prompted by struggles over leadership in the early Church. Third, resurrection is one—but only one—of the metaphors used to express the sense of Jesus' continuing presence with his followers and friends.... Is the story of the empty tomb historical? No, I've already explained why I doubt there was any tomb for Jesus in the first place. I don't think any of Jesus' followers even knew where he was buried—if he was buried at all. And the gospel writers don't come close to agreeing with each other on what they report. So my conviction is that motives other than just history writing are clearly at work here.... Paul is the earliest writer we have on resurrection... and he nowhere shows awareness of having heard an empty tomb story.[8]

This statement by Crossan and Watts makes no sense without a common knowledge of terminology and biblical concepts. Here, Crossan contradicts his definition of history as reconstructive interactivism by asking if the empty tomb was historical, by which he understands that "I doubt there was any tomb for Jesus in the first place." This is the traditional understanding of history and not that of reconstruction. Crossan repeats such a view with this statement: "Jesus' burial by his friends was totally unhistorical," by which he refers to the tomb hewn out of stone and the alleged shallow grave where the body was a prey for scavenging dogs.

He needs his readers to understand what the Easter story means (resurrection of Jesus) and then reverts to a postmodern interpretation that

---

8. Crossan and Watts, *Who Is Jesus*, 152–54.

repudiates the understanding he gave of the empty tomb by making Easter mean that "it is not about events of a single day, but reflects the struggle of Jesus' followers" and "their continuing experience of empowerment by him." Thus, in the space of three pages in this publication, he commits the philosophical crusher with his self-contradiction regarding the nature of history. Ben Meyer explains one of the principles of the philosophical crusher is "the reduction of implicit to explicit self-contradiction."[9] What self-contradiction do we find in Crossan's view of history?

Also, in the above statement, the normal, plain meaning of these words and phrases needs to be understood. In this case, the nature of the crucifixion of Jesus is described. It is not as stated in Martin Hengel's exposition of crucifixion in the first century.[10]

As to Crossan's statement that "Paul is the earliest writer we have on resurrection . . . and he nowhere shows awareness of having heard an empty tomb story,"[11] there was no need for Paul to record the empty tomb and bodily resurrection, because Paul was a Pharisaic Jew who believed in the resurrection.[12]

Crossan has to refute the statements of Paul in 1 Corinthians 15:12–21, with emphasis added by me:

> 12 Now if *Christ is proclaimed as raised from the dead*, how can some of you say that there is no resurrection of the dead? 13 But *if there is no resurrection of the dead, then not even Christ has been raised*. 14 And *if Christ has not been raised*, then our preaching is *in vain* and your faith is *in vain*. 15 We are even found to be misrepresenting God, because *we testified about God that he raised Christ, whom he did not raise if it is true that the dead are not raised. 16 For if the dead are not raised, not even Christ has been raised. 17 And if Christ has not been raised*, your *faith is futile* and *you are still in your sins*. 18 Then those also who have fallen asleep in Christ have perished. 19 If in Christ we have hope in this life only, we are of all people most to be pitied. 20 But *in fact Christ has been raised from the dead*, the firstfruits of those who have fallen asleep. 21 For as by a man came death, by *a man has come also the resurrection of the dead*.

9. Meyer, "Philosophical Crusher."
10. Hengel, *Crucifixion in Ancient World*.
11. Crossan, and Watts, *Who Is Jesus*, 122.
12. "From all that we can work out (the evidence is found in various places, from Maccabees to Acts to Josephus to the Rabbis) that the Pharisees in Jesus' day believed in bodily resurrection" (Wright, "Resurrection and Afterlife").

Crossan is to be commended for his advocacy of the position that one "should first read the text and get the story right."[13] This is fundamental to understanding any written material. It also is as essential for reading Crossan's own publications and Gospel materials as it is for understanding the content of the film *The Passion of the Christ*, for which Crossan offers the challenge "Read the text and get the story right." To him, I reciprocate the plea "Read the text (of the New Testament Gospels) to obtain the meaning of the passion accounts." Of course, the challenge to Crossan is "Read the Gospel texts without a priori assumptions that engage in textual free play."

(A) SAMPLES OF JESUS'S BURIAL AND RESURRECTION

These following statements by Crossan concerning the passion-resurrection accounts are indicators of the philosophical crusher's application to Crossan's writings. His view is that one should read the text (in this case, the New Testament Gospels) to get the correct story. What does Crossan state about Jesus's burial and resurrection in comparison with the Gospel accounts? These are samples and not comprehensive examples from Crossan's writings:

"The story of Jesus' burial by his friends was totally unhistorical. If he was buried at all, he was buried not by his friends but by his enemies." Jesus "was buried not in a tomb hewed out of stone, but in a shallow grave that would have made his body easy prey for scavenging animals."[14] This is a radical departure from that which the Gospels portray in Matthew 27:57–59; Mark 15:43–46; Luke 23:50–56; and John 19:38–40. By contrast, the biblical text states that Joseph of Arimathea "who was also a disciple of Jesus" asked Pilate for the body of Jesus, "and Joseph took the body and wrapped it in a clean linen shroud and laid it in his own new tomb, which he had cut in the rock."[15] Thus, Crossan commits another philosophical crusher by not following his own exhortation about Mel Gibson's movie that one "should first read the text and get the story right," and here there are multiple attestations in the Gospel texts.

As for the existence of Joseph of Arimathea and Jesus's tomb, Crossan states that "Joseph of Arimathea *could* have buried Jesus, perhaps out of personal piety or communal duty"; but Crossan is persuaded, based on several points that he argues, that "Mark *created* that burial by Joseph of Arimathea in 15:42–47. It contains no pre-Markan tradition." Even further, "Mark

---

13. Crossan, *God and Empire*, 138.
14. Crossan, and Watts, *Who Is Jesus*, 154–55.
15. Matthew 27:57–59.

created the empty-tomb story just as he created the sleeping disciples in Gethsemane."[16] Of Jesus's burial, Crossan writes that "this deliberate, almost desperate, but terribly understandable defensiveness about the nonburial of Jesus [by Joseph of Arimathea] comes to a magnificent climax in John 19:38–42."[17] He then cites this passage from John in full, in which it is stated that Joseph of Arimathea was a secret disciple of Jesus who asked Pilate to permit him to take the body of Jesus, permission that Pilate granted. Because "there was a garden in the place where he was crucified, and in the garden there was a new tomb in which no one had ever been laid," Joseph, accompanied by Nicodemus, "came and removed his body . . . . And so, because it was the Jewish day of Preparation, and the tomb was nearby, they laid Jesus there."[18]

The contradiction in this kind of statement is that Crossan has stated that this is "the nonburial of Jesus" by Joseph of Arimathea, but then he immediately cites the passage from John 19:42 where it is stated that "the tomb was nearby, they laid Jesus there" (NRSV). He cannot have it both ways. Was there a non-burial of Jesus? Was Jesus laid in the tomb, or was Joseph of Arimathea part of the FC creation? Crossan uses his FC understanding, which is not critiqued in this project but is treated as having, in the words of John Nolland,

1. an appreciative dimension in its "stimulating an imaginative engagement with dimensions of the life of the early church in a period largely otherwise inaccessible to us," and

2. a negative component that is quite "speculative."[19]

Crossan moves beyond FC to declare that the tomb of Jesus was unhistorical. He is responding to some of Raymond Brown's material: "Brown comments that 'there is nothing implausible in John's scenario that there was a garden in the area north of Jerusalem where Jesus was crucified, and that he was buried in that tomb.'[20] . . . That is absolutely correct: nothing implausible. *Nothing historical either.*"[21] Here again Crossan is using historical in the traditional sense and not according to his postmodern, reconstructed, interactive definition.[22]

---

16. Crossan, *Birth of Christianity*, 555, 557 (emphasis in original); Crossan, "Historical Jesus as Risen Lord," 12.

17. Crossan, *Jesus*, 157.

18. As cited in Crossan, *Jesus*, 157–58.

19. Nolland, "Form Criticism," 233.

20. R. Brown, *Death of the Messiah*, 1270.

21. Crossan, *Who Killed Jesus?* 176 (emphasis added).

22. Crossan, *Birth of Christianity*, 20.

(B) Enter Reconstruction

Crossan's view is that "the Easter story is not about events of a single day, but reflects the struggle of Jesus' followers over a period of months and years to make sense of both his death and their continuing experience of empowerment by him."[23] To the contrary, the Easter story of the death of Jesus Christ, according to Matthew 27:45–46, 50, happened this way: "Now from the sixth hour there was darkness over all the land until the ninth hour. And about the ninth hour Jesus cried out with a loud voice, saying, 'Eli, Eli, lema sabachthani?'[24] that is, "My God, my God, why have you forsaken me" . . . . And Jesus cried out again with a loud voice and yielded up his spirit." What are the time factors here? Robertson explains the meaning of "from the sixth hour" (Matt 27:45):

> Curiously enough McNeile takes this to mean the trial before Pilate (John 18:14). But clearly John uses Roman time when the trial occurred before Pilate. The crucifixion began at the third hour (Mark 15:25) Jewish time or nine A.M. The darkness began at noon, the sixth hour Jewish time and lasted till 3 P.M. Roman time, the ninth hour Jewish time (Mark 15:33 = Matt. 27:45 = Luke 23:44). The dense darkness for three hours could not be an eclipse of the sun and Luke (23:45) does not so say, only "the sun's light failing." Darkness sometimes precedes earthquakes and one came at this time or dense masses of clouds may have obscured the sun's light.[25]

On which day was Jesus crucified? Mark 15:42–43 states: "When evening had come, since it was the day of Preparation, that is, the day before the Sabbath, Joseph of Arimathea, a respected member of the Council, who was also himself looking for the kingdom of God, took courage and went to Pilate and asked for the body of Jesus" (see also Matt 27:57; Luke 23:54; John 19:42). Mark's explanation is that Jesus's death was on the day of Preparation, which is the day before the Sabbath, the Sabbath beginning at sunset Friday. So Jesus was crucified on the Friday. Robertson explains, based on Matthew 27:57, that the Preparation (*paraskeuē*) "is the name in modern

---

23. Crossan and Watts, *Who Is Jesus*, 153.

24. Robertson explained the divergence in MSS evidence: "Matthew first transliterates the Aramaic, according to the Vatican manuscript (B), the words used by Jesus: *Elōabachthanei*; some of the MSS give the transliteration of these words from Psa. 22:1 in the Hebrew (*Eli, Eli, lama Zaphthanei*)" (Robertson, *Matthew and Mark*, 234).

25. Robertson, *Matthew and Mark*, 233–34.

Greek today for Friday. 'The Jews were anxious that these bodies should be taken down before the sabbath began at 6 P.M.'"[26]

On which day was Jesus's resurrection? Mark 16:1–6 states that it happened "when the Sabbath was past," and it was "very early on the first day of the week, when the sun had risen," when Mary Magdalene and Mary, the mother of James, and Salome, "brought spices so that they might go and anoint him," the buried Jesus. They did not find the body of Jesus, but "they saw that the stone had been rolled back," and in the tomb, they saw a young man sitting, dressed in white, who told them, "Do not be alarmed. You seek Jesus of Nazareth, who was crucified. He has risen; he is not here. See the place where they laid him" (Mark 16:6).

The time factor is that Jesus was crucified and buried by sunset on the Friday, and he had risen from the dead by sunrise Sunday. This is in accordance with Jesus's prophecy: "For just as Jonah was three days and three nights in the belly of the great fish, so will the Son of Man be three days and three nights in the heart of the earth" (Matt 12:40), and "as they were gathering in Galilee, Jesus said to them, 'The Son of Man is about to be delivered into the hands of men, and they will kill him, and he will be raised on the third day.' And they were greatly distressed" (Matt 17:22–23). According to Matthew 16:21, Jesus began to show his disciples that he would go to Jerusalem, suffer, be killed, and on the third day be raised.

Robertson's comment on Matthew 12:40 is: "'Three days and three nights' may simply mean three days in popular speech. Jesus rose 'on the third day' (Mt 16:21), not 'on the fourth day.' It is just a fuller form for 'after three days.'"[27]

Therefore, the text of Scripture provides opposing evidence to that of Crossan's reconstruction. Jesus's resurrection happened three days after his crucifixion, according to Jewish reckoning, and the Easter story was not about a single day or the struggle of Jesus's followers for their continuing experience and empowerment over months and years, as in Crossan and Watts. It was about a historical event that happened, that can be verified by deduction from the evidence, by multiple attestation in Scripture. The historicity or otherwise of the empty tomb will be examined in the nature of Jesus's resurrection.

According to Crossan and Watts, "Stories of the resurrected Jesus appearing to various people are not really about 'visions' at all, but are literary fiction prompted by struggles over leadership in the early Church."[28]

26. Robertson, *Matthew and Mark*, 237–38.
27. Robertson, *Matthew and Mark*, 98.
28. Crossan and Watts, *Who Is Jesus*, 153.

This position emerges from Crossan's commitment to FC and RC and their explanation of how the Gospel accounts were written or compiled. In Jesus's post-resurrection appearances, the Scriptures record that "Jesus met them and said, 'Greetings!' And they came up and took hold of his feet and worshipped him" (Matt 28:9); Jesus spoke with them (Matt 28:10; John 20:15-19) and told Mary Magdalene, "Do not cling to me" (John 20:17). Further discussion is in an examination of the nature of the resurrection, but it should be obvious Jesus's resurrected body was a physical one that could speak to and cling to—physically. Crossan denigrates Scripture for him to arrive at his post-resurrection conclusions.

(c) Barabbas as Mark's Creation

One of Crossan's classic reconstructions is what he does with the release of Barabbas from prison (Mark 15:6-15): "I judge that narrative to be absolutely unhistorical, a creation most likely of Mark himself."[29] Note his use of "unhistorical," with a traditional understanding of history and not his commitment to a definition of history as reconstructed interactivism. His interpretation is that Mark's narrative about Barabbas was "a symbolic dramatization of Jerusalem's face, *as he saw it.*" Authorial creations, he claims, are not primarily for literary embellishment but are for "*symbolic dramatization, . . . or prophetic fulfillment*, as with the Triumphal Entrance, or both, as with the infancy stories."[30] Elsewhere, he asks whether the use of names such as Barabbas (Mark 15:7); Simon of Cyrene, father of Alexander and Rufus (Mark 15:21); and Joseph of Arimathea (Mark 15:43) would "preclude fictional creation, not only of those names but of the actions and events associated with them." His working hypothesis is that Barabbas, Simon, and Joseph are "all so Markan . . . . He himself created both names and events."[31]

This creative explanation by Crossan casts doubts on the historicity of people associated with Jesus's passion. John Meier's assessment is that "if the Barabbas incident, historical or not, was in an early form of the Passion Narrative, then that form of the Passion Narrative would naturally give the impression that the Barabbas incident took place on the morning of the fourteenth of Nissan, when there was still time for Barabbas to take part in the Passover meal, and not on the morning of the fifteenth of Nisan, when the meal was already over." Therefore, Meier understands "'the presence of the Barabbas incident is some early form of the Passion Narrative,' which

---

29. Crossan, *Jesus*, 141.
30. Crossan, *Jesus*, 141-43 (emphasis in original).
31. Crossan, *Who Killed Jesus*, 177.

agrees, implicitly, with the John (18:38-40) and not the Synoptic (Matt 27:15-26; Mark 15:6-15; Luke 23:18-25) chronology."[32]

Leon Morris, after examining the Barabbas evidence in the four Gospels, concludes that while "the custom of releasing a prisoner at Passover is not attested elsewhere," he finds "nothing inherently unlikely about it." His conclusion is that Barabbas seems to have been a member of the local resistance movement and would have been a hero to many Jews because of his opposition to the Romans.[33]

(D) Parables

The claim by Crossan is that parables *about* Jesus presume historical characters and invented stories about John and Jesus, Annas and Caiaphas, Antipas and Pilate, and the incident on the road to Emmaus. If that were not provocative enough, he widens his "case to think of each entire gospel version as a book-length *megaparable* about the life, death and resurrection of the historical character Jesus of Nazareth."[34]

Crossan's understanding of parables is that they are "invented stories" and "parables *about* Jesus" that involved "*fictional* events about *factual* characters," and this extended to "each entire gospel version" where the life, death, and resurrection of the historical Jesus of Nazareth was "a book-length *megaparable*."[35] Thus, Crossan has made up his own version of the meaning of parable. He summarizes his view:

> Parable = Metaphoricity + Narrativity[36]

He tries to base his understanding of parable (which he extends to each entire New Testament Gospel) on etymology: "Metaphor means 'carrying something over' from one thing to another and thereby 'seeing something as another' or 'speaking of something as another'.... A metaphor is 'seeing as' or 'speaking as' and we have, of course, no problem with recognizing *small* metaphors.... It is the *big* ones that are as dangerous as they are inevitable. When a metaphor gets big, it is called 'tradition'; when it gets

---

32. Meier, *Marginal Jew*, 1:400.
33. Morris, *Gospel According to John*, 772-74.
34. Crossan, *Power of Parable*, 5-6 (emphasis in original).
35. Crossan, *Power of Parable*, 5-6 (emphasis in original).
36. Crossan, *Power of Parable*, 8.

bigger, it is called 'reality'; when it gets biggest of all, it is called 'evolution' or even 'god.'"[37]

So, Crossan's postmodernism has run amuck with his redefining parable and metaphor according to his peculiar, personal understanding. Crossan has the power of a producer; that's what he seems to be trying to achieve with his redefinition of parables. Here, producer is used as synonymous with creator, innovator, originator, and inventor. Therefore, in light of Crossan's view of parables as "invented stories" about "presumed historical characters," the conclusion must be that the entire Gospels are megaparables containing invented stories about presumed historical characters. Thus, there is no reliable historical record of what is recorded in the Gospels.

Jesus made it specific when he was using parables in the New Testament (see Matt 13:3, 10, 34–35, 53; 21:45; 22:1; Mark 3:23; 4:2, 11, 13, 33; 12:1; Luke 8:10). He left no doubt that this was a parable, as the text labelled his stories as parables. Based on the Greek New Testament lexicon, Arndt, Gingrich, and Bauer define *parabolē* as meaning "type, figure," indicating "a symbol (pointing) to the present age." In the Synoptics, "the word denotes a characteristic form of the teaching of Jesus" that was "a short discourse that makes a comparison; it expresses a (single) complete thought. The evangelists considered that it needed interpretation because it presented teaching in obscure fashion."[38] This last sentence is a bowing of the head to FC, as the intimation here is that the evangelists created the "needed interpretation" because of what they considered was "teaching in obscure fashion."[39] That is not what the texts state, but it is a presupposition of FC.

Friedrich Hauck's word study explains that in the New Testament, parable is used forty-eight times in the Synoptic Gospels and twice in Hebrews. The Synoptic use "corresponds fully to the broad use" in the Old Testament and rabbinic literature. In the Synoptics, *parabolē* means "a short saying which is combined with a comparison or figure of speech" and is "a proverbial saying." He explains that the New Testament parable means more than a "mere metaphor" such as "leaven of the Pharisees" (Matt 16:6) or simile, "clever as serpents" (Matt 10:16). Instead, "it is an independent similitude in which an evident or accepted truth from a known field (nature, human life) is designated to establish or illustrate a new truth in the preaching of Jesus (kingdom of God, God's nature and action, piety)." Formally, one might be able to differentiate, firstly, "true parables, which are distinguished from figures of speech and similes only by the more extended development of the

---

37. Crossan, *Power of Parable*, 8 (emphasis in original).
38. Arndt and Gingrich, *Greek-English Lexicon*, 617.
39. Arndt and Gingrich, *Greek-English Lexicon*, 617.

image, and which may sometimes grow out of metaphors (Mt. 18:12–14; 24:43 f.), sometimes out of similes (Mt. 13:31f., 33, 44, 45f.)." The "obvious truth . . . of the parable constitutes its power to convince."[40]

Secondly, "parables may consist of a story, often with subsidiary details, to which the comparative material is adapted. The story is in the past tense, as with Mk. 4:3–9; Mt 21:39; 22:2; 25:1," but the distinction between these two elements "is fluid, and the characteristic narrative form is plain to see" (see Mark 4:3–9; Luke 11:5–8; 13:6–9; 18:1–8).

Thirdly, they are "illustrative stories in which the idea is presented without figurative garb. Lk. alone offers this type of parable in the 4 passages 10:30–37; 12:16–21; 16:19–31; 18:9–14." Hauck notes that Jesus took his parabolic material "partly from nature (Mk. 4:26–29; 13:28 f.; Lk. 12:54–56 etc.) and partly from the manifold relationships of human life as He knew them from His Palestinian background (householder, servant, moneylender, merchant, friend, widow, shepherd, housewife, judge, bridegroom, house-building etc.). In part He uses regular occurrences (leaven, grain of mustard-seed), in part typical incidents (quarrelling, children, sower), in part exceptional situations (the workers in the vineyard, Mt. 20:1–16)."[41]

A biblical example of the meaning of parable, in contrast to that by Crossan, could be summarized as:

> Parable is an extended metaphor (contemporary symbol from a known field?) with application to God's truth or Christian living (to teach one truth/theme).

Such an example is the parable of the sower, where the extended metaphor was a contemporary symbol that was well known in the first century—a sower sowing seed in the field (Matt 13:1–9), with the application to the seed of Jesus's word—the message—and how it is received by various people (Matt 13:18–23).

This explanation of *parabolē*, based on New Testament Greek usage, demonstrates how Crossan has placed his own, innovative meaning on parable and made it apply to the New Testament, even to designating entire Gospels as megaparables. Thus, Crossan has imposed a meaning on parable that is not exegetically based on the New Testament's original language. This makes it impossible to compare Crossan's view with a biblical understanding of parable.

Crossan's stated accusation against Mel Gibson's movie and the promotion of substitutionary atonement was that Gibson "should first read the

---

40. Hauck, "Parabolē," 752.
41. Hauck, "Parabolē," 752.

text and get the story right."[42] When this principle is applied to Crossan and a sample of examples related to Christ's resurrection, Crossan's own philosophy of textual fidelity is found wanting. Crossan clearly demonstrates he engages in textual free play with the biblical text.

In his writings, does Crossan reveal any data that could explain how or why he has perpetrated these anomalies of self-contradiction? Three possibilities emerge, the first two being closely connected. They are:

- a priori premises or assumptions,
- the imposition of personal interpretations on the data; and
- speculation and opinion.

Here data are gathered to support Crossan's possible explanations:

A Priori Assumptions

What is an a priori assumption? The definition adopted here is that of Bruce Russell:

> Roughly speaking, *a priori* justification provides reasons for thinking a proposition is true that comes from merely understanding, or thinking about, that proposition.... Philosophers argue that we can also be *a priori* justified in believing a false proposition.... A type of justification is defeasible[43] if and only if that justification could be overridden by further evidence that goes against the truth of the proposition or undercut by considerations that call into question whether there really is justification.[44]

What are some of Crossan's a priori premises that he brings to the study of the historical Jesus and especially to his interpretation of Jesus's resurrection that can be defeated by further knowledge?

---

42. Crossan, *God and Empire*, 138.
43. Defeasible means "capable of being annulled or made void" ("Defeasible," in *M-WD*).
44. Russell, "*A Priori* Justification."

(a) Postmodernism: The Object and Subject Will Challenge and Change the Other

In the context of discussing archaeology, Crossan quotes British archaeologists Michael Shanks and Christopher Tilley, who have led a new postmodern movement, "post-processual archaeology."[45] They state that "archaeology, as cultural practice, is always a politics, a morality" and "is nothing if not critique."[46] Shanks and Tilley state that in the seven years before their publication, for the first time, archaeologists were faced with different theoretical perspectives on the past for their discipline. Their claim is that there was a gap to be filled of "the perceived fundamental isolation of past from the present" and that this was "to reinscribe the past into the present, to realize their interaction." This impetus had come almost entirely from outside the discipline, through debates in social theory. Archaeology is being taken "into the realm of structuralism, semiotics, post-structuralism and deconstruction."[47] In their conclusion, they state: "We might also make reference to the idea of an avant-garde, or the debate over socialist realism, or the emergence of a so-called post-modernist culture."[48]

Therefore, Crossan has called on these two postmodern scholars advocating post-processual archaeology to bolster his a priori commitment to postmodern epistemology for the historical Jesus. He admits that this understanding of archeology is identical to his understanding of history that *"history is the past reconstructed interactively by the present through argued evidence in public discourse."*[49] He admits that both disciplines are attempting "to wrestle closely and honestly with *postmodernism's correct assertion that the object known is changed by the subject knowing it*," and this means charting a course between objectivism and subjectivism, historicism and relativism, positivism and narcissism. His answer is "that the present must reconstruct the past in openly admitted interaction so that each will challenge and change the other."[50]

Crossan cites philosopher Marianne Sawicki's definition that "post-processualists assert that historical agency and self-interested strategy are the key terms in archeological understanding and that reconstruction of the past is a component of the social construction of the present." Crossan

---

45. Crossan, *Birth of Christianity*, 212.
46. Shanks and Tilley, as cited in Crossan, *Birth of Christianity*, 211.
47. Shanks and Tilley, *Social Theory and Archaeology*, 99.
48. Shanks and Tilley, *Social Theory and Archaeology*, 208.
49. Crossan, *Birth of Christianity*, 20.
50. Crossan, *Birth of Christianity*, 211–12 (emphasis added).

acknowledges one of Sawicki's conclusions: "Post-structuralism does not offer an internally coherent theory and does not seem able on its own to escape a debilitating relativism." He continues: "That is, of course, the moral black hole threatening all of postmodernism."[51]

I would add to the description of a debilitating relativism that Crossan has raised it already in that he engages in free play of concepts and content. Is it any wonder he arrives at a debilitating relativism when he has cast aside the biblical moral foundation, based on the Sermon on the Mount (Matt 5–7), supported by the Old Testament's Ten Commandments (Exod 20:1–17)?

This is one of Crossan's major problems with his postmodern definition of history. It cannot escape from debilitating relativism and thus proves to be the moral black hole of his own making. Could Jesus's resurrection being described as an apparition be associated with Crossan's promotion of debilitating relativis"? However, while admitting that he is not a field archaeologist, he states that his present disagreements with such archaeologists "are with their social conclusions, which seem to contradict general anthropological ones and which would therefore need specific arguments and proofs to substantiate them."[52] However, how does Crossan's interactive reconstruction of postmodernism avoid Sawicki's assessment of "subjective factors" associated with the "debilitating relativism" of postmodernism? At least, he admits his problem. Why should archaeologists be restricted to using Crossan's view of anthropology, when relativism is one philosophy driving the content of postmodernism?

Crossan further illustrates his postmodern interpretation when he asks his readers: "Locate yourself on the first Holy Saturday, *a day that is going to last about, say, five or ten years* . . . . You search for texts that show death not as end but as beginning, not as divine judgment but as divine plan, not as ultimate defeat but as postponed victory for Jesus. You are, therefore, especially looking for texts with a certain duality, a certain hint of two stages, two moments, two phases, or two levels."[53] Note his imposition of two stages, two moments, two phases, or two levels on the text. Instead of allowing the text to interpret itself through plain understanding of the text, he encourages the reader to especially go "looking for texts with a certain debilitating relativism." In this manner, he is asking for a postmodern hermeneutic to be read into the text. This is eisegesis rather than exegesis.

---

51. Crossan, *Birth of Christianity*, 212–13.

52. Crossan, *Birth of Christianity*, 214.

53. Crossan, *Jesus*, 146. A duality is "the quality or state of having two different or opposite parts or elements" ("Duality," in *M-WD*).

There is further postmodern, reconstructed interactivism with Crossan's view that "the last chapters of the New Testament gospels" are not "entranced revelations" but are "quite deliberate political dramatizations of the priority of one *specific leader* over another, of this *leadership group* over that *general community*. Those stories are not primarily interested in trance and apparition but in power and authority."[54] Says who? That's Crossan's projection of a presupposition.

Again, his unusual postmodern interpretation of Matthew 27:19 is that "Pilate's wife had troubled dreams the previous night. That never happened, of course, but it was true nonetheless. It was a most propitious time for the Roman Empire to start having nightmares."[55] Something did not happen factually, but it was true, nevertheless, because of his postmodern reconstruction (seen as a metaphor) of the text's referring to the nightmares happening in the Roman Empire. This is relativism and illogical madness in action.

Crossan's statement that "postmodernism's correct assertion of the object known being changed by the subject knowing it"[56] is the a priori affirmation he maintains; but he commits a philosophical crusher when he attempts to comprehensively adopt his postmodern meaning of history in his own publications, as we saw earlier.

(b) A Postmodern Working Definition of History

Crossan's definition of history is articulated with postmodern epistemology: "*History is the past reconstructed interactively by the present through argued evidence in public discourse*. There are times we can get only alternative perspectives on the same event. (There are *always* alternative perspectives, even when we do not hear them.) But history as argued public reconstruction is necessary to reconstruct *our* past in order to project *our* future."[57] He affirms that "any reconstruction of the past is interactive with the present. Our own personal and individual, social and cultural positions in terms of race, color, creed, gender, class, and everything else as well, are at play in such reconstruction."[58] This is an a priori assumption by Crossan that is yet to be proven with evidence. How can an interactive view of history be applied to specifics, even of recent history, such as the war in

---

54. Crossan, *Jesus*, 169 (emphasis in original).
55. Crossan, *Historical Jesus*, 394.
56. Crossan, *Birth of Christianity*, 211.
57. Crossan, *Birth of Christianity*, 20 (emphasis in original).
58. Crossan, *Birth of Christianity*, 213.

Afghanistan? Would Crossan apply such a conjecture to the suicide bombers in Afghanistan?

Crossan draws four corollaries from this definition of history, the last of which "concerns method. I insist that Jesus-reconstruction, like all such reconstruction, is always a creative interaction of past and present. But what keeps the dialectic of us and them as even and honest as possible? Method, method, and, once again, method. It will not guarantee the truth because nothing can do that. But method, as self-conscious and self-critical as we can make it, is our only discipline." He claims "it is our one best hope for honesty," as "it is the due process of history," which cannot take a person out of their present bodies, minds, hearts, societies and cultures.[59] Try that approach in a historical investigation of Hitler, the Nazis, and the death ovens in Europe during World War II.

Crossan's postmodern, interactive reconstruction of the evidence from the past, to deal with the present and the future in Jesus-reconstruction, is his method. He claims that methodologies "will not guarantee the truth because nothing can do that."[60]

Does Crossan want his readers to accept this as a truthful statement by Crossan about his own method of research and his writing from that research? Crossan is stating that no method will guarantee the truth, but surely he wants the readers of this statement of his methodology of Jesus's reconstruction to be taken seriously as a truthful assessment about what he means by postmodern, interactive, reconstruction?

This is another example of a philosophical crusher in Crossan's works. Crossan cannot be consistent. He wants to deny truth as emanating from methodology, but surely he also wants his writings to be read so that what he says is a truthful representation of his own method. Or does he want this writer to place his own meaning from the present circumstances onto Crossan's statements? What is the meaning of *"history is the past reconstructed interactively by the present through argued evidence in public discourse,"*[61] when it is given a postmodern contemporary twist by this researcher?

Borg and Crossan give an example of how their understanding of reconstruction applies to the biblical texts articulating the Last Supper. In the Gospel accounts of the Last Supper (Matt 26:27–28; Luke 22:20; Mark 14:22–24) and in Paul's version (1 Cor 11:24–25), "the different versions indicate a degree of fluidity in how the Last Supper was remembered and celebrated."[62]

---

59. Crossan, "Historical Jesus as Risen Lord," 5.
60. Crossan, "Historical Jesus as Risen Lord," 5.
61. Crossan, "Historical Jesus as Risen Lord," 3 (emphasis in original).
62. Borg and Crossan, *Last Week*, 117–20.

They state that "the Last Supper is about bread for the world, God's justice against human injustice, a New Passover from bondage to liberation, and participation in the path that leads through death to new life."[63] This is imposing a postmodern, subjective interpretation on the text, a hermeneutic that does not arise from an inductive analysis of the biblical texts.

Crossan explains that "Christianity is historical reconstruction interpreted as divine manifestation. It is not (in a postmodern world) that we find once and for all who the historical Jesus was way back then. It is that each generation and century must redo that historical work and establish its best reconstruction, a reconstruction that will be and must be in some creative interaction with its own particular needs, visions, and programs." He explains further that this "historical reconstruction, in principle, is available to any researcher" who wants to undertake the task within "disciplined constraints." Within the "dialogues, debates, controversies and conclusions of contemporary scholarship," there are challenges to "faith to see and say how that is for now the Christ, the Lord, the Son of God."[64]

I could apply Crossan's scholarship of deconstruction to a song, like the chorus of "Keep the Home-Fires Burning":[65]

> Keep the Home Fires Burning,
> While your hearts are yearning,
> Though your lads are far away
> They dream of home.
> There's a silver lining
> Through the dark clouds shining,
> Turn the dark cloud inside out
> 'Til the boys come home.

Surely, using Crossan's reconstructive and interactive methodology, there should be no objection to such a personal interpretation, based on a postmodern reconstructed interactivism that uses free play in its interpretations. Therefore, this writer's interpretation of the song "Keep the Home-Fires Burning" is not unlike Crossan's hermeneutics on Jesus's resurrection as apparition.

However, the truth is that I invented what I wanted Crossan's story line to mean. Crossan's story line does not relate to the lyrical meaning of the song's text. This researcher created the eccentric meaning he wanted it to have. This postmodern, reconstructive, interactive understanding of the Lena

---

63. Borg and Crossan, *Last Week*, 120.
64. Crossan, *Who Killed Jesus*, 17.
65. Ford, "Keep the Home-Fires Burning" (public domain). This is the chorus of the song.

Ford lyrics "Keep the Home-Fires Burning" was a fictitious invention that is, nonetheless, valid when using Crossan's interactive free play. It amounts to creative invention of my own, not a valid method in historical research.

Would Crossan place my interpretation—to use his words—in the category of a "lethal deceit that too often renders savage the heart of Christianity," where Christians argue that they have facts, not interpretation, and where Christians "have history not myth, that *we* have truth and *you* have lies. That will not work any longer."[66] Why not? My postmodern reconstruction of the lyrics is designed to "work" for this researcher. Who is Crossan to say "that will not work any longer"?

Thus, Crossan's postmodern reconstruction of the definition of history becomes farcical when it can be made to mean so many interpretations by various people throughout history. It causes any writing, whether of history by Josephus, Tacitus, the author of Luke-Acts, or the local newspaper's reporting of ten years ago to lose sense of factual meaning. It is a failure as an interpretative method of history.

(c) Self-Contradiction and Lack of Systematic Consistency

In the above exposition of Crossan's self-contradictions, he has demonstrated a lack of systematic consistency in the foundation of historical investigation. This has been exposed in the abduction and Crossan's philosophical crusher in this and the previous chapter.

In the same document in which Crossan affirms his postmodern definition of history, how does he approach other evidence from history? He writes that "Roman crucifixion normally involved leaving the condemned person on the cross for carrion birds and prowling dogs to consume," and he calls upon Martin Hengel's evidence:

> Crucifixion was aggravated further by the fact that quite often its victims were never buried. It was a stereotyped picture that the crucified victim served as food for wild beasts and birds of prey. In this way his humiliation was made complete. What it meant for a man in iniquity to be refused burial, and the dishonour which went with it, can hardly be appreciated by modern man.[67]

Crossan's comment is that "crucifixion was not just about physical pain or social shame. It was, like condemnation to the arena beasts or the grilled fire, an attempt to annihilate the individual as fully and completely

---

66. Crossan, *Who Killed Jesus*, 217–18.
67. Hengel, *Crucifixion in Ancient World*, 87–88.

as possible." Then he adds: "We know from both textual and archaeological sources that exceptions to that ultimate fate were possible." He proceeds to give historical examples, including Philo from Alexandria, Egypt, Jesus's contemporary Jehochanan, and Paul on Jesus's burial tradition. The horrific alternative to "the body abandoned on the cross is the body dumped in a limed pit."[68]

What is unmistakable in Crossan's citing this historical evidence is that he is not following his own theory that "*history is the past reconstructed interactively by the present through argued evidence in public* discourse."[69] On a page after this definition, he discusses "the difference between history and story," explaining that "both contemporary North American culture and current scholarly exegetical discussion often speak too easily about story without distinguishing between historical narrative and fictional narrative." After giving "a particularly horrible example" of a woman who recovered memories of satanic ritual abuse by her parents in therapy, he comments that "it is worst of all, for herself, for her family, for her society, if her therapist finds the distinction between fact and fiction, fantasy and history, of no importance whatsoever." In that context, he writes that "history matters. And history is possible because its absence is intolerable. History is not the same as story. *Even if all history is story, not all story is history.*"[70] However, to which meanings of history and historical narrative is he referring? Is it a traditional understanding or his postmodern reconstruction?

In the very article in which he declares this definition of history, he violates his own theory of the nature of history. In these examples, he often pursues a definition of history similar to that of Tudor historian Sir Geoffrey Elton (1921–1994). Elton states that "history deals with events, not states; it investigates things that happen and not things that are." Elton's definition of history includes "the transformation of things (people, institutions, ideas and so on) from one state into another" as well as "those human sayings, thoughts, deeds and sufferings which occurred in the past and have left a present deposit; and it deals with them from the point of view of happening, change and the particular."[71]

Elton also writes of the historian's case:

> Just because historical matter is in the past, is gone, irrecoverable and unrepeatable, its objective reality is guaranteed: it is

---

68. Crossan acknowledges this information from Sawicki, *Seeing the Lord*, 180, 257, in Crossan, "Historical Jesus as Risen Lord," 17–18.
69. Crossan, "Historical Jesus as Risen Lord," 3 (emphasis in original).
70. Crossan, "Historical Jesus as Risen Lord," 4–5 (emphasis added).
71. Elton, *Practice of History*, 10–12.

beyond being altered for any purpose whatsoever. Let it be noted that what is in question here is the subject matter of history, the events of the past, not the evidence they have left behind or the product of the historian's labours. However biased, prejudiced, incomplete and inadequate that product may be, it embodies an account of events that happened quite independent of the existence of him who now looks at them.[72]

This definition also is consonant with that given by historian Paul Barnett. Barnett states that "history is not concerned with things that *are* so much as with things that *happen* and with the new directions that occur as a consequence. Understood this way, history deals with phenomena and, where possible, seeks an explanation for these phenomena."[73]

Therefore, Crossan has committed the philosophical crusher in his "reduction of implicit to explicit self-contradiction" in his definition and practice of history.[74]

As indicated in chapter 3, the interrelated indices used here to test the validity or otherwise of all hypotheses are that only those will be accepted that are

1. noncontradictory,
2. supported by adequate evidence, and
3. affirmable without hypocrisy.[75]

In his self-contradictions, Crossan has violated one of these fundamentals, which Edward Carnell frames in terms of the criterion of "systematic consistency." By consistency as a test of truth, Carnell refers to the law of noncontradiction that means that A is not non-A at the same time and in the same respect. This is based on Aristotle's sharpening of Plato's statement. "The logical law of noncontradiction" means "both the affirmation and the denial of the same thing cannot be true at the same time in the same respect."[76] The law of noncontradiction is critical in understanding Crossan's claims about history and his appraisal of Jesus's resurrection.

---

72. Elton, *Practice of History*, 52–53.
73. Barnett, *Jesus and the Rise*, 14 (emphasis in original).
74. Meyer, "Philosophical Crusher."
75. Lewis and Demarest, *Integrative Theology*, 1:25.
76. Lewis and Demarest, *Integrative Theology*, 1:73.

Carnell's evaluation is that "without consistency in our meaning, we cannot tell the lunatic from the expert. The former is known by his frequent violation of the law of contradiction."[77]

"Consistency is our surest test for the absence of truth. It is the test of consistency that the jury applies to the evidence during the trial. It is consistency that we apply in daily contact one with the other."[78] There is a qualification: "'Sheer consistency in the use of our terms, however, is not proof that we have truth. It only means that where we are not consistent, there we are involved in error' as it deals with formal truth, exemplified in mathematics and logic."[79]

According to Carnell, systematic consistency also includes

> material truth, the truth which we seek in Christianity, [which] pertains always to the totality of what is real. The real is whatever is, that is, whatever may be brought into our experience . . . . Systematic consistency is the combination of formal and material truth. It is a *consistency* because it is based upon a rigid application of the law of contradiction,[80] and it is *systematic* consistency because the data which are formed into this consistent system are taken from the totality of our experience, within and without.[81]

Carnell explicates systematic consistency as having negative and positive dimensions, the negative being that it does not violate the law of contradiction (a.k.a., the law of noncontrradiction) and the positive that it includes the facts of experience.[82]

Carnell notes that "the rock-bottom fact upon which Christianity rests is the Person, death, and resurrection of Jesus Christ,"[83] and then he calls upon Gresham Machen for support of Christianity as a historical religion: "The great weapon with which the disciples of Jesus set out to conquer the world was not a mere comprehension of eternal principles; it was an historical message, an account of something that had recently happened, it was the

---

77. Carnell, *Introduction to Christian Apologetics*, 57.
78. Carnell, *Introduction to Christian Apologetics*, 57.
79. Carnell, *Introduction to Christian Apologetics*, 58–59.
80. "The law of non-contradiction (LNC) ([is] also called the law of contradiction)" (Horn, "Contradiction").
81. Carnell, *Introduction to Christian Apologetics*, 59 (emphasis in original).
82. Carnell, *Introduction to Christian Apologetics*, 60–61.
83. Carnell, *Introduction to Christian Apologetics*, 114.

message, 'He is risen.'"[84] When determining whether Jesus did or did not rise from the grave, Carnell maintains,

> by no presently known manipulation of symbols can one demonstrate either that Christ did rise from the grave or that He did not. Systematic consistency is our only means for proving or disproving either theory of the resurrection. We must set up that hypothesis which is based upon a careful sifting and screening of the relevant data. When one shows that Julius Caesar was born 100 B. C., he does not take down a volume of higher calculus and pore over it; he goes to the painful work of evaluating the actual evidence of what happened in history. A coherent hypothesis, let us recall, is one which can smoothly lead us into the totality of our experience inside and outside.[85]

Geisler rightly affirms systematic consistency as a test for truth *within* a worldview system but rejects it "as a test *between* worldviews." This is primarily because "more than one system might be equally systematically consistent and . . . the facts within a system are given meaning by that system."[86] However, since the Christian worldview examined in this project is exploring Jesus's resurrection as an important dimension of worldview, it is appropriate that systematic consistency be used as one test of truth *within* this worldview.

Crossan demonstrates- through his self-contradictions in the philosophical crusher (see especially (a), (b), (c) above) that he has violated a fundamental of historical investigation—systematic consistency within his own worldview.

(d) Anti-Supernaturalism

It is expected that Crossan would have major difficulties in accepting Jesus's supernatural resurrection because of his a priori commitment against supernatural interventions within history and the present world. He states, "It's a theological presupposition of mine that God does not operate that way [by performing supernatural miracles]."[87] In the context of Jesus bringing Lazarus back to life, Crossan states, "I do not think that anyone, anywhere, at any time

---

84. Machen, *Christianity and Liberalism*, 28–29.
85. Carnell, *Introduction to Christian Apologetics*, 114.
86. Geisler, *Christian Apologetics*, 145 (emphasis in original).
87. Crossan, as cited in Copan, *Will the Real Jesus*, 61.

brings dead people back to life."[88] These two statements by Crossan about the supernatural commit the erroneous reasoning of begging the question where "the conclusion is assumed in one of the premises . . . . *Begging the question* is a form of *circular reasoning*" (it is also known as "assuming the initial point, assuming the answer, chicken and the egg argument").[89] It's a stubborn fixation by Crossan that miracles do not happen. He hasn't proved that is the case.

In analyzing the records of Jesus walking on water in the Gospels of Matthew, Mark, and John (multiple attestation), Crossan writes that "the 'nature' miracles of Jesus are actually credal statements about ecclesiastical authority, although they all have as their background Jesus' resurrectional victory over death, which is, of course, the supreme 'nature' miracle."[90] He presents not a shred of evidence from the biblical text to support his personal view.

This is exposed in Crossan's redefinition of miracles and his presupposition where this fundamental a priori premise is stated by him: "I believe that miracles are not changes in the physical world so much as changes in the social world."[91] Also, "the so-called *nature miracles* . . . are not about Jesus' physical power over the world but about the apostles' spiritual power over the community."[92] These are Crossan's inventions. He has not demonstrated these statements to be true according to the biblical data available.

This decided antagonism towards the supernatural is evident in Crossan's following Geza Vermes's "strong case for a 'holy man' or *hasid* tradition within 'charismatic Judaism,'" in which Crossan writes of the traditions involving Elijah and Elisha, Honi and Hanina, "We are dealing with a type of wonder worker who operates with certain and secure divine authority not mediated through or dependent on the normal forms, rituals, and institutions through which that divine power usually operates." He expresses concern that "the evidence concerning Honi and Hanina is very doubtful," and "once the healings, multiplications, and even miraculous trivializations of Elijah and Elisha stories were made part of the Great Tradition, it would be much more difficult to erase magic completely from the Little Tradition." For Crossan, "I presume, therefore, that Jewish magic and miracle working were widespread on the popular and oral levels among the lower classes."[93]

---

88. Crossan, *Jesus*, 95.
89. "Begging the Question."
90. Crossan, *Historical Jesus*, 404.
91. Crossan and Watts, *Who Is Jesus*, 88.
92. Crossan, *Jesus*, 170 (emphasis in original).
93. Crossan, *Historical Jesus*, 156–57.

There is no systematic consistency with affirming the biblical data by bringing into the mix the miracle-working powers of Honi and Hanina. Crossan has not assessed the biblical data on its own criteria. He has introduced foreign "miracle workers" when he hasn't consistently interpreted the biblical data.

(e) Scholarly Presuppositions Regarding Canonical Independence

Crossan is overt in his statement: "I accept, as scholarly presuppositions, both the canonical independence of the *Gospel of Thomas* and the written existence of the *Q Gospel*. If those positions are basically invalid—if the *Q Gospel* does not exist or the *Gospel of Thomas* is canonically dependent—then so is this section [a comparison of two early Gospels] completely invalid."[94]

This canonical independence also extends to the Gospel of Peter that Crossan claims "is exactly the story needed to explain how Jesus died and why his tomb needed guarding.... There may be, I repeat, another and now completely lost first part of that consecutive and independent source in *Gospel of Peter* 8:28–11:49, but the most economical solution is that it is *Gospel of Peter* 1:1–6:22."[95] He names the proposed source in the Gospel of Peter as the Cross Gospel. However, those who represent his "intellectual debt" in the Jesus Seminar voted on the statement "The earliest written version of the passion story is found in the *Gospel of Peter*"—and 74 percent disagreed, while 60 percent agreed that "the earliest written version of the passion story is found in the Gospel of Mark."[96]

(f) Triadic Methodology and Reconstruction

Crossan claims that his 1991 publication "had to raise most seriously the problem of methodology and then follow most stringently whatever theoretical model was chosen." His method was triadic, involving the interplay of "cross-cultural and cross-temporal social *anthropology*," "Hellenistic or Greco-Roman *history*," and "the *literature* of specific sayings and doings, stories and anecdotes, confessions and interpretations concerning Jesus." His statement is that "all three levels, anthropological, historical, and literary, must cooperate fully and equally for an effective synthesis.... Weakness

---

94. Crossan, *Birth of Christianity*, 239 (emphasis in original).
95. Crossan, *Birth of Christianity*, 492.
96. Jesus Seminar, "Voting Records," 227.

in any element imperils the integrity and validity of the others."[97] The data from (a), (b), and (c) above demonstrate a substantial literary weakness in the implementation of his postmodern, reconstructionist interactivism of history. He has not been able to consistently apply this model to his own work, and this compromises the integrity of his reconstruction.

Crossan "presumes that there will always be divergent historical Jesuses, that there will always be divergent Christs built upon them, but above all, it argues that the structure of a Christianity will always be: *this is how we see Jesus-then as Christ-now.*"[98] The evolution of his view of history is reiterated with this definition: "*History is the past reconstructed interactively by the present through argued evidence in public discourse.*"[99] This definition is at the beginning of a massive inventory of over 650 pages of historical data and analysis on "the birth of Christianity." He repeats it over and over in some of his publications. The data above have demonstrated that Crossan finds it impossible to fulfill his postmodern, reconstructed, interactive view of history in a systematically consistent manner.

For him, "the Gospels are neither histories nor biographies, even within the ancient tolerances for those genres. They are what were eventually called Gospels or good newses, and thereby comes a double warning. 'Good' is always such within some individual's or community's opinion or interpretation. And 'news' is not a word we usually pluralize again as 'newses.'"[100] If they are not histories, why has Crossan spent so much time and energy on many publications in analyzing the data from these nonhistories? Why does he define history as "*the past reconstructed interactively by the present*" if there is no intent to examine history (traditional history) associated with the life of Jesus and reconstruct it?

(g) Plural Attestation Jettisoned When Another Agenda Is Promoted

Crossan states that he completely avoids "any unit found only in single attestation within the first stratum," but "plural attestation in the first stratum pushes the trajectory back as far as it can go with at least formal objectivity."[101]

Is he consistent in this application? There are examples where, in order to support his FC a priori presumption, he rejects plural attestation, as he does with the Lord's Prayer, "Two as One," and "Supper and Eucharist" cases

---

97. Crossan, *Historical Jesus*, xxviii–xxix.
98. Crossan, *Historical Jesus*, 423 (emphasis in original).
99. Crossan, *Birth of Christianity*, 20 (emphasis in original).
100. Crossan, *Birth of Christianity*, xxviii–xxix.
101. Crossan, *Historical Jesus*, xxxii–xxxiii.

"that, although they are plurally attested in the first stratum and although they summarize principles or practices, themes or emphases, of the historical Jesus, stem not from him but from the liturgical creativity of the early communities."[102] Who determined so? Which evidence supports such a position?

We find that an a priori commitment to an FC principle (creativity of the Christian community) takes precedence over plural attestation. An application of the creative Christian community principle is Mark's solution in the passion account: "It is impossible *in my mind* to overestimate the creativity of Mark" in the twin trials in which Mark creates "consummate theological fictions," and "Mark's solution is to create the Barabbas incident in 15:6–15. I do not believe for a second that it actually happened."[103]

Crossan has no qualms in adding "*in my mind*" for him to violate his own principles and add data. Systematic consistency is violated.

(h) Commitment to FC Principles

Crossan's a priori assumption is that "the Jesus tradition . . . contains three major layers." These are:

1. Retention, which is "recording the essential core of words and deeds, events and happenings"
2. Development, which is applying "such data to new situations, novel problems, and unforeseen circumstances"
3. Creation, which is "not only composing new sayings and new stories, but, above all, composing larger complexes that changed their contents by that very process"[104]

He supports Koester's summary of this FC view concerning Gospel composition: "Everybody could and did rewrite, edit, revise, and combine, however he saw fit,"[105] but Crossan, in talking of "original, developmental, and compositional layers, or of retention, development and creation," rejects any presumption that these were referring to illicit or inauthentic layers or that he was using pejorative language.[106]

---

102. Crossan, *Historical Jesus*, 360 (emphasis in original).
103. Crossan, *Historical Jesus*, 390 (mphasis added).
104. Crossan, *Historical Jesus*, xxxi.
105. Koester, "History and Development," 77.
106. Crossan, *Historical Jesus*, xxxi.

(i) Citing Secondary Literature

Another of Crossan's a priori premises is that "in quoting *secondary* literature I spend no time citing other scholars to show how wrong they are. Those who are cited represent my intellectual debt."[107] As indicated already, he violates this within seven pages with his taking John Davis to task for castigating an anthropological peer, Julian Pitt-Rivers.[108] If he cites primarily those who represent his intellectual debt, how does this deal with the objections to his views that come from those outside of his circle of "intellectual" scholarly colleagues? As discussed earlier in this chapter, Crossan opposes some of the content of Johnson's publication *The Real Jesus*.

This seems to be a myopic scholarly viewpoint. In later publications, Crossan does interact with the works of Wright in which the views on Christ's resurrection are markedly different from Crossan's.[109] In appealing to those representing his intellectual debt, Crossan has committed the erroneous reasoning of an "appeal to authority," which is "insisting that a claim is true simply because a valid authority or expert on the issue said it was true, without any other supporting evidence offered."[110]

Crossan especially takes to task British novelist, playwright, and Christian apologist Dorothy Sayers over statements concerning her acceptance of differences in Gospel "parables and sayings" as being associated with their being "repeated over and over again" and not evidence of "any inaccuracy and contradiction." His claim is that the "two processes—source-criticism and redaction-criticism—were the twin sides of the same coin. They stood or fell together; they confirmed or disconfirmed one another." His view is that the basic validity of that double process is "the major presupposition" in his section on "gospels and sources." He concludes that "if it is wrong, any historical reconstruction of Jesus and his followers built upon it is methodologically invalid. Ditto, of course, for any alternative hypothesis." He denigrates Sayers's view with this sarcasm: "The scholarly conclusions of *tradition-criticism*, hard won by gospel scholarship over the last two hundred years (but also confirmed by my own personal study) . . . separates me from the simplicity of common sense that here, as elsewhere, can become *un*common *non*sense."[111] This is

---

107. Crossan, *Historical Jesus*, xxxiv.
108. Crossan, *Historical Jesus*, 7.
109. See Crossan, *Birth of Christianity*, 44, 49, 95–99, 104, 258; Wright and Crossan, "Resurrection."
110. "Appeal to Authority."
111. Crossan, *Birth of Christianity*, 91, 93 (emphasis in original).

hardly a demonstration of his personal humility in addressing the scholarship of another from whom he differs.

He responds to some of the content of Johnson's book *The Real Jesus* "as a Christian to a fellow Christian." His critique of Johnson is that Johnson, in opposing Crossan's methodology, "negates the possibility not only of historical Jesus reconstruction but, in effect, of all past and even present history."[112]

This shows that the assertion "I spend no time citing other scholars to show how wrong they are" is not practiced consistently and coherently with the critique of Johnson and Sayers. In this publication, Crossan cites other scholars with whom he disagrees, including Wright and Brown.[113]

There is not systematic consistency by Crossan in applying his stated premise with regard to his use of secondary literature and not challenging scholars about whether their conclusions are wrong. He does the opposite of what he states.

(j) Metaphorical Interpretation

There are numerous assumed metaphorical interpretations throughout Crossan's publications. This is a typical example, where he is in dialogue with Wright on the nature of Jesus's resurrection in an appendix titled "Bodily-Resurrection Faith." Here, Crossan states that throughout Wright's book *The Resurrection of the Son of God*, Wright argues, according to Crossan, "clearly that the only sufficient and necessary *historical* explanation for Christian Judaism's stunning mutation of Pharisaic Judaism's resurrection is twofold":

1. "The *historical* discovery of Jesus' empty tomb," and
2. "The *historical* experience of Jesus' bodily presence."[114]

Crossan's dissenting explanation is: "I do not for here and now debate the historicity of either Jesus' burial or the empty tomb's discovery. Instead, for here and now (*dato non concesso*, to be sure) *I take the Gospel stories of the empty tomb's discovery and of all those risen apparitions as historically factual in their entirety*."[115] Wright's perspective is bodily resurrection of

---

112. Crossan, *Birth of Christianity*, 30–31.

113. Crossan, *Birth of Christianity*, 103–20.

114. Crossan is citing Wright, *Resurrection of the Son*, and is himself cited in Stewart, *Quest of Hermeneutical Jesus*, 176 (emphasis in original).

115. Crossan, as cited in Stewart, *Quest of Hermeneutical Jesus*, 176 (emphasis in original.) The meaning of *dato non concesso* is "conceding (for the sake of argument)"

Jesus as historically factual, but Crossan's a priori understanding of "historically factual" was the stores were about "risen apparitions" and not bodily appearances after Jesus's resurrection.

Crossan's description of Christ's resurrection being an apparition begins appearing in some of his early publications without exposition of his position, an example being *Four Other Gospels* (1985), in which he has a chapter that examines "Resurrection and Confession" from the Gospel of Peter. A section of this Gospel has a designated heading "Disciples and Apparition," in which, without justification for his use of the designation, Crossan labels Jesus's resurrection as an "apparition."[116] Concerning the resurrection in Christian tradition, he writes that the four intracanonical Gospels agree on the sequence and detail of the passion narrative, "but they disagree almost totally on the place and time, the setting and content of Jesus' apparition to the apostles to give them their missionary mandate for the world."[117] Here again, the resurrection apparition is assumed a priori. There is no grappling with *sōma* (body) in association with Jesus's resurrection.

By contrast, Wright deals with the biblical and cultural data in light of the apostle Paul's statements in Romans 8. Paul believed this from his Jewish worldview:

> "The resurrection" had divided, as a historical moment, into two: the resurrection would not only be bodily (the idea of a non-bodily resurrection would have been as much an oxymoron to him as it would be to both Jews and pagans of his day; whether you believed in resurrection or not, the word meant bodies), but that it would also involve *transformation*. The present body is corruptible, decaying and subject to death; but death, which spits in the face of the good creator God, cannot have the last word. The creator will therefore make a new world, and new bodies, proper to the new age.[118]

Another a priori assumption continues in Crossan's *The Cross That Spoke*[119] with his assessment of the Gospel of Peter, disciples and apparition,

---

(Meltzer, *Thinker's Thesaurus*, 105). It is assumed that this is a position adopted only for pursuit of an argument and is not the actual position of the debater or scholar making the concession.

116. Crossan, *Four Other Gospels*, 165.

117. Crossan, *Four Other Gospels*, 179.

118. Wright, *Resurrection of the Son*, 372 (emphasis in original).

119. Crossan, *Cross That Spoke*, 20. Crossan here gives two of his "major propositions": (1) "I prefer my proposed theory of Mark and the Cross Gospel as the twin sources of Matthew, Luke, and John in the Passion and Resurrection sections." (2) "My second major proposition, then, is that an intracanonical stratum was combined with

and argument for a redactor creating a scene in Gospel of Peter 7:26–27 in preparation, to facilitate the later insertion of Jesus's apparition to the twelve (Gos. Pet. 14:60).[120]

Crossan writes "that no distinction is made in the *Cross Gospel* (the earliest alleged stage of GPet) between the phenomena of resurrection and ascension."[121] He also writes "of epiphany and apparition" without an apologetic for his declaration that the resurrection of Jesus was an apparition and not a bodily resurrection, except to say that his "proposal builds on those earlier studies, but is much more precise in its explanation."[122]

Thus, Crossan is making the resurrection an epiphany,[123] an apparition. However, it is his a priori requirement for the integration of the texts of the intracanonical Gospels and the Gospel of Peter, to make them assimilate "resurrection and transfiguration,"[124] so he can arrive at his assumed understanding that Jesus's resurrection was an apparition and not a bodily resurrection.

This leads to his pointed diagnosis: "It is the resurrectional apparition of a dead man that explains the power of Christianity's birth and growth, spread and triumph, across the Roman empire."[125] For Crossan, it is historical apparition and not bodily resurrection that birthed Christianity and led to its spread. More recently, Crossan admitted that the story of the discovery of Jesus's empty tomb "was created by Mark precisely to avoid any apparitions to the (by him) discredited outer Twelve or inner Three or, especially, Peter himself."[126] In addition, "the apparition stories present in our gospels are about authority rather than apparition, or, better, about authority by apparition. But, of course, both those conclusions point to original risen apparitions as taken absolutely for granted and I fully accept them as historical events even though details are now lost to us forever."[127]

These are his personal projections, without evidence to prove them.

---

that original Cross Gospel in the formation of the Gospel of Peter."

120. Crossan, *Cross That Spoke*, 291.

121. Crossan, *Cross That Spoke*, 347. Crossan provides his analysis of the "three distinguishable strata" in Gos. Pet. in Crossan, *Birth of Christianity*, 409–13.

122. Crossan, *Cross That Spoke*, 348, 350.

123. An epiphany is "a powerful religious experience" ("Epiphany," in *CD*).

124. Crossan, *Cross That Spoke*, 359.

125. Crossan, "Historical Jesus as Risen Lord," 32.

126. Crossan, as cited in Stewart, *Quest of Hermeneutical Jesus*, 177. The parenthesis was in the original.

127. Crossan, as cited in Stewart, *Quest of Hermeneutical Jesus*, 177.

IMPOSITION OF PERSONAL INTERPRETATION ON THE DATA

Again, these will be samples and not comprehensive examples of this suggested reason for the self-contradiction in some of Crossan's data. The indication by this subtitle is that there are examples where a unique interpretation seems to be forced on the data. These include the following:

(A) SACROPHILIA AND NOT SACROPHOBIA

Crossan proposes two categories, which he acknowledges are "deliberately provocative," for the spirit and flesh dimensions in Jesus's person. One, he calls a "monism of enfleshed spirit *sacrophilia*" and the other, "dualism of flesh against spirit *sacrophobia*, from the Greek roots for 'flesh' (*sarx*), 'love' (*philia*), and 'fear' (*phobos*)." His position is "monistic rather than dualistic," and he concludes, "We are spiritual flesh or fleshly spirit and we flee that amalgam at our peril." How does this monism apply to Jesus? "We might think to ourselves: of course Jesus was human. The question is: was he divine? They had the opposite problem. If they believed Jesus was divine, the question became: how could he be human? How could his body be real rather than apparitional and illusional? Was it not just a seem-to-be body?"[128]

Crossan applies this view to Jesus's resurrection: "There was no point in responding that people saw, heard, or even touched his body," and this is what is said to have occurred in the post-resurrection appearances.[129] Why not? If some people saw, heard, and touched his body, it demonstrated the resurrection was that of a body and not of an apparition or epiphany. That's common sense.

Therefore, this Crossan perspective directly opposes any view that would support Jesus's bodily resurrection and post-resurrection appearances in the flesh. Crossan does not deal with the biblical, physical evidence of Jesus appearing to his disciples and Jesus's physical actions among them.

Crossan adopts a view he says was "brilliantly explored by Gregory Riley. Jesus could be explained not as *god* or *spirit* but as *hero*, as the offspring of a divine and human conjunction, himself therefore half-human and half-divine but really and truly each half."[130] The Riley view, supported by Crossan, is that with this perspective of the half-human, half-divine Jesus, Jesus could "ascend after a real and true death and take his place

---

128. Crossan, "Historical Jesus as Risen Lord," 39.
129. Crossan, "Historical Jesus as Risen Lord," 40.
130. Crossan, "Historical Jesus as risen Lord," 40 (emphasis in original).

among the heavenly immortals. But if one ever wished to move beyond Jesus as hero to Jesus as spirit or Jesus as god, the unreality of his flesh and the apparitional illusion of his body would have seemed inevitable concomitants in the ancient world." So Crossan supports the view of Christianity as "sacrophilic and/or incarnational as distinct from sacrophobic and/or docetic Christianity."[131]

It is difficult to know exactly what Crossan is teaching in his view of the divine-human Jesus with his support for "monism of enfleshed spirit." It seems to be a version of Nestorianism where there are "two separate persons in Christ, a human person and a divine person, a teaching that is distinct from the biblical view that sees Jesus as one person."[132] Do not confuse this statement about Jesus with three persons in the Godhead—the Trinity. Historically, Crossan's view was not accepted as orthodox Christianity, as Scripture does not teach that "Christ was two distinct persons. Nowhere in Scripture do we have an indication that the human nature of Christ, for example, is an independent person, deciding to do something contrary to the divine nature of Christ."[133]

Crossan's sacrophilic view of Jesus as enfleshed spirit is a heretical interpretation that he has imposed on the biblical material. In so doing, he has created his own way of defining the divine-human Jesus and reconstructing the post-resurrection appearances of Jesus to mean other than that there were those who actually "saw, heard, or even touched his body" (see Matt 28:1–20; Luke 24:1–49; John 20:1–21:19; Acts 1:1–5). Grudem diagrammed Nestorianism and its view of Christ as containing two persons.[134] This is a diagrammatic form of the Nestorian view, where the human and divine persons of Christ are separate.

---

131. Crossan, "Historical Jesus as Risen Lord," 40–41.
132. Grudem, *Systematic Theology*, 555.
133. Grudem, *Systematic Theology*, 555.
134. Grudem, *Systematic Theology*, 555.

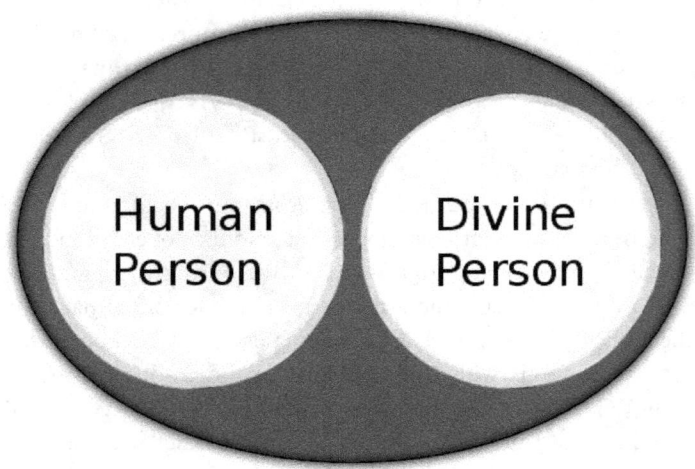

A historical misinterpretation of the Nestorian view was that it taught that the human and divine persons of Christ were separate.[135]

There is controversy as to whether Nestorius believed the view that has been attributed to him. Harold O. J. Brown, an Evangelical, maintains that Nestorius's incarnate person was a single person, not two, as his critics thought, but Brown could not convince others that it was so. Consequently, Nestorius has gone down in history as a heretic, although what he actually believed was reaffirmed at Chalcedon. The Council of 451 really was far more compatible with the formulations of Nestorius, the heretic, than with those of Cyril, the doctor of the church.[136] Nowhere does Scripture affirm Christ was two persons in one body rather than one person.[137]

What makes Crossan difficult to categorize is his imprecision in articulating the person(s) and nature of Christ, by his accepting Jesus as half-God, half-man. This does seem to place him into what has become known as the Nestorian camp. Or could it be a unique, heretical, Crossan designation of sacrophilic, enfleshed spirit that is meant to be nebulous? Werner Kelber, in dialogue with Crossan and Johnson, responded to my concerns with Crossan's lack of exactitude in defining the relationship of God and human being in Jesus: "Crossan's thesis is not without irony because it decries the anthropological binary divide of soul versus body only to reinvoke a historical

---

135. Image courtesy of Noapaniers, http://thoughtfulfaith.wordpress.com/, available at https://commons.wikimedia.org/wiki/File:Nestorianism.svg/.

136. H. Brown, *Heresies*, 176.

137. See Grudem, *Systematic Theology*, 242.

binary divide between sacrophobic versus a sacrophilic typology. Why reimagine Christianity in the traditional metaphors of truth versus falsehood? *More finely tuned responses to the concreteness of multiple distinctions are required.*"[138] Kelber then observed Crossan's theological justification as a historical Jesus quester: "The reasons he advances for his work cause one to wonder why his *re*construction of the historical Jesus is associated with a serious *mis*judgment of the tradition."[139]

The orthodox understanding of the two natures of Christ in the one person is defined by Lewis and Demarest "as the personal (hypostatic) union" of *"two distinct natures* [deity and humanity]. The two sets of attributes are neither mixed nor confounded. No attribute of the one nature is transferred to the other. Neither is a third hybrid produced. What unites the two natures is that both may be predicated of the one actual person. The two natures exist not merely in a functional harmony, nor are they in a nonmetaphysical way merely communicated to each other."[140]

Explained further, it is not a union between deity and the human, as nominalists maintain. "It was not a merely relational union like the oneness of mind among friends." Instead, the most coherent proposal suggests a personal union of the divine and human natures in one *hypostasia*. Both natures are predicated of the one person. Some of Jesus's attributes are divine, and some of them are human. "Hence we speak of the *hypostatic or personal union* of the two distinct natures."[141] So, from conception and birth, Jesus possessed two natures: "The second person of the Trinity condescended to partake in or share our humanity."[142] This is affirmed in Luke 1:43; John 1:1, 14; Acts 13:35–37; Philippians 2:5–11; Colossians 2:9; Hebrews 2:14; and 1 John 4:1–3.

A foretaste of this doctrine is seen in Ignatius of Antioch, Syria (ca. first to second centuries), in his letter to the Ephesians, with a glimpse of the Lord Jesus's hypostatic or personal union: "God Himself being manifested in human form for the renewal of eternal life."[143] Another is in Irenaeus's work, *Against Heresies*, in which he states, "He, therefore, who was known, was not a different being from Him who declared 'No man knows the

---

138. Kelber, *Jesus Controversy*, 98 (emphasis added).
139. Kelber, *Jesus Controversy*, 102 (emphasis in original).
140. Lewis and Demarest, *Integrative Theology*, 2:343.
141. Lewis and Demarest, *Integrative Theology*, 2:343.
142. Lewis and Demarest, *Integrative Theology*, 2:343 (emphasis in original).
143. Ignatius, "Epistle of Ignatius," ch. 19.

Father,' but one and the same, while He received testimony from all that He was very man, and that He was very God."[144]

(b) Intersection of Three Independent Vectors

If one wanted to move "behind the screen of credal interpretation" to "give an accurate but impartial account of the historical Jesus as distinct from the confessional Christ," what would one do? Crossan considers that is what is pursued through an "academic or scholarly study of the historical Jesus." He understands that is what it does, when it is not "a disguise for doing theology and calling it history," not "doing autobiography and calling it biography," and "not doing Christian apologetics and calling it academic scholarship." He maintains that results and conclusions "are only as good as the theory and method on which they are based."[145]

So what is Crossan's methodological approach in his academic and scholarly study of the historical Jesus? He locates the historical Jesus where three independent vectors intersect. These vectors are cross-cultural anthropology, Graeco-Roman and especially Jewish history, and literary text.[146]

This approach is here considered to be an imposition of a chosen, a priori methodology on the biblical data. Why does Crossan not pursue only an inductive study of what the text says, in light of historical and cultural context, and interpret the Scriptures as he would when reading literature from scholarly sources or the local newspaper or viewing the evening television news? Why does he not use the standard methods of hermeneutics by accepting the plain (literal) meaning of the text with its metaphors, symbols, and other inductive characteristics? Instead, he imposes two other vectors of understanding on the text, the literary text being only one vector.

(c) The Supernatural as Process

While Crossan rejects any concept of supernatural intervention, he understands Lazarus's being raised from the dead "as process incarnated in event and not the reverse." According to his understanding of John 11:21–27, the movement from process to event was that "the process of general resurrection is incarnated in the event of Lazarus's resuscitation." He imagines that the peasants of lower Galilee would have been thinking of their present

---

144. Irenaeus, *Against Heresies*, 4.6.7.
145. See Crossan, *Jesus*, xi, and Crossan, *Historical Jesus*, xxviii.
146. Crossan, *Jesus*, xi–xii.

earthly existence and not a heavenly future. Therefore, "life out of death is how they would have understood the Kingdom of God, in which they began to take back control over their own bodies, their own hopes, and their own destinies."[147] This metaphorical interpretation of the supernatural event, the supernatural being denied by Crossan, is an example of how Crossan interprets another supernatural event—the resurrection of Jesus.

The outrageous title of a Crossan chapter is "How Many Years Was Easter Sunday?"[148] Here, Crossan is precise about how his metaphorical, postmodern hermeneutic applies to Jesus's resurrection: "What we have here [Luke 24:13–46] is not an event from Easter Sunday but a process that happened over many years. The presence and empowerment of Jesus remain in the community as it studies the scriptures 'about' him and shares a meal of bread and fish together. This is not trance but exegesis, not ecstasy but eucharist."[149] This kind of interpretation makes me embarrassed over being a historical Jesus scholar when Crossan invents such outlandish conclusions.

This aspect will be analyzed when testing hypothesis 2 in another book: "The divine manifestation for Christianity is interpreted by reconstruction for a postmodern world." Can that hypothesis be verified? Was it an apparition, fantasy, an invention by the Gospel writers, or was it a bodily resurrection?

(D) Resurrection and the Cross Gospel

Crossan places so much emphasis on the role of the Cross Gospel from the Gospel of Peter as the foundation of the passion accounts in the New Testament that he states: "The signal achievement of the Cross Gospel to move from the *prophetic passion* to the *narrative passion*" was "to create from discrete prophetic allusions and composite prophetic fulfillments a coherent and sequential story."[150]

How does this prominence influence the resurrection accounts in the Gospels? Crossan promotes the view that "the first writer to use and develop the Cross Gospel composition was, in my judgment on the extant texts, the evangelist Mark himself. I see no convincing evidence that Mark has any other basis for his passion narrative than that source and his own theological creativity."[151]

---

147. Crossan, *Jesus*, 95.
148. Crossan, *Jesus*, 159.
149. Crossan, *Jesus*, 172.
150. Crossan, *Historical Jesus*, 389 (emphasis in original).
151. Crossan, *Historical Jesus*, 389.

How does that apply to the resurrection? Mark "made three profound changes" to the Cross Gospel. "The first and most basic one was to change the overarching model from *innocence rescued to martyrdom vindicated*. No salvific miracle here below would save Jesus before, during, or after death. Only at the parousia would the resurrectional victory become visible, according to Mark 13:26 and 14:62." Therefore, "Mark had . . . to negate completely both the visible resurrection and the subsequent Roman confession from the Cross Gospel. He did it by retrojecting both back into preceding sections of his Gospel. These were in Mark 9:2–8 and Mark 15:39."[152]

(e) Prophecy Historicized Rather Than History Remembered

This will not be a significant emphasis pursued in this project, but it is given prominence in publications where Crossan states that many of the passion-resurrection details did not come from history but from a prophetic understanding of the Old Testament read back into the New Testament texts. The following provides samples of his statements:

- "The details [of Jesus' passion] in our gospels are, in any case, *prophecy historicized* and not *history memorized*."[153]
- "The passion narratives are prophecy historicized rather than history remembered."[154]
- "By 'prophecy historicized' I mean that no such historical three-hour-long midnight at noon accompanied the death of Jesus, but that learned Christians searching their Scriptures found this ancient description of future divine punishment, maybe facilitated by its mention of 'an only son' in the second-to-last line, and so created that fictional story about darkness at noon to assert that Jesus died in fulfillment of prophecy."[155]
- Luke's Gospel "is interested in portraying Jesus in close interaction with major events of 'Roman history,' interest, that is, in the historicization of prophecy, or rephrasing prophetic allusion as 'historical' narrative."[156]

---

152. Crossan, *Historical Jesus*, 389 (emphasis in original).
153. Crossan, *Jesus*, 152 (emphasis in original).
154. Crossan, *Jesus*, 119.
155. Crossan, *Who Killed Jesus*, 19, 4.
156. Crossan, *Jesus*, 162 (emphasis in original).

- "Hide the prophecy, tell the narrative, and invent the history."[157]
- The model used to organize "all those discrete prophetic applications to a full passion narrative" was what Crosan calls "*innocence rescued*" and "that process not only 'historicized' the prophetic passion, it allowed the 'historicization' of *passion and resurrection* so that resurrection, which was of course taken for granted in earlier dyadic *passion and parousia* prophecies, could now become part of the story and receive full focus in its own right."[158]

Crossan writes of the "validity of the hypothesis that the passion narratives are prophecy historicized rather than history remembered."[159] His conclusion about the execution of Jesus is:

> I cannot find any detailed historical information about the crucifixion of Jesus. Every item we looked at was prophecy historicized rather than history recalled. There was one glaring exception. The one time the *narrative passion* broke away from its base in the *prophetic passion*, that is, from the single, composite trial in Psalm 2, was to assert Jewish responsibility and Roman innocence. But those motifs were neither prophecy nor history but Christian propaganda, a daring act of public relations faith in the destiny of Christianity not within Judaism but within the Roman Empire. In a way, that *was* history, not past history but future history.[160]

It is again noticed that Crossan uses the term history in a contradictory way by using its traditional sense and not according to his own definition of history as reconstructed interactivism. When he states, "I cannot find any detailed historical information about the crucifixion of Jesus," he deliberately rejects the material in the four Gospels. "I cannot find" is a statement of his presuppositional ignorance or of deliberate intention to cover up, especially in light of the crucifixion details recorded in Matt 27:1–56; Mark 15:6–41; Luke 23:13–49; and John 19:1–37.

Barnett's review of Crossan highlights Crossan's failure "to observe one of the basic principles of historiography, namely to use the earliest and best sources and to exercise critical caution with historically remote texts." Therefore, Barnett finds it puzzling that Crossan writes of "dark decades ... cloaked in silence" in the years after the execution of Jesus, but Crossan's

---

157. Crossan, *Historical Jesus*, 372.
158. Crossan, *Historical Jesus*, 385 (emphasis in original).
159. Crossan, *Who Killed Jesus*, 119.
160. Crossan, *Who Killed Jesus*, 159 (emphasis in original).

biblical indices do not include a single reference to the Book of Acts until one gets to the co-authored book by Crossan and Reed, *In Search of Paul*.[161]

Crossan also dispenses with the early church fathers who affirmed Jesus's death and resurrection in agreement with the Gospel accounts. Justin Martyr (ca. 100–165), in his "Dialogue with Trypho," writes, "Since those who did that which is universally, naturally, and eternally good are pleasing to God, they shall be saved through this Christ in the resurrection equally with those righteous men who were before them, namely Noah, and Enoch, and Jacob."[162] There is no claiming a resurrection apparition here. Irenaeus (ca. 120–190) writes that Polycarp, Christian bishop at Smyrna, Asia Minor was "instructed" and "appointed" by the apostles and "conversed with many who had seen Christ . . . *having always taught the things which he had learned from the apostles*."[163] These are early statements after the Gospel passion accounts, and they do not confirm the content of Crossan's view of the passion.

Craig Evans has two main criticisms of Crossan's favoring the Gospel of Peter as containing the earliest passion-resurrection account and of Crossan's stating that the New Testament Gospels were generated by Christians who found that information in the Old Testament. They are:

1. Crossan's "contention that Old Testament prophecy is what underlies the Gospels' passion story is not persuasive. It is gratuitous to assert that Jesus' friends and followers did not know and did not find out what happened. It is much more probable that they did find out what happened, even if only in bits and pieces, and then did their best to show that what happened was 'according to the scriptures.'"

2. The Gospel of Peter is a late writing with a mixture of details from the four canonical Gospels and that of "pious Christian imagination (complete with a talking cross and two angels whose heads reach the heavens) and not-so-pious Christian criticism of the Jewish people."[164]

The Gospel of Peter comes with historical inaccuracies that even Crossan acknowledges, and it "strikes most scholars as far removed from the authentic Jesus tradition and its setting in first-century Jewish Palestine."[165]

---

161. Barnett, *Birth of Christianity*, 211, 215. See the index in Crossan and Reed, *In Search of Paul*, 427.

162. Martyr, "Dialogue with Trypho," ch. 45.

163. Irenaeus, *Against Heresies*, 3:3:4 (emphasis added). Irenaeus also claims to have spoken with Polycarp when Irenaeus was "in my early youth."

164. Evans, "Passion of Jesus,"161.

165. Evans, "Passion of Jesus," 161–62.

Craig Blomberg points to a "docetic tendency"[166] in the Gospel of Peter 4 where it is stated, "They brought two malefactors, and they crucified the Lord between them. But he held his peace, as though having no pain." There also are some additions surrounding Jesus's resurrection: the soldiers "see three men come forth from the tomb, and two of them supporting one, and a cross following them: and of the two the head reached unto the heaven, but the head of him that was led by them overpassed the heavens. And they heard a voice from the heavens, saying, You have preached to them that sleep. And a response was heard from the cross, Yea" (Gos. Pet. 10). Blomberg labels these as "more obviously legendary elements."[167] Evans explains in more detail why these two criticisms of Crossan's promotion of "prophecy historicized" make Crossan's view problematic.

Instead of Crossan's contrast between history remembered and prophecy historicized, Mark Goodacre gives an alternate perspective, borrowing Judith Newman's understanding of *scripturalization*[168] and applying it to Mark's passion narrative. Goodacre sees many echoes of biblical themes and allusions to scriptural precedent, which he considers "can be explained on the basis of intimate interaction between the tradition and the Scriptural reflection. The traditions generated Scriptural reflection, which in turn influenced the way the traditions were recast."[169] How did scripturalization take place?

Goodacre's claim is that there exists both internal and external evidence to suggest that it happened during worship, and this could have been the context for the development of Mark's passion narrative. First Corinthians 11 and the Eucharist provide examples external to the Gospels where liturgy provides a context for the earliest known version of the retelling of the passion story. Goodacre maintains one advantage to his claim is that there might be "footprints" of the liturgy in Mark's passion narrative. "It provides us with a plausible context for the creation of the first Passion Narrative, with its marked scripturalizing tendency, and so—ultimately—it sheds light on the genesis of the Gospels themselves."[170] At least Goodacre is providing a suggestion for the how-to of obtaining Mark's passion narrative and is not

---

166. Doceticism was a variety of the teaching of Gnosticism by which Jesus Christ was denied as the divine Redeemer who was the subject of human experiences, but the application of the term to Jesus Christ is disputed by patristic scholars (D. F. Wright, "Doceticism," 306).

167. Blomberg, *Historical Reliability of Gospels*, 217.

168. Newman borrowed the term from her teacher James L Kugel, where Kugel used the term in perceiving the Psalms as Scripture (Goodacre, "Scripturalization," 40–41n21).

169. Goodacre, "Quest to Digest Jesus."

170. Goodacre, "Scripturalization," 40, 42–43, 45.

redefining or destroying any concept of Mark's Gospel containing a historical narrative, as with Crossan.

(F) There Is More!

One can find a diverse array of examples of Crossan's imposition of his own interpretation on the biblical data. These are, briefly, some further samples.

"I understand the virginal conception of Jesus to be a confessional statement about Jesus' status and not a biological statement about Mary's body. It is later faith in Jesus as an adult retrojected mythologically onto Jesus as an infant." This leads to two understandings for Crossan: "Four unnamed brothers, and at least two unnamed sisters are Jesus' natural siblings," and Jesus "is not necessarily the firstborn child of Joseph and Mary."[171]

Regarding Josephus as a witness to Jesus, Crossan's position is that "the problem is that Josephus's account is too good to be true, too confessional to be impartial, too Christian to be Jewish. There are sentences in it that could hardly have been written by a Jewish writer, sentences that assert Christian beliefs, sentences that could have been written only by a Christian believer. Remember that Josephus's works were preserved and copied by Christian rather than Jewish editors." Josephus's text regarding Jesus states: "Caiaphas, being high priest that year, prophesied that Jesus should die for that nation, and not for that nation only."[172] Scholars question the authenticity of this quote, assuming it may be an interpolation by a Christian-friendly copyist. Yet, of Josephus, Crossan writes that "a prudently neutral Jewish historian reported, at the end of the first century" about Pilate.[173] I ask: which is it— "too good to be true" or that of "a prudently neutral Jewish historian"? Those two designations create a paradox.

Crossan states that "an arrogant Roman historian [Tacitus] reported, at the start of the second century" about Christus, founder of the name of Christian, and includes his death penalty during the reign of Tiberius, sentenced by the procurator, Pontius Pilate, and how the "pernicious superstition" of Christians broke out in a number of places.[174]

---

171. Crossan, *Jesus*, 23.
172. Josephus, *Antiquities*, ch. 11n10.
173. Crossan, *Jesus*, 197.
174. Crossan, *Jesus*, 197.

Speculation and Opinion

These are pointed samples of some statements of how Crossan speculates, presumes, and gives opinions, beginning with his 1988 publication *The Cross That Spoke*:

- "*I consider* that those closest to Jesus had fled his Crucifixion and had no idea how or where he was buried."[175]
- Regarding the Mount of Transfiguration, "*I presume* that it was Mark himself who first transformed those 'two men' [from Gos. Pet. 9:36] into Moses and Elijah for his newly created Transfiguration narrative."[176]
- "Matthew is, *in my view*, conflating two sources in his account of the angel and guards in 28:2–4, that of the 'two men' from the *Cross Gospel* and that of the 'young man' from Mark 16:1–8."[177]
- "Matthew, *in my opinion*, knows both the Transfiguration story from Mark 9:2–7 and the Epiphanic Resurrection story from *Gospel of Peter* 9:35–10:42)."[178]
- "While *I am more certain* of the cross as symbol of the common Passion of Israel and Jesus, *I think it might be just possible* that the author visualizes them following Jesus in a great cruciform procession. Maybe."[179]
- "Notice, however, that *I determine that sequence* [in the Honi and Hanina traditions] along a documentary trajectory but by successive stages along a rabbinization trajectory."[180]
- "Those mothers *might be* simply Josephus' own invention intended to heighten the human theater of the trial."[181]
- "That is *an unfortunate scholarly construct based on Josephan disinformation*."[182]

---

175. Crossan, *Cross That Spoke*, 248 (emphasis added).
176. Crossan, *Cross That Spoke*, 350 (emphasis added).
177. Crossan, *Cross That Spoke*, 352 (emphasis added).
178. Crossan, *Cross That Spoke*, 358 (emphasis added).
179. Crossan, *Cross That Spoke*, 387 (emphasis added).
180. Crossan, *Historical Jesus*, 149 (emphasis added).
181. Crossan, *Historical Jesus*, 175 (emphasis added).
182. Crossan, *Historical Jesus*, 218 (emphasis added).

- "*I prefer to think*, however, that the detailed narrative of Mark 6:14–29 is his own creation."[183]

- "*I presume* that, to make sense of 'coming up out of the water,' some account of John's baptism must have preceded that section, but *the power of its mythological presentation* would have negated any problems about superiority or inferiority."[184]

- "*It is quite likely, it seems to me*, that those cases are not at all a movement from event to process but actually from process to event. Early Christian communities symbolically *retrojected their own activities back into* the life of Jesus."[185]

Further examples of speculation and opinion are in the Crossan publications listed in the footnote.[186]

Why the Resurrection Narratives Are Not Historical for Crossan.

The primary reason found in this assessment for why the resurrection narratives cannot be affirmed as historical for Crossan is because historical, in the traditional sense, has been redefined by him to mean a postmodern, reconstructed interactivism that is not harmonious with the elements of traditional historiography affirmed by historians, Christian and non-Christian, throughout human history.

This is confounded by Crossan's

1. self-contradiction in not being consistent in his application of his own definition of history,
2. imposing a priori premises on some of the data,
3. not inductively accepting the literal meaning of the text, and
4. imposing his opinionated reason on some of the biblical texts associated with the historical Jesus and Jesus's resurrection.

---

183. Crossan, *Historical Jesus*, 232 (emphasis added).
184. Crossan, *Historical Jesus*, 233 (emphasis added.)
185. Crossan, *Historical Jesus*, 328 (emphasis added).
186. Crossan, *Jesus*, 24, 94–95, 99, 152; Crossan, *Who Killed Jesus*, 71, 73, 78, 81, 132, 177, 188, 220; Crossan, and Watts, *Who Is Jesus*, 40; Crossan, *Birth of Christianity*, 521, 524, 532; Borg and Crossan, *Last Week*, 213; Crossan in conversation with Wright, as cited in Stewart, *Quest of Hermeneutical Jesus*, 33.

Richard R. Niebuhr, although addressing metaphysical issues of a previous generation, has exposed one of Crossan's major difficulties with the biblical resurrection narratives and his postmodern a priori approach:

> When history is dissolved by meta-history, it forgets that we do not have the option of thinking either historically or metaphysically. We have only the option to think historically about historical events, or historically about the metaphysical implications of such events . . . . Neither the *a priori* metaphysical approach nor the historical critical method as hitherto encountered has shown itself adequate to the peculiar problems raised by the necessity of interpreting the resurrection of Jesus.[187]

By application, when Crossan defines history as postmodern, reconstructed interactivism and then concludes accordingly (on many occasions), he commits the logical fallacy of begging the question. He does not answer the historical issue: was Jesus's resurrection a historical resurrection in the traditional sense? Instead, he provides his postmodern views of history (but not consistently).

Geisler and Brooks explain that begging the question is a stacking the deck fallacy in which "the conclusion is sneaked into the premises. . . . It is a circular argument, where the conclusion actually becomes the premise . . . . If you start out with the conclusion as the first premise, it really doesn't matter what the second premise is, you can still reach the conclusion you want." Therefore, "the question being asked is given the desired answer before any reasoning is done."[188]

The fallacy with the postmodern approach is that Crossan presumes a postmodern definition of history and concludes with many postmodern examples (but not consistently applied), as shown in this chapter. Readers of Crossan are exposed to his premise as conclusion. Instead of reading a text inductively and allowing the text to provide the definition of the nature of history for itself, readers have Crossan's postmodern epistemology of history imposed on the conclusion. In addition, Crossan excludes miracles in his a priori presuppositions. God does not do it that way is Crossan's profoundly pompous statement.

Evidence was provided on a priori assumptions on the nature of the resurrection that an a priori postmodern approach and the historical critical method of applying such postmodernism to the data show itself to have the peculiar problems associated with postmodern epistemology and its application to the events of Jesus's resurrection.

187. Niebuhr, *Resurrection and Historical Reason*, 22–23.
188. Geisler and Brooks, *Come, Let Us Reason*, 100.

Niebuhr's assessment of the resurrection and history applies to Crossan's understanding when Niebuhr states that if theologians want "to abandon the realm of ordinary history, when they speak of the resurrection of Jesus," then "they must also abandon these narratives of recognition, for non-historical revelation can make no use of historical signs." He acknowledges that for some, the bodily resurrection has questions, because the meaning of resurrection faith was associated with Jesus's resurrection appearances being "independently and tangibly present to the disciples." His response is: "Apart from that, common sense argues, the resurrection is meaningless." He then states that if his argument is valid, "that the narratives are about encounters centered in recognition and identification—then we can affirm that the resurrection appearances shared in the same kind of independence as all historical events."[189]

Wright notes that "in the various works of the brilliant writer J. Dominic Crossan, Stephen Moore's assessment was that Crossan's 'work subverts itself through his insistence on trying, at the same time as he is deconstructing the texts, to discover the historical Jesus through and behind them. The way is hard that leads to genuine deconstructionism, and those who follow it consistently are few.'"[190] Wright asks: "Can one, as a good deconstructionist, ever hope to find *any* historical referent, even another deconstructionist (as Crossan supposes Jesus to have been)."[191]

The evidence provided throughout this chapter has reached a reasonable conclusion.

WAS HYPOTHESIS 1 CONFIRMED OR FALSIFIED?

Crossan has demonstrated:

1. Self-contradiction in not being consistent in the application of his own definition of history

2. Imposition of a priori premises on some of the data, including his presuppositions.

3. Not inductively accepting the literal meaning of the text but engaging in deconstructionist free play, imposing his concepts and meaning

---

189. Niebuhr, *Resurrection and Historical Reason*, 74.

190. Wright, *New Testament*, 60. Stephen Moore is a New Testament scholar who currently is professor of New Testament at Drew Theological School, Madison, NJ.

191. Wright, *New Testament*, 60, n 34.

4. Imposition of his opinionated reason on some of the biblical texts associated with the historical Jesus and Jesus's resurrection

I find it impossible to reach a reasoned decision on Crossan's consistency of interpretation when Crossan engages in such free play. One of the greatest challenges for Crossan is for him to practice what he preaches with "First, read the text." He has not chosen so to do, demonstrated by numerous examples of imposing his presuppositions on the text and adding to the text. He uses a question-begging logical fallacy in defining history, so adding to the previous evidence that causes the hypothesis to be falsified.

SUMMARY OF CHAPTER 6

The test for this chapter was to examine if Crossan could be consistent with his own proclamation "First, read the text." His self-contradictions were exposed. He violates two fundamentals: (1) first, read the text in the context of its literal meaning (with figures of speech included); (2) second, to determine the meaning of a biblical statement, the statement must fit the historical and cultural setting of the writer and the first readers. These fundamentals of reading were also applied to all of Crossan's writings.

When Crossan interprets with reconstruction, his free play enters with its diverse additions to the text. I surveyed some of Crossan's reconstructions to show their historical multiplicity of meanings. He was provocative in thinking of an entire Gospel as a book-length megaparable. His a priori presumptions were exposed to show that he is not following his own proclamation of "Anyone who wants to dramatize the death of Jesus in play or film, should first read the text and get the story right." He was referring to *The Passion of the Christ*.[192] His postmodern working definition of history deconstructs the nature of history to make it something that must happen over and over. That view crashes on the reality of, say, the 9/11 terrorism attacks in the USA; the suicide bombers who exploded bombs at Kabul airport;[193] and the content of his autobiography, *A Long Way from Tipperary*, where he uses a traditional approach to history.

As indicated in chapter 3, the interrelated indices used to test the validity or otherwise of all hypotheses are that only those will be accepted that are (1) noncontrradictory, (2) supported by adequate evidence, and (3) affirmable without hypocrisy.

---

192. Crossan, *God and Empire*, 138.
193. Kottasová et al., "US Troops."

Crossan's anti-supernaturalism automatically excludes the supernatural resurrection. His placing the Gospel of Peter in the first stratum, AD 30–60, puts him in company with his fellows in the Jesus Seminar but is at odds with many in the scholarly historical community. Throughout his writings, he doesn't allow the New Testament text to speak for itself but imposes his personal interpretation (opinion) on the text. This is seen, for example, in his causing the supernatural to be process in the Gospels.

He places great emphasis and early dating on the Gospel of Peter, but his view is replaced by the researched date of rational conclusions. There is too much speculation and opinion in Crossan to treat him seriously as a historical scholar. His presuppositions have provoked a nonhistorical view of his data because of

1. self-contradiction in not being consistent in his application of his own definition of history,
2. imposition of a priori premises on some of the data,
3. not inductively accepting the literal meaning of the text, and
4. imposition of his opinionated reason on some of the biblical texts associated with the historical Jesus and Jesus's resurrection.

It is impossible to reach a reasoned decision on Crossan's consistency of interpretation when Crossan engages in such free play. One of the greatest challenges for Crossan is for him to practice what he preaches with "First, read the text." In this chapter, Crossan's self-contradiction and lack of systematic consistency were shown in his various definitions and examples of two kinds of history: his reconstruction intermingled with traditional history.

Therefore, hypothesis 1 was falsified.

SEVEN

Conclusion: A Front-to-Back Evaluation

This is not only a conclusion but also a response to the back-to-front chapter 1.

Crossan's definition of history is "*History is the past reconstructed interactively by the present through argued evidence in public discourse.*"[1] Instead, as has been the case since the beginning of historical investigation, history involves an examination of the past with interpretation. It does not involve interactivity in argued public evidence. That is Crossan's deconstruction, which is his invention.

For Crossan, interpretation must be redone for each generation. This is based on his definition of history. It has been shown in this book that this unconventional theory grows out of his commitment to postmodern, deconstructionist, reader-response interpretation.

The view that historical information is not factual as fixed facts that don't exist is a creation of Crossan and the theory he promotes. The outlook that your interpretation is all that matters grows out of his postmodern, deconstructive, reader-response theory that engages in such language. Reader-response theory means I decide the meaning of a text, and my meaning is as valid as yours. It overrides the intended meaning by the author.

Reader-response theory collides with the facts of history. Try telling your history class that George Washington, Christopher Columbus, Captain James Cook, the 9/11 terrorism attack, Hitler and the Nazis, and personal conversation allow you to engage in free play with use of language.

---

1. Crossan, "Historical Jesus as Risen Lord," 3 (emphasis in original).

You will find yourself being laughed at in the class. "There are no facts" is a basic reader-response theory, but reader-response clashes with the intended meaning by any author.

Don't believe the biblical account of Jesus's resurrection, as it was an apparition—says Crossan. Crossan engages in free play to decide what it means, and your view is as good as mine. That's Crossan's unconventional approach and creation of meaning.

This book has shown Jesus's resurrection was a bodily resurrection that happened in history, where people could touch Jesus, eat with him, have conversations with him, and be asked by Jesus to thrust a hand in the wound in his side—demonstrating Jesus's body was physical.

"Jesus's burial in a shallow grave meant he was eaten by dogs, scratching about for a feed"—this was a creation by Crossan.

"The books of the Apocrypha and Pseudepigrapha (the Gospel of Peter especially) are as valid as the New Testament Gospels in determining the passion details about Jesus." Those are assertions, but this book has shown that they were proven false when compared with the New Testament Gospels' resurrection accounts as being historical.

In assessing Crossan's multiple writings, I found he invented much of the Gospel in his postmodern deconstructionism. However, he did not do this when writing his autobiography, *A Long Way from Tipperary*. He did not ask us to read his own publications that way. If it's fair enough for Crossan to impose his meaning on the Bible, it's reasonable to engage in that interpretation with meanings in Crossan's own writings.

Bibliography

"Ad Hominem (Abusive)." Logically Fallacious, n.d. https://www.logicallyfallacious.com/logicalfallacies/Ad-Hominem-Abusive.

Allison, Gregg R. "Speech Act Theory and Its Implications for the Doctrine of the Inerrancy/Infallibility of Scripture." Conference paper, Theological Research Exchange Network, 1993. https://place.asburyseminary.edu/trenpapers/1268/.

"Ancient Greece, Rome, Egypt, Israel and the Near East." Macquarie University, accessed 9 June 2021. https://www.mq.edu.au/faculty-of-arts/departments-and-schools/department-of-ancient-history. Site updated since access date.

"Appeal to Authority." Logically Fallacious, n.d. https://www.logicallyfallacious.com/logicalfallacies/Appeal-to-Authority.

Arndt, William F., and F. W. Gingrich. *A Greek-English Lexicon of the New Testament and Other Early Christian Literature*. Translated and adapted from Walter Bauer's *Griechisch-Deutsches Wörtbuch zu den Schriften des Neuen Testaments und der übrigen urchristlichen Literatur*, 4th rev. and aug. ed., 1952. Chicago: University of Chicago Press, 1957.

Athanasius. "Four Discourses against the Arians." Translated by John Henry Newman and Archibald Robertson. In *Nicene and Post-Nicene Fathers*, edited by Philip Schaff and Henry Wace, 2nd ser., 4. Buffalo, NY: Christian Literature, 1892. Revised and edited for New Advent by Kevin Knight. http://www.newadvent.org/fathers/2816.htm.

Aune, David E., ed. *The Blackwell Companion to the New Testament*. Chichester, UK: Blackwell, 2010.

———. "Oral Tradition and the Aphorisms of Jesus." In *Jesus and the Oral Gospel Tradition*, edited by H. Wansbrough, 211–65. Sheffield, UK: Sheffield Academic, 1991.

"Australian Curriculum in Queensland." Queensland Government, Queensland Curriculum and Assessment Authority, n.d. https://www.qcaa.qld.edu.au/p-10/aciq.

Barnett, Paul W. *The Birth of Christianity: The First Twenty Years*. Vol. 1 of *After Jesus*. Grand Rapid.: Eerdmans, 2005.

———. *Is the New Testament History?* 2nd ed. Sydney South: Aquila, 2003.

———. *Jesus and the Logic of History*. Leicester, UK: Inter-Varsity, 1997.

———. *Jesus and the Rise of Early Christianity: A History of New Testament Times*. Downers Grove, IL: InterVarsity, 1999.

———. *Finding the Historical Christ*. Vol. 3 of *After Jesus*. Grand Rapids: Eerdmans, 2009.

Barr, James. "Abba Isn't 'Daddy.'" *Journal of Theological Studies* 39 (1988) 28–47.

Bartholomew, Craig G. "Deconstruction." In *Dictionary for Theological Interpretation of the Bible*, edited by Kevin J. Vanhoozer, 163–65. London: SPCK, 2005.

Bauckham, Richard J. "Gospels (Apocryphal)." In *Dictionary of Jesus and the Gospels*, edited by Joel B. Green and Scot McKnight, 286–91. Downers Grove, IL: InterVarsity, 1992.

———. *Jesus and the Eyewitnesses: The Gospels as Eyewitness Testimony*. Grand Rapids: Eerdmans, 2006.

Beaver, David Ian. "Presupposition." CiteSeerX, Feb. 1996. http://citeseerx.ist.psu.edu/viewdoc/download?doi=10.1.1.136.6336&rep=rep1&type=pdf.

———, et al. "Presupposition." Stanford Encyclopedia of Philosophy, 1 Apr. 2011, revised Spring 2021. http://plato.stanford.edu/archives/sum2011/entries/presupposition/.

"Begging the Question." Logically Fallacious, n.d. https://www.logicallyfallacious.com/logicalfallacies/Begging-the-Question.

Beilby, James K., and Paul R. Eddy. "The Quest for the Historical Jesus: An Introduction." In *The Historical Jesus: Five Views*, edited by James K. Beilby and Paul R. Eddy, 9–54. Downers Grove, IL: IVP, 2009.

Benson, Bruce E. "Structuralism." In *Dictionary for Theological Interpretation of the Bible*, edited by Kevin J. Vanhoozer, 772–73. London: SPCK, 2005.

Best, Victoria. "Derrida for Dummies." Tales from the Reading Room, 1 Dec. 2011. http://litlove.wordpress.com/2011/12/01/derrida-for-dummies/.

Betz, Otto. *What Do We Know about Jesus?* Translated by M. Kohl. London: SCM, 1968.

Bevans, Rebecca. "A Step-by-Step Guide to Hypothesis Testing." Scribbr, 8 Nov. 2019, revised 29 Oct. 2021. https://www.scribbr.com/statistics/hypothesis-testing/.

Bietenhard, Hans. "Amēn." In *The New International Dictionary of New Testament Theology*, edited by C. Brown, 1:97–99. Exeter, UK: Paternoster, 1975.

Blomberg, Craig L. "Form Criticism." In *Dictionary of Jesus and the Gospels*, edited by Joel B. Green et al., 243–50. Downers Grove, IL: InterVarsity, 1992.

———. *The Historical Reliability of the Gospels*. Leicester, UK: Inter-Varsity, 1987.

———. "The Legitimacy and Limits of Harmonisation." In *Hermeneutics, Authority and Canon*, edited by in Don A. Carson and John D. Woodbridge, 137–74. Leicester, UK: Inter-Varsity, 1985.

———. "Where Do We Start Studying Jesus?" In *Jesus under Fire: Modern Scholarship Reinvents the Historical Jesus*, edited by Michael J. Wilkins and James P. Moreland, 17–50. Grand Rapids: Zondervan, 1995.

Bock, Darrell L. *Jesus According to Scripture: Restoring the Portrait from the Gospels*. Grand Rapids: Baker, 2002a.

———. *The Missing Gospels: Unearthing the Truth behind Alternative Christianities*. Nashville: Thomas Nelson, 2006.

———. *Studying the Historical Jesus: A Guide to Sources and Methods*. Grand Rapids: Baker, 2002.

———. "The Words of Jesus in the Gospels: Live, Jive or Memorex." In *Jesus under Fire: Modern Scholarship Reinvents the Historical Jesus*, edited by Michael J. Wilkins and James P. Moreland, 73–99. Grand Rapids: Zondervan, 1995.
Borg, Marcus. *Conflict, Holiness, and Politics in the Teachings of Jesus*. New York: Edwin Mellen, 1984.
———. "David Friedrich Strauss: Miracle and Myth." Westar, May–June 1991. https://www.westarinstitute.org/resources/the-fourth-r/david-friedrich-strauss/.
———. *The God We Never Knew*. New York: HarperSanFrancisco, 1997.
———. *Jesus: A New Vision*. San Francisco: Harper & Row, 1987.
———. *Jesus in Contemporary Scholarship*. Valley Forge, PA: Trinity International, 1994.
———. *Meeting Jesus Again for the First Time: The Historical Jesus and the Heart of Contemporary Faith*. New York: HarperSanFrancisco, 1994.
Borg, Marcus J., and John Dominic Crossan. *The Last Week: A Day-by-Day Account of Jesus's Final Week in Jerusalem*. New York: HarperSanFrancisco, 2006.
Bornkamm, Günther. *Jesus of Nazareth*. Translated by I. McLuskey et al. New York: Harper & Row, 1960.
Boyd, Gregory A. *Cynic, Sage, or Son of God?* Wheaton, IL: BridgePoint, 1995.
Brandon, Samuel G. F. *Jesus and the Zealots: A Study of the Political Factor in Primitive Christianity*. New York: Charles Scribner's, 1967.
Britannica, The Editors of Encyclopaedia, et al. "Gospel of Peter." Britannica, 20 July 1998, last updated 23 Apr. 2020. https://www.britannica.com/to pic/Gospel-of-Peter.
———. "Hans-Georg Gadamer." Britannica, 20 July 1998, last updated 10 Mar. 2021. https://www.britannica.com/biography/Hans-Georg-Gadamer.
———. "List of Roman Emperors." Britannica, 11 Nov. 2015. https://www.britannica.com/topic/list-of-Roman-emperors-2043294.
———. "Praetorian Guard." Britannica, 20 July 1998, last updated 29 Mar. 2018. https://www.britannica.com/topic/Praetorian-Guard.
Brown, Harold O. J. *Heresies: The Image of Christ in the Mirror of Heresy and Orthodoxy from the Apostles to the Present*. Garden City, NY: Doubleday, 1984.
Brown, Raymond E. *The Birth of the Messiah: A Commentary on the Infancy Narratives in the Gospels of Matthew and Luke*. Rev. ed. Anchor Bible Reference Library. New York: Doubleday, 1993.
———. *The Death of the Messiah: From Gethsemane to the Grave*. 2 vols. Anchor Bible Reference Library. New York: Doubleday, 1994.
Bruce, Frederick F. *The New Testament Documents: Are They Reliable?* Rev ed. Leicester, UK: Inter-Varsity, 1960.
Bultmann, Rudolf. *Faith and Understanding*. Translated by Louise Pettibone Smith. London: SCM, 1969.
———. *The Gospel of John: A Commentary*. Translated by G. R Beasley-Murray et al. Oxford, UK: Basil Blackwell, 1971.
———. *The History of the Synoptic Tradition*. Translated by J. Marsh. Oxford, UK: Basil Blackwell, 1963.
———. *Jesus and the Word*. Translated by L. P. Smith and E. H. Lantero. New York: Charles Scribner's Sons, 1934. https://www.religion-online.org/book/jesus-and-the-word/.
Bultmann, Rudolf, et al. *Kerygma and Myth*. Translated by R. H. Fuller. London: SPCK, 1953. https://www.religion-online.org/book/kerygma-and-myth/.

———. "The Mythological Element in the Message of the New Testament and the Problem of Its Re-Interpretation Part II." Religion Online, n.d. https://www.religion-online.org/book-chapter/the-mythological-element-in-the-message-of-the-new-testament-and-the-problem-of-its-re-interpretation-part-ii/.

———. *New Testament and Mythology and Other Basic Writings*. Philadelphia: Fortress, 1984.

Byrskog, Samuel. *Story as History—History as Story: The Gospel Tradition in the Context of Ancient Oral History*. Leiden, Neth.: Brill Academic, 2002.

Caird, George B. *Jesus and the Jewish Nation*. London: Penguin, 1965.

Cairns, Earle E. *Christianity through the Centuries: A History of the Christian Church*. Grand Rapids: Zondervan, 1981.

"Canegrubs." Sugar Research Australia, n.d. https://sugarresearch.com.au/pest/canegrubs/.

Caputo, John D. "Jacques Derrida (1930–2004)." *Journal for Cultural and Religious Theory* 6, no. 1 (Dec. 2004) 6–9. http://www.jcrt.org/archives/06.1/caputo.pdf.

Carnell, Edward J. *An Introduction to Christian Apologetics*. Grand Rapids: Eerdmans, 1948.

Carson, Donald A. "Five Gospels, No Christ." *Christianity Today* (25 Apr. 1994) 30–33. http://s3.amazonaws.com/tgc-documents/carson/1994_five_gospels_no_Christ_Jesus_Seminar.pdf.

———. *The Gagging of God*. Grand Rapids: Zondervan, 1996.

———. "Redaction Criticism: On the Legitimacy and Illegitimacy of a Literary Tool." Difa3iat, n.d. https://www.difa3iat.com/8939.html/redaction-criticism-legitimacy-illegitimacy-literary-tool-d-carson/.

Carson, Donald A., and John D. Woodbridge, eds. *Hermeneutics, Authority, and Canon*. Leicester, UK: Inter-Varsity, 1986.

———. *Scripture and Truth*. Grand Rapids: Baker, 1992.

Charles, R. H., trans. "Second Baruch." In *The Apocrypha and Pseudepigrapha of the Old Testament in English*, 2:481–524. Oxford, UK: Oxford University Press, 1913. Edited and adapted by George Lyons for the Wesley Center for Applied Theology at Northwest Nazarene University. http://www.pseudepigrapha.com/pseudepigrapha/2Baruch.html.

Charlesworth, James H. *Jesus within Judaism*. New York: Doubleday, 1988.

Chilton, Bruce D. *The Galilean Rabbi and His Bible*. Wilmington, DE: Michael Glazier, 1984.

———. "Regnum Dei Deus Est." *Scottish Journal of Theology* 31 (1978) 261–70.

———. *The Temple of Jesus: His Sacrificial Program within a Cultural History of Sacrifice*. University Park: Pennsylvania State University Press, 1992.

Christmass, Pip. "Margaret Court Defends Views on Gay Marriage amid Renewed Tennis Australia Drama." *Seven News*, 11 July 2019, updated 7 Nov. 2019. https://7news.com.au/sport/tennis/i-have-nothing-against-homosexuals-margaret-court-defends-views-on-gay-marriage-c-545514.

Clarke, Rachel Ivy. "Librarianship and Democracy: Creating an Informed Citizenry." Syracuse University School of Information Studies, 14 Nov. 2016. https://ischool.syr.edu/librarianship-democracy-creating-informed-citizenry/.

Collingwood, Robin G. *The Idea of History*. Rev. ed. Oxford, UK: Clarendon, 2019.

"Convict Cargo." National Museum Australia, updated 31 Aug. 2021. https://www.nma.gov.au/defining-moments/resources/convict-cargo.

"Convicts: Bound for Australia." State Library New South Wales, 15 Oct. 2021. https://guides.sl.nsw.gov.au/convicts-bound-for-australia/first_fleet.

Copan, Paul, ed. *Will the Real Jesus Please Stand Up? A Debate between William Lane Craig and John Dominic Crossan.* Grand Rapids: Baker, 1998.

Copan, Paul, and Ronald K. Tacelli, eds. *Jesus' Resurrection: Fact or Figment? A Debate between William Lane Craig and Gerd Lüdemann.* Downers Grove, IL: IVP, 2000.

"Country Analysis Executive Summary: Japan." U.S. Energy Information Administration, last updated Oct. 2020. https://www.eia.gov/international/content/analysis/countries_long/Japan/japan.pdf.

Craig, William L. "Did Jesus Rise from the Dead?" In *Jesus Under Fire: Modern Scholarship Reinvents the Historical Jesus*, edited by Michael J. Wilkins and James P. Moreland, 141–76. Grand Rapids: Zondervan, 1995.

———. "John Dominic Crossan on the Resurrection of Jesus." In *The Resurrection: An Interdisciplinary Symposium on the Resurrection of Jesus*, edited by Stephen T. Davis et al., 249–71. Oxford, UK: Oxford University Press, 1997.

———. "Rediscovering the Historical Jesus: Presuppositions and Pretensions of the Jesus Seminar." *Faith and Mission* 15 (1998) 3–15. http://www.leaderu.com/offices/billcraig/docs/rediscover1.html.

Craig, William L., and Bart D. Ehrman. "Is There Historical Evidence for the Resurrection of Jesus? The Craig-Ehrman Debate." Reasonable Faith, Mar. 2006. http://www.reasonablefaith.org/is-there-historical-evidence-for-the-resurrection-of-jesus-the-craig-ehrman.

Crossan, John Dominic. *The Birth of Christianity: Discovering What Happened in the Years Immediately after the Execution of Jesus.* New York: HarperSanFrancisco, 1998.

———. *The Cross That Spoke: The Origins of the Passion Narrative.* Eugene, OR: Wipf & Stock, 1988.

———. *The Dark Interval: Towards a Theology of Story.* Sonoma, CA: Polebridge, 1988.

———. "Difference and Divinity." *Semeia 23: Derrida and Biblical Studies* (Jan. 1982) 29–40.

———. *The Essential Jesus: What Jesus Really Taught.* San Francisco: HarperSanFrancisco, 1994.

———. *Four Other Gospels: Shadows on the Contours of Canon.* Minneapolis: Winston, 1985.

———. *God and Empire: Jesus against Rome, Then and Now.* New York: HarperSanFrancisco, 2007.

———. "Historical Jesus as Risen Lord." In *The Jesus Controversy: Perspectives in Conflict*, by John Dominic Crossan et al., 1–47. Harrisburg, PA: Trinity International, 1999.

———. *The Historical Jesus: The Life of a Mediterranean Jewish Peasant.* New York: HarperSanFrancisco, 1991.

———. "Historical Jesus Theories: J. D. Crossan." Early Christian Writings, n.d. http://www.earlychristianwritings.com/jesus/johndominiccrossan.html.

———. *In Fragments: The Aphorisms of Jesus.* San Francisco: Harper & Row, 1983.

———. *In Parables: The Challenge of the Historical Jesus.* San Francisco: Harper & Row, 1973.

———. *Jesus: A Revolutionary Biography.* New York: HarperSanFrancisco, 1994.

———. *A Long Way from Tipperary: A Memoir.* New York: HarperSanFrancisco, 2000.

———. "An Odyssey." Westar Institute, Sept.–Oct. 1993. http://www.westarinstitute.org/resources/the-fourth-r/almost-the-whole-truth/.

———. *The Power of Parable: How Fiction by Jesus Became Fiction about Jesus*. New York: HarperOne, 2012.

———. *Raid on the Articulate: Comic Eschatology in Jesus and Borges*. Eugene, OR: Wipf and Stock, 1976.

———. "What Victory? What God? A Review Debate with N. T. Wright on Jesus and the Victory of God." *Scottish Journal of Theology* 50, no. 3 (1997) 345–79. https://www.cambridge.org/core/journals/scottish-journal-of-theology/article/abs/what-victory-what-god-a-review-debate-with-n-t-wright-on-jesus-and-the-victory-of-god1/8481D0C55BBC0C72DD0242A3ABDA40F4.

———. *Who Killed Jesus? Exposing the Roots of Anti-Semitism in the Gospel Story of the Death of Jesus*. New York: HarperSanFrancisco, 1995.

Crossan, John Dominic, and Jonathan L. Reed. *Excavating Jesus: Beneath the Stones, Behind the Texts*. New York: HarperSanFrancisco, 2001.

———. *In Search of Paul: How Jesus's Apostle Opposed Rome's Empire with God's Kingdom*. New York: HarperSanFrancisco, 2004.

Crossan, John Dominic, and Richard G. Watts. *Who Is Jesus? Answers to Your Questions about the Historical Jesus*. New York: Harper Paperbacks, 1996.

Davids, P. H. "Tradition Criticism." In *Dictionary of Jesus and the Gospels*, edited by Joel B. Green et al., 831–34. Downers Grove, IL: InterVarsity, 1992.

Davis, Roger B., and Kenneth J. Mukamal. "Hyphothesis Testing." *Circulation* 114, no. 10 (5 Sept. 2006) 1078–82. https://www.ahajournals.org/doi/full/10.1161/circulationaha.105.586461/.

Davis, Stephen T., et al. "The Resurrection: An Interdisciplinary Symposium on the Resurrection of Jesus." Oxford Scholarship Online, Nov. 2003; orig. 1998. https://oxford.universitypressscholarship.com/view/10.1093/0198269854.001.0001/acprof-9780198269854.

De Jonge, Marinus. *Jesus, the Servant-Messiah*. New Haven, CT: Yale University Press, 1991.

Denton, Donald L., Jr. *Historiography and Hermeneutics in Jesus Studies: An Examination of the Work of John Dominic Crossan and Ben F. Meyer*. London: T&T Clark International, 2004.

Department of the Environment, Water, Heritage and the Arts. "The Cane Toad (Bufo marinus): Fact Sheet." Australian Government, Department of Agriculture, Water and the Environment, 2010. https://www.awe.gov.au/biosecurity-trade/invasive-species/publications/factsheet-cane-toad-bufo-marinus.

Derrida, Jacques. *The Ear of the Other: Texts and Discussions with Jacques Derrida*. Edited by Christie V. McDonald. Translated by Peggy Kamuf. New York: Shocken, 1985.

Eddy, Paul Rhodes, and Gregory A Boyd. *The Jesus Legend*. Grand Rapids: Baker Academic, 2007.

Editors, History.com. "September 11 Attacks." History, 25 Aug. 2018, updated 24 Aug. 2021. https://www.history.com/topics/21st-century/9-11-attacks.

Edwards, Lucy Emily. "Lessing and the Reimarus Manuscript." MA thesis, State University of Iowa, 1913. https://iro.uiowa.edu/esploro/outputs/graduate/Lessing-and-the-Reimarus-manuscript/9983776763402771?institution=01IOWA_INST.

"Egerton Gospel." Early Christian Writings, AD 70–120. http://www.earlychristianwritings.com/egerton.html.

Elton, Geoffrey R. *The Practice of History*. Sydney: Sydney University Press, 1967.

"Endeavour Cannon." National Museum Australia, n.d. https //www.nma.gov.au/explore/collection/highlights/endeavour-cannon.

Enochs, Kevin. "The Real Story: Who Discovered America." Voice of America, 10 Oct. 2016. https://www.voanews.com/usa/real-story-who-discovered-america.

Evans, Craig A. *Ancient Texts for New Testament Studies: A Guide to the Background Literature*. Peabody, MA: Hendrickson, 2005.

———. *Fabricating Jesus: How Modern Scholars Distort the Gospels*. Nottingham, UK: Inter-Varsity, 2007.

———. "The Passion of Jesus: History Remembered or Prophecy Historicized?" *Bulletin for Biblical Research* 6 (1996), 159–65.

Flint, Valerie I. J. "Christopher Columbus." Britannica, 16 May 2021. https://www.britannica.com/biography/Christopher-Columbus.

Ford, Lena Guilbert. "Keep the Home-Fires Burning (Till the Boys Come Home)." PICRYL, Jan. 1915. https://picryl.com/media/keep-the-home-fires-buring-till-the-boys-come-home-song-7.

"Fraser Island Shipwrecks." Frasier Island, n.d. https://www.fraserisland.net/fraser-island-history/fraser-island-shipwrecks.

Freyne, Seán. *Galilee, Jesus and the Gospels: Literary Approaches and Historical Investigations*. Philadelphia: Fortress, 1988.

———. "The Geography, Politics, and Economics of Galilee and the Quest for the Historical Jesus." In *Studying the Historical Jesus: Evaluations of the State of Current Research*, edited by Bruce D. Chilton and Craig A. Evans, 75–121. New Testament Tools, Studies and Documents 19. Leiden, Neth.: Brill, 1994. https://brill.com/view/book/9789004379893/B9789004379893_s008.xml.

Fukuda, Shin. "Two Syntactic Positions for English Aspectual Verbs." In *Proceedings of the Twenty-Sixth West Coast Conference on Formal Linguistics*, edited by Charles B. Chang and Hannah J. Haynie, 172–80. Somerville, MA: Cascadilla Proceedings Project., 2008. http://www.lingref.com/cpp/wccfl/26/paper1670.pdf.

"Fukushima Daiichi Accident." World Nuclear Association, updated Apr. 2021. https://www.world-nuclear.org/information-library/safety-and-security/safety-of-plants/fukushima-daiichi-accident.aspx.

Funk, Robert W. *Honest to Jesus: Jesus for a New Millennium*. Rydalmere, Aus.: Hodder & Stoughton, 1996.

———. "Jesus Seminar Opening Remarks." Westar Institute, 21 Mar. 1985. https://www.westarinstitute.org/projects/jesus-seminar-opening-remarks/.

Funk, Robert W., et al. *The Five Gospels: The Search for the Authentic Words of Jesus*. New York: Macmillan, 1993.

———. *The Gospel of Mark: Red Letter Edition*. Sonoma, CA: Polebridge, 1991.

Gadamer, Hans-Georg. *Truth and Method*. Translated by Joel Weinsheimer and Donald G. Marshall. 2nd ed. London: Continuum, 1989.

Gear, Spencer D. "Crossan and the Resurrection of Jesus: Rethinking Presuppositions, Methods and Models." PhD diss., University of Pretoria, 2015. https://repository.up.ac.za/handle/2263/50510.

Geisler, Norman L. *Christian Apologetics*. Grand Rapids: Baker, 1976.

———. "Is It Just a Matter of Interpretation, Not of Inerrancy? Examining the Relationship between Inerrancy and Hermeneutics." *Journal of the International Society of Christian Apologetics* 8, no. 1 (Apr. 2015) 5–50. https://theologicalstudies.org.uk/pdf/jisca/08-1_005.pdf.

Geisler, Norman L., and Ronald M. Brooks. *Come, Let Us Reason: An Introduction to Logical Thinking.* Grand Rapids: Baker, 1990.

Gerhardsson, Birger. *Memory and Manuscript.* In *Memory and Manuscript: Tradition and Transmission in Early Christianity with Tradition and Transmission in Early Christianity*, 1–379. Combined vol. Grand Rapids: Eerdmans, 1998.

———. *The Reliability of the Gospel Tradition.* Peabody, MA: Hendrickson, 2001.

———. *Tradition and Transmission in Early Christianity.* In *Memory and Manuscript: Tradition and Transmission in Early Christianity with Tradition and Transmission in Early Christianity*, 1–47. Combined vol. Grand Rapids: Eerdmans, 1998.

Gibbon, Edward. *The History of the Decline and Fall of the Roman Empire.* 6 vols. Gutenberg, 7 June 2008, last updated 14 Mar. 2021. https://www.gutenberg.org/files/25717/25717-h/25717-h.htm.

Glanzberg, Michael. "Truth." Stanford Encyclopedia of Philosophy, 13 June 2006, last revised 16 Aug. 2018. https://plato.stanford.edu/entries/truth/.

Goodacre, Mark. "Jesus Seminar as Renewed New Quest." Yahoo Groups: Crosstalk, 2000. http://groups.yahoo.com/group/crosstalk2/message/3854. Site discontinued.

———. "The Quest to Digest Jesus: Recent Books on the Historical Jesus." *Reviews in Religion and Theology* 7 (2000) 156–61. http://www.markgoodacre.org/digest.htm.

———. "Scripturalization in Mark's Crucifixion Narrative." In *The Trial and Death of Jesus: Essays on the Passion Narrative in Mark*, edited by Geert van Oyen and Tom Shepherd, 33–47. Leuven, Belg.: Peeters, 2006. http://markgoodacre.org/Markcrucif.pdf.

Gopnik, Adam. "What Did Jesus Do? Reading and Unreading the Gospels." *New Yorker*, 17 May 2010. https://www.newyorker.com/magazine/2010/05/24/what-did-jesus-do.

"Gospel of the Hebrews." Early Christian Writings, AD 80–150. http://www.earlychristianwritings.com/gospelhebrews.html.

Gowler, David B. *What Are They Saying About the Historical Jesus?* Mahwah, NJ: Paulist, 2007.

Green, Joel B. "Peter, Gospel of." In *Dictionary of the Later New Testament and Its Developments*, edited by Ralph P. Martin and Peter H. Davids, 927–29. Downers Grove, IL: InterVarsity, 1997.

Grudem, Wayne. *Systematic Theology: An Introduction to Biblical Doctrine.* Leicester, UK: Inter-Varsity, 1994.

Gundry, Robert H. *Sōma in Biblical Theology: With Emphasis on Pauline Anthropology.* Grand Rapids: Academie, 1987.

Gustafson, Cole. "History of Ethanol Production and Policy." North Dakota State University, n.d. https://www.ag.ndsu.edu/energy/biofuels/energy-briefs/history-of-ethanol-production-and-policy.

Habermas, Gary R. *The Historical Jesus: Ancient Evidence for the Life of Christ.* Joplin, MO: College Press, 1996.

Hagner, Donald A. "Foreword." In *The Reliability of the Gospel Tradition*, by Birger Gerhardsson, vii–xvi. Peabody, MA: Hendrickson, 2001.

———. "The New Testament, History and the Historical-Critical Method." In *New Testament Criticism and Interpretation*, edited by David A. Black and David S. Dockery, 73–96. Grand Rapids: Zondervan, 1991.
Harvey, Anthony E. *Jesus and the Constraints of History: The Bampton Lectures, 1980.* London: Duckworth, 1982.
———. *Strenuous Commands: The Ethic of Jesus.* London: SCM, 1990.
Hauck, Friedrich. "Parabolē." In *Theological Dictionary of the New Testament*, edited by G. Friedrich, translated by G. W. Bromiley, 5:744–61. Grand Rapids: Eerdmans, 1967.
Hawthorne, Gerald F. "Amen." In *Dictionary of Jesus and the Gospels*, edited by Joel B. Green et al., 7–8. Downers Grove, IL: InterVarsity, 1992.
Hays, Richard B. "The Corrected Jesus." *First Things*, May 1994. https://www.firstthings.com/article/1994/05/the-corrected-jesus.
Heidegger, Martin. *An Introduction to Metaphysics.* Translated by R. Manheim. Garden City, NY: Anchor Doubleday, 1961.
———. *An Introduction to Metaphysics.* Translated by G. Fried and R. Pold. 2nd ed. New Haven, CT: Yale University Press, 2014.
Henderson, Timothy P. "'The People Believe That He Has Risen from the Dead': The Gospel of Peter and Early Christian Apologetics." PhD diss., Marquette University, 2010. https://epublications.marquette.edu/cgi/viewcontent.cgi?article=1053&context=dissertations_mu.
Hengel, Martin. *Acts and the History of Earliest Christianity.* Translated by John Bowden. Eugene, OR: Wipf and Stock, 1979.
———. *The Atonement: The Origins of the Doctrine in the New Testament.* London: SCM, 1981.
———. *The Charismatic Leader and His Followers.* New York: Crossroad, 1981.
———. *Crucifixion in the Ancient World and the Folly of the Message of the Cross.* Translated by John Bowden. Philadelphia: Fortress, 1977.
———. *The Four Gospels and the One Gospel of Jesus Christ: An Investigation of the Collection and Origin of the Canonical Gospels.* Translated by John Bowden. Harrisburg, PA: Trinity, 2000.
———. *Victory over Violence: Jesus and the Revolutionists.* Philadelphia: Fortress, 1973.
———. *Was Jesus a Revolutionist?* Philadelphia: Fortress, 1971.
Herodotus. *The History of Herodotus: Parallel English/Greek.* Translated by G. C. Macaulay. London: Macmillan, 1890. https://www.sacred-texts.com/cla/hh/index.htm.
Hick, John. *The Fifth Dimension: An Exploration of the Spiritual Realm.* Oxford, UK: Oneworld, 1999.
"Historiography." Definitions, n.d. https://www.definitions.net/definition/historiography.
"History: Connecting the Past with the Present." University of San Francisco, College of Arts and Sciences, n.d. https://www.usfca.edu/arts-sciences/undergraduate-programs/history.
"History Education." Universität Hamburg, last updated 4 Feb. 2021. https://www.ew.uni-hamburg.de/en/einrichtungen/ew5/didaktik-geschichte.html.
Hodge, Charles. *Systematic Theology.* 3 vols. Grand Rapids: Eerdmans, 1979.
Hoeber, Karl. "Flavius Josephus." In *The Catholic Encyclopedia* 8. New York: Appleton, 1920. http://www.newadvent.org/cathen/08522a.htm.

Hofius, O. "Abba." In *The New International Dictionary of New Testament Theology*, edited by Colin Brown, 1:614–21. Exeter, UK: Paternoster, 1975.

Horn, Laurence R. "Contradiction." Stanford Encyclopedia of Philosophy, 28 June 2006. https://stanford.library.sydney.e

Horsley, Richard A. *Jesus and the Spiral of Violence: Popular Jewish Resistance in Roman Palestine*. San Francisco: Harper & Row, 1987.

"How Do I License the NIV?" Biblica, n.d. https://www.biblica.com/resources/bible-faqs/how-do-i-license-the-niv/.

"How Sugar Is Made." Sugar Cane Growers Cooperative of Florida, n.d. https://www.scgc.org/sugar-process/.

"How Was Australia Named?" National Library of Australia, n.d. https://www.nla.gov.au/faq/how-was-australia-named. du.au/archives/spr2008/entries/contradiction/.

Hurtado, Larry W. "God." In *Dictionary of Jesus and the Gospels*, edited by Joel B. Green et al., 270–82. Downers Grove, IL: InterVarsity, 1992.

Ignatius. "The Epistle of Ignatius to the Ephesians." Translated by Alexander Roberts and James Donaldson. In *Ante-Nicene Fathers*, edited by Alexander Roberts et al., 1. Buffalo, NY: Christian Literature, 1885. Revised and edited for New Advent by Kevin Knight. http://www.newadvent.org/fathers/0104.htm.

Ingraffia, Brian D. *Postmodern Theory and Biblical Theology: Vanquishing God's Shadow*. Cambridge, UK: Cambridge University Press, 1995.

Irenaeus. *Against Heresies*. Translated by Alexander Roberts and William Rambaut. In *Ante-Nicene Fathers*, edited by Alexander Roberts et al., 1. Buffalo, NY: Christian Literature, 1885. Revised and edited for New Advent by Kevin Knight. http://www.newadvent.org/fathers/0103.htm.

"James Cook and His Voyages." National Library of Australia, 2008, revised 2019. https://www.nla.gov.au/collections/guide-selected-collections/james-cook-and-his-voyages.

James, M. R., trans. "The Gospel of Peter." Oxford, UK: Clarendon, 1924. http://gnosis.org/library/gospete.htm.

"Jesus: Just Another Wonder-Worker?" BeliefNet, n.d. https://www.beliefnet.com/faiths/2005/03/jesus-just-another-wonder-worker.aspx.

Jesus Seminar. "Voting Records: The Passion Narratives." *Forum* 1, no. 1 (Spring 1998) 227–33.

Johnson, Luke T. *The Real Jesus: The Misguided Quest for the Historical Jesus and the Truth of the Traditional Gospels*. New York: HarperSanFrancisco, 1996.

Josephus. *Antiquities of the Jews*. Translated by William Whiston. Christian Classics Ethereal Library, n.d. http://www.ccel.org/j/josephus/works/JOSEPHUS.HTM.

Kähler, Martin. *The So-Called Historical Jesus and the Historic Biblical Christ*. Philadelphia: Fortress, 1964.

Kelber, Werner H. *The Jesus Controversy: Perspectives in Conflict*. Harrisburg, PA: Trinity International, 1999.

Kierstead, Raymond. "Herodotus and the Invention of History." *Reed Magazine* 90, no. 3 (Sept. 2011) n.p. http://www.reed.edu/reed_magazine/september2011/articles/features/classiclecture/classiclecture.html.

Kittel, Gerhard. "Abba." In *Theological Dictionary of the New Testament*, edited by Gerhard Kittel, translated by Geoffrey W. Bromiley, 1:5–6. Grand Rapids: Eerdmans, 1964.

Kloppenborg, John S. *The Formation of Q: Trajectories in Ancient Wisdom Collections*. Studies in Antiquity and Christianity. Philadelphia: Fortress, 1987.

———. "Sayings Gospel Q." Oxford Bibliographies. *Biblical Studies*, Oxford University Press, last reviewed 7 June 2019. https://www.oxfordbibliographies.com/view/document/obo-9780195393361/obo-9780195393361-0101.xml. Site discontinued.

Kloppenborg, John S., et al. *Q Thomas Reader*. Sonoma, CA: Polebridge, 1990.

Koay, Jeremy. "What Is Reader-Response Theory?" Edumaxi, 22 Oct. 2021. https://www.edumaxi.com/blog/what-is-reader-response-theory.

Koester, Helmut. *Ancient Christian Gospels: Their History and Development*. London: SCM, 1990.

———. "History and Development of Mark's Gospel: From Mark to Secret Mark and Canonical Mark." In *Colloquy on New Testament Studies: A Time for Appraisal and Fresh Approaches*, edited by Bruce Corley, 35–57. Macon, GA: Mercer University Press, 1983.

———. *Introduction to the New Testament*. 2 vols. Philadelphia: Fortress, 1982.

Kohn, Rachel. "John Dominic Crossan and the Historical Jesus." *ABC Radio International*, 18 July 1999. https://www.abc.net.au/radionational/programs/archived/spiritofthings/john-dominic-crossan-and-the-historical-jesus/3568360.

Köstenberger, Andreas J., and Kruger, Michael J. *The Heresy of Orthodoxy: How Contemporary Culture's Fascination with Diversity Has Shaped Our Understanding of Early Christianity*. Wheaton, IL: Crossway, 2010.

Kottasová, Ivana, et al. "US Troops and Afghans Killed in Suicide Attacks outside Kabul Airport." *CNN*, updated 27 Aug. 2021. https://edition.cnn.com/2021/08/26/asia/afghanistan-kabul-airport-blast-intl/index.html.

Kraft, Robert. "History and Historiography in Early Judaism and Early Christianity, with Special Focus on Josephus and Eusebius." Syllabus for Religious Studies 735, 27 Mar. 2007. http://ccat.sas.upenn.edu/rak/courses/735/Historiography/historiography.html.

Krammer, Florian. "SARS-CoV-2 Vaccines in Development." *Nature* 586 (Oct. 2020) 516–27. https://www.nature.com/articles/s41586-020-2798-3.

Kuhn, Thomas S. *The Structure of Scientific Revolution*. 2nd ed. Chicago: University of Chicago Press, 1970.

Kulikovsky, Andrew S. "An Evaluation of Historical-Critical Methods: With Special Reference to Source Criticism, Tradition Criticism, Form Criticism and Redaction Criticism." Kulikovsky Online, 20 Jan. 1997 http://hermeneutics.kulikovskyonline.net/hermeneutics/critmeth.htm.

Ladd, George E. *I Believe in the Resurrection of Jesus*. Grand Rapids: Eerdmans, 1975.

———. *The New Testament and Criticism*. Grand Rapids: Eerdmans, 1967.

Lambdin, Thomas O., trans. "Gospel of Thomas." Marquette, n.d. https://www.marquette.edu/maqom/Gospel%20of%20Thomas%20Lambdin.pdf.

Latourette, Kenneth S. *To A.D. 1500*. Vol. 1 of *A History of Christianity*. Rev. ed. New York: Harper & Row, 1975.

Layt, Stuart. "'This Is Not Normal': Australian Cane Toad Tadpoles Have Become Cannibals." *Age*, 27 Aug. 2021. https://www.theage.com.au/national/queensland/this-is-not-normal-toad-tadpoles-are-eating-each-other-research-confirms-20210827-p58mgh.html.

Lenski, Gerhard. *Power and Privilege: A Theory of Social Stratification*. New York: McGraw-Hill, 1966.
Lewis, Gordon R. "Schaeffer's Apologetic Method." In *Reflections on Francis Schaeffer*, edited by Ronald W. Ruegsegger, 69–104. Grand Rapids: Academie, 1986.
Lewis, Gordon R., and Bruce A. Demarest. *Integrative Theology*, vol. 1. Grand Rapids: Academie, 1987.
———. *Integrative Theology*, vol 2. Grand Rapids: Academie, 1990.
Lightfoot, J. B. *Biblical Essays*. London: Macmillan, 1893. http://www.archive.org/stream/biblicalessaysoolighgoog#page/n7/mode/2up.
Linnemann, Eta. *Biblical Criticism on Trial: How Scientific Is "Scientific Theology"?* Grand Rapids: Kregel, 2001.
———. *Historical Criticism of the Bible: Methodology or Ideology*. Translated by Robert W. Yarbrough. Grand Rapids: Baker, 1990.
———. *Is There a Synoptic Problem? Rethinking the Literary Dependence of the First Three Gospels*. Translated by Robert W. Yarbrough. Grand Rapids: Baker, 1992.
Lohfink, Gerhard. *Jesus and Community*. Translated by J. P. Galvin. Philadelphia: Fortress, 1984.
Lonergan, Bernard J. F. *Insight: A Study of Human Understanding*. London: Longmans, 1958.
———. *Method in Theology*. London: Darton, Longman & Todd, 1972.
Long, Jimmy. "Generating Hope: A Strategy for Reaching the Postmodern Generation." In *Telling the Truth: Evangelizing Postmoderns*, edited by Don A. Carson, 322–35. Grand Rapids: Zondervan, 2000.
"The Lost Sayings Gospel Q." Early Christian Writings, AD 40–80. http://www.earlychristianwritings.com/q.html.
Lüdemann, Gerd. *The Resurrection of Jesus: History, Experience, Theology*. London: SCM, 1994.
Machen, J. Gresham. *Christianity and Liberalism*. Grand Rapids: Eerdmans, 1923.
Mack, Burton L. *The Lost Gospel: The Book of Q and Christian Origins*. New York: HarperSanFrancisco, 1993.
———. *A Myth of Innocence: Mark and Christian Origins*. Philadelphia: Fortress, 1988.
———. *Who Wrote the New Testament?* New York: HarperSanFrancisco, 1995.
Malpas, Jeff. "Hans-Georg Gadamer." Stanford Encyclopedia of Philosophy, 3 Mar. 2003, revised 17 Sept. 2018. http://plato.stanford.edu/entries/gadamer/.
Manson, Thomas W. "The Failure of Liberalism to Interpret the Bible as the Word of God." In *The Interpretation of the Bible*, edited by C. W. Dugmore, 92–107. London: SPCK, 1944.
Marlowe, Michael D. "J. B. Lightfoot on the Semitic Style of John's Gospel." Bible Researcher, Mar. 2004. http://www.bible-researcher.com/lightfoot.html.
Marshall, I. Howard. "An Evangelical Approach to 'Theological Criticism.'" *Themelios* 13, no. 3 (Jan. 1988) 79–85. http://www.biblicalstudies.org.uk/article_criticism_marshall.html.
———. *I Believe in the Historical Jesus*. Grand Rapids: Eerdmans, 1977.
———. *Luke: Historian and Theologian*. Grand Rapids: Zondervan, 1970.
Martin, Sarah. "Australia Plans to Shelve AstraZeneca Covid Vaccine by October 2021." *Guardian*, 23 June 2021. https://www.theguardian.com/business/2021/jun/23/australia-plans-to-shelve-astrazeneca-covid-vaccine-by-october.
Martin, Walter. *Exorcism: Fact or Fable*. Santa Ana, CA: Vision House, 1975.

Martyr, Justin. "Dialogue with Trypho (Chapters 31–47)." Translated by Marcus Dods and George Reith. In *Ante-Nicene Fathers*, edited by Alexander Roberts et al., 1. Buffalo, NY: Christian Literature, 1885. Revised and edited for New Advent by Kevin Knight. https://www.newadvent.org/fathers/01283.htm.

Massola, James. "Liberal and Labor MPs Back Changes to Australia Day Honours System." *Sydney Morning Herald*, 24 Jan. 2021. https://www.smh.com.au/politics/federal/liberal-and-labor-mps-back-changes-to-australia-day-honours-system-20210123-p56wd2.html.

McEleney, Neil J. "Authenticating Criteria and Mark 7:1–23." *Catholic Biblical Quarterly* 34, no. 4 (Oct. 1972) 431–60. https://www.jstor.org/stable/43713354?refreqid=exc elsior%3A31c1061adc20926d6b2a8b32f76b6253.

McGaughy, Lane C. "Why Start with the Sayings?" Westar Institute, Sept.–Dec. 1996. https://www.westarinstitute.org/resources/the-fourth-r/the-search-for-the-historical-jesus/.

McKenzie, Steven L. "What Is Source Criticism?" Bible Odyssey, n.d. https://www.bibleodyssey.org/tools/bible-basics/what-is-source-criticism-mckenzie.

McKirdy, Lachlan. "No Moves to Rename Margaret Court Arena Despite Petition Gaining Traction to Honour Evonne Goolagong." *Sporting News*, 25 Jan. 2021. https://www.sportingnews.com/au/featured-content-sport/news/tennis-margaret-court-australia-day-arena-petition-evonne-goolagong-australian-open/10conf4006hqt16u9ctoh8c1pw.

Meier, John Paul. *Mentor, Message, and Miracles*. Vol. 2 of *A Marginal Jew*. Anchor Bible Reference Library. New York: Doubleday, 1994.

———. *Rethinking the Historical Jesus: The Roots of the Problem and the Person*. Vol. 1 of *A Marginal Jew*. Anchor Bible Reference Library. New York: Doubleday, 1991.

Meltzer, Peter E. *The Thinker's Thesaurus: Sophisticated Alternatives to Common Words*. 2nd ed. New York: Norton, 2010.

Menni, Cristina, et al. "Vaccine Side-Effects and SARS-CoV-2 Infection after Vaccination in Users of the COVID Symptom Study App in the UK: A Prospective Observational Study." *Lancet Infectious Diseases* 21, no. 7 (1 July 2021) 939–49. https://www.thelancet.com/journals/laninf/article/PIIS1473-3099(21)00224-3/fulltext.

Metzger, Bruce M., ed. *The Apocrypha of the Old Testament (Revised Standard Version)*. New York: Oxford University Press, 1973.

———. *The Canon of the New Testament: Its Origin, Development, and Significance*. Oxford, UK: Clarendon, 1987.

Meyer, Ben F. *The Aims of Jesus*. Princeton Theological Monograph Series. Eugene, OR: Pickwick, 2002.

———. *Christmas Father: The Master-Builder and the House of God*. Allison Park, PA: Pickwick Publications, 1992.

———. "Jesus Christ." In *Anchor Bible Dictionary*, edited by D N. Freedman, 3:773–96. New York: Doubleday, 1992b.

———. "The Philosophical Crusher." *First Things*, Apr. 1991. https://www.firstthings.com/article/1991/04/the-philosophical-crusher.

———. Review of *The Historical Jesus*, by John Dominic Crossan. *Catholic Biblical Quarterly* 55 (1993) 575–76.

Mickelsen, A. Berkeley. *Interpreting the Bible*. Grand Rapids: Eerdmans, 1963.

Miller, Robert J., ed. *The Complete Gospels: Annotated Scholars Version*. Sonoma, CA: Polebridge, 1992.

Minitab Blog Editor. "Understanding Hypothesis Tests: Why We Need to Use Hypothesis Tests in Statistics." Minitab, 5 Mar. 2015. https://blog.minitab.com/en/adventures-in-statistics-2/understanding-hypothesis-tests-why-we-need-to-use-hypothesis-tests-in-statistics.

Mitchell, Stephen. *The Gospel According to Jesus: A New Translation and Guide to His Essential Teachings for Believers and Unbelievers*. San Francisco: HarperCollins, 1991.

Mokyr, Joel, et al. "Great Famine." Britannica, 5 Feb. 2000, last updated 27 July 2021. https://www.britannica.com/event/Great-Famine-Irish-history.

Montgomery, John W. *Faith Founded on Fact: Essays in Evidential Apologetics*. Newburgh, IN: Trinity, 1978.

———. *The Suicide of Christian Theology*. Minneapolis: Bethany Fellowship, 1970.

———. *Where Is History Going? A Christian Response to Secular Philosophies of History*. Minneapolis: Bethany House, 1969.

Moritz, Thorsten. "Critical Realism." In *Dictionary for Theological Interpretation of the Bible*, edited by Kevin J. Vanhoozer, 147–50. London: SPCK, 2005.

Morris, Leon. *The Gospel According to John*. Grand Rapids: Eerdmans, 1971.

"Mouth of Baffle Creek Conservation Park." Queensland Government, Department of Environment and Science, last updated 14 July 2020. https://parks.des.qld.gov.au/parks/mouth-of-baffle-creek.

Nelson, Randy Wayne. "The Jesus Seminar's Search for the Authentic Sayings of Jesus: An Examination of Phase One of the Seminar's Quest for the Historical Jesus." PhD diss., Rice University, 1999. https://scholarship.rice.edu/handle/1911/19426.

"Nestorianism." Wikipedia, last edited 2 Aug. 2021. https://en.wikipedia.org/wiki/Nestorianism.

"New English-Language Study Programmes at UW." University of Warsaw, 30 Apr. 2021. https://en.uw.edu.pl/new-english-language-study-programmes-at-uw/.

Nguyen, Kevin, and Sarah Thomas. "Sydney's Northern Beaches Coronavirus Cluster Grows to Ninety after Eight New Infections Recorded." *ABC News*, updated 22 Dec. 2020. https://www.abc.net.au/news/2020-12-22/sydney-nsw-northern-beaches-coronavirus-cluster-grows-to-90/13006258.

Niebuhr, Richard R. *Resurrection and Historical Reason: A Study in Theological Method*. New York: Charles Scribner's Sons, 1957.

Nolland, John. "Form Criticism and the NT." In *Dictionary for Theological Interpretation of the Bible*, edited by Kevin J. Vanhoozer, 232–33. London: SPCK, 2005.

"Null Hypothesis." Corporate Finance Institute, n.d. https://corporatefinanceinstitute.com/resources/knowledge/other/null-hypothesis-2/.

Oakman, Douglas E. *Jesus and the Economic Questions of the Day*. Studies in the Bible and Early Christianity 8. Lewiston, NY: Mellen, 1986.

O'Collins, Gerald, and Daniel Kendall. "Did Joseph of Arimathea Exist?" *Biblica* 75 (1994) 235–41.

Origen. *Commentary on the Gospel of Matthew (Book X)*. Translated by John Patrick. In *Ante-Nicene Fathers*, edited by Allan Menzies, 9. Buffalo, NY: Christian Literature, 1896. Revised and edited for New Advent by Kevin Knight. http://www.newadvent.org/fathers/101610.htm.

---. *De Principiis.* Translated by Frederick Crombie. In *Ante-Nicene Fathers*, edited by Alexander Roberts et al., 4. Buffalo, NY: Christian Literature, 1885. Revised and edited for New Advent by Kevin Knight. http://www.newadvent.org/fathers/0412.htm.
Osborne, Grant R. "Redaction Criticism." In *Dictionary for Theological Interpretation of the Bible*, edited by Kevin J Vanhoozer, 663–66. Grand Rapids: Baker Academic, 2005.
Oswalt, John N. *The Bible among the Myths.* Grand Rapids: Zondervan, 2009.
Owende, P. M. O., et al. "Comparison of Options for Sugarcane (Saccharum officinarum L.) Stool Destruction [1995]." *Soil and Tillage Research* 33, nos. 3–4 (1995) 185–95. https://agris.fao.org/agris-search/search.do?recordID=NL9503542.
Pagels, Elaine. *The Gnostic Gospels.* New York: Random House, 1979.
Pankhurst, Clive. "Effects of Pesticides Used in Sugarcane Cropping Systems on Soil Organisms and Biological Functions associated with Soil Health." GBP Qld, Apr. 2006. http://www.grazingbestprac.com.au/research/chemicals/060701%2520-%2520YDV002%2520-%2520Pankhurst%2520Pesticide%2520Report.pdf.
Patterson, Stephen J. *The Gospel of Thomas and Jesus.* Foundations and Facets Reference Series. Sonoma, CA: Polebridge, 1993.
Peter, Laurence. "Auschwitz Inmate's Notes from Hell Finally Revealed." *BBC News*, 1 Dec. 2017. https://www.bbc.com/news/world-europe-42144186.
Poland, Lynn M. *Literary Criticism and Biblical Hermeneutics: A Critique of Formalist Approaches.* AAR Academy 48. Chicago: Scholars, 1985.
"Presupposition." SIL, 2003. https://glossary.sil.org/term/presupposition.
"Presupposition Trigger." SIL, 2003. https://glossary.sil.org/term/presupposition-trigger.
Probyn, Andrew. "The Afghanistan Mission Was Always Going to End in Failure. A Rifle from 1880 Could Have Told Us That." *ABC News*, 29 Aug. 2021. https://www.abc.net.au/news/2021-08-30/afghanistan-taliban-tarin-kot-rifle-failure/100416590.
Quarles, Charles. "The Gospel of Peter." North American Mission Board, 30 Mar. 2016. https://www.namb.net/apologetics/resource/the-gospel-of-peter/.
"Reader-Response Criticism in Brief." Lumen, n.d. https://courses.lumenlearning.com/introliterature/chapter/reader-response-criticism-suggested-replacement.
Reid, David E. "The Problem with Allegory in Preaching." Preaching, n.d. https://www.preaching.com/articles/the-problem-with-allegory-in-preaching/.
Reimarus, Hermann S. *Fragments.* Edited by C. H. Talbert. 2nd ed. Philadelphia: Fortress, 1970.
Riches, John K. *Jesus and the Transformation of Judaism.* London: Darton, Longman & Todd, 1980.
Riddle, M. B., trans. *The Didache.* In *Ante-Nicene Fathers*, edited by Alexander Roberts et al., 7. Buffalo, NY: Christian Literature, 1886. Revised and edited for New Advent by Kevin Knight. http://www.newadvent.org/fathers/0714.htm.
Robertson, Archibald T. *Matthew and Mark.* Vol. 1 of *Word Pictures in the New Testament.* Nashville: Broadman, 1930.
Robinson, James M., ed. and trans. *The Nag Hammadi Library.* Rev ed. Leiden, Neth.: Brill, 1984.
---. *A New Quest for the Historical Jesus.* Missoula, MT: Scholars, 1979.
Robinson, J. Armitage, trans. "The Gospel According to Peter." In *Ante-Nicene Fathers*, edited by Allan Menzies, 9. Buffalo, NY: Christian Literature, 1896. Revised and

edited for New Advent by Kevin Knight. http://www.newadvent.org/fathers/1001.htm.

Rogerson, John W. "Slippery Words: V. Myth." *Expository Times* 110 (1978) 10–14.

Russell, Bruce. "A Priori Justification and Knowledge." Stanford Encyclopedia of Philosophy, 9 Dec. 2007, last revised 6 May 2020. http://plato.stanford.edu/entries/apriori/.

Sanders, E. P. *The Historical Figure of Jesus*. London: Penguin, 1993.

———. *Jesus and Judaism*. Philadelphia: Fortress, 1985.

Sanders, E. P., and Margaret Davies. *Studying the Synoptic Gospels*. London: SCM, 1989.

Santos, Amanda Proença. "The Witch Doctors of Northern Peru." *BBC Travel*, 18 Feb. 2017. https://www.bbc.com/travel/article/20170214-the-witch-doctors-of-northern-peru.

Sawicki, Marianne. *Seeing the Lord: Resurrection and Early Christian Practices*. Minneapolis: Fortress, 1994.

Schaberg, J. *The Illegitimacy of Jesus: A Feminist Theological Interpretation of the Infancy Narratives*. New York: Crossroad, 1990.

Schaff, Philip. *Apostolic Christianity: AD 1–100*. Vol. 1 of *History of the Christian Church*. Christian Classics Ethereal Library, 1998. https://ccel.org/ccel/schaff/hcc1/hcc1.

Schweitzer, Albert. *The Quest of the Historical Jesus: A Critical Study of Its Progress from Reimarus to Wrede*. Translated by W. Montgomery. 2nd ed. London: Black, 1911. https://www.gutenberg.org/files/45422/45422-pdf.pdf.

Scott, James C. *Domination and the Arts of Resistance: Hidden Transcripts*. New Haven, CT: Yale University Press, 1990.

Shanks, Michael, and C. Tilley. *Social Theory and Archaeology*. Albuquerque: University of New Mexico Press, 1988.

Sheehan, Thomas. *The First Coming: How the Kingdom of God became Christianity*. New York: Random House, 1986.

Silva, Moises. "The Place of Historical Reconstruction in New Testament Criticism." In *Hermeneutics, Authority and Canon*, edited by Donald A. Carson and John D. Woodbridge, 103–33. Leicester, UK: Inter-Varsity, 1986.

Simons, Mandy. "On the Conversational Basis of Some Presuppositions." In *Proceedings of Semantics and Linguistic Theory* 11, edited by B. Hastings et al., 431–48. Ithaca, NY: Cornell University Press, 2001. https://www.researchgate.net/publication/228586746_On_the_Conversational_Basis_of_Some_Presuppositions.

———. "Presupposition and Cooperation." CiteSeerX, Aug. 2007. https://citeseerx.ist.psu.edu/viewdoc/download?doi=10.1.1.206.2349&rep=rep1&type=pdf.

———. "Presupposition without Common Ground." Carnegie Mellon University, Sept. 2006. https://www.cmu.edu/dietrich/philosophy/docs/simons/Presupposition%20without%20Common%20Ground.pdf.

Sinnerton, Jackie, and Rachael Rosel. "State on High Alert as Delta Outbreak Sparks Strict Lockdown." *Courier-Mail*, 2 Aug. 2021. https://www.couriermail.com.au/coronavirus/state-on-high-alert-as-delta-outbreak-sparks-strict-lockdown-news-story/e94d7fc898c7e2a46906d489c090bf49.

Sire, James W. *The Universe Next Door: A Basic Worldview Catalog*. 4th ed. Downers Grove, IL: IVP 2004.

Smith, David Woodruff. "Phenomenology." Stanford Encyclopedia of Philosophy, 16 Nov. 2003, last revised 16 Dec. 2013. http://plato.stanford.edu/entries/phenomenology/.

Soulen, Richard N., and R. Kendall Soulen. *Handbook of Biblical Criticism.* 3rd ed. London: Westminster John Knox, 2001.

Spong, John S. *Born of a Woman: A Bishop Rethinks the Birth of Jesus.* New York: HarperSanFrancisco, 1992.

———. *Rescuing the Bible from Fundamentalism: A Bishop Rethinks the Meaning of Scripture.* San Francisco: HarperSanFrancisco, 1990.

———. *Resurrection: Myth or Reality? A Bishop's Search for the Origins of Christianity.* San Francisco: HarperSanFrancisco, 1994.

Stanton, Graham N. "Presuppositions in New Testament Criticism." In *New Testament Interpretation: Essays on Principles and Methods*, edited by I. Howard Marshall, 60–71. Rev. ed. Carlisle, UK: Paternoster, 1979. https://biblicalstudies.org.uk/pdf/nt-interpretation/nti_03.pdf.

Stewart, Robert B., ed. *The Resurrection of Jesus: John Dominic Crossan and N. T. Wright in Dialogue.* Minneapolis: Fortress, 2006.

———. *The Quest of the Hermeneutical Jesus: The Impact of Hermeneutics on the Jesus Research of John Dominic Crossan and N. T. Wright.* Lanham, MD: University Press of America, 2008.

Stiver, Dan R. "Method." In *Dictionary for Theological Interpretation of the Bible*, edited by Kevin J. Vanhoozer, 510–12. London: SPCK, 2005.

Strauss, David Friedrich. *The Life of Jesus Critically Examined.* Translated by Marian Evans. New York: Blanchard, 1860. http://www.earlychristianwritings.com/strauss/.

Stroll, Avrum, et al. "Epistemology." Britannica, 20 July 1998, last updated 11 Feb. 2021. https://www.britannica.com/topic/epistemology/additional-info#contributors.

Svennevig, Jan. "Abduction as a Methodological Approach to the Study of Spoken Interaction." BI Norwegian Business School, n.d. http://home.bi.no/a0210593/Abduction%20as%20a%20methodological%20.pdf.

Svoboda, Elizabeth. "Typhus." WebMD, 28 Sept. 2020. https://www.webmd.com/a-to-z-guides/what-is-typhus.

Swales, Jon. "Gerd Theissen and the Criterion of Historical Plausibility." Theological Ramblings, Apr. 2008. http://ordinand.files.wordpress.com/2008/04/chapter-6-historical-plausibility1.pdf.

Tacitus. *The Works of Tacitus: The Annals.* Translated by Alfred John Church and William Jackson Brodribb. Sacred Texts, 1864–1877. http://www.sacred-texts.com/cla/tac/.

Tatum, W. Barnes. *In Quest of Jesus: A Guidebook.* Atlanta: John Knox, 1982.

———. *John the Baptist and Jesus: A Report of the Jesus Seminar.* Sonoma, CA: Polebridge, 1993.

Theissen, Gerd. *The First Followers of Jesus: A Sociological Analysis of the Earliest Christianity.* London: SCM, 1978.

———. *The Shadow of a Galilean.* Philadelphia: Fortress, 1987.

Theissen, Gerd, and Annette Merz. *Historical Jesus: A Comprehensive Guide.* Translated by J. Bowden. Minneapolis: Augsburg Fortress, 1998.

Theissen, Gerd, and Dagmar Winter. *The Quest for the Plausible Jesus: The Question of Criteria*, Translated by M. Eugene Boring. Louisville, KY: Westminster/John Knox, 2002.

Thiessen, Henry C. *Introductory Lectures in Systematic Theology.* Grand Rapids: Eerdmans, 1949.

Thiselton, Anthony C. *A Concise Encyclopedia of the Philosophy of Religion*. Oxford, UK: Oneworld, 2002.

———. *New Horizons in Hermeneutics: The Theory and Practice of Transforming Biblical Reading*. Grand Rapids: Zondervan, 1992.

———. *The Two Horizons: New Testament Hermeneutics and Philosophical Description with Special Reference to Heidegger, Bultmann, Gadamer and Wittgenstein*. Grand Rapids: Eerdmans, 1980.

Thomas, Robert L. "Impact of Historical Criticism on Theology and Apologetics." In *The Jesus Crisis: The Inroads of Historical Criticism into Evangelical Scholarship*, edited by Robert L. Thomas and F. David Farnell, 356–77. Grand Rapids: Kregel, 1998.

———. "Redaction Criticism." In *The Jesus Crisis: The Inroads of Historical Criticism into Evangelical Scholarship*, edited by Robert L. Thomas and F. David Farnell, 233–67. Grand Rapids: Kregel, 1998.

Threatened Species Scientific Committee. "The Biological Effects, Including Lethal Toxic Ingestion, Caused by Cane Toads (Bufo marinus)." Australian Government. Department of Agriculture, Water and the Environment, 12 Apr. 2005. https://www.environment.gov.au/biodiversity/threatened/key-threatening-processes/biological-effects-cane-toads.

Torres, Hazel. "Witch Finally Turns to Christ after a Year of Hearing Gospel from Southern Baptist Missionaries." Christian Today, 21 Dec. 2016. https://www.christiantoday.com/article/witch.finally.turns.to.christ.after.a.year.of.hearing.gospel.from.southern.baptist.missionaries/103187.htm.

"Trailer Vertical as Crash Cuts Highway Traffic." *ABC News*, 30 Sept. 2013; updated 1 Oct. 2013. https://www.abc.net.au/news/2013-10-01/trailer-vertical-as-crash-cuts-highway-traffic/4990826.

Travis, Stephen H. "Form Criticism." In *New Testament Interpretation: Essays on Principles and Methods*, edited by I. Howard Marshall, 153–64. Rev. ed. Carlisle: Paternoster, 1979.

Turner, Debra L. "How to Get Sugarcane Cuttings." SFGate, n.d. https://homeguides.sfgate.com/sugarcane-cuttings-42979.html.

"Vaccine Testing and the Approval Process." Centers for Disease Control and Prevention, 1 May 2014. https://www.cdc.gov/vaccines/basics/test-approve.html.

Vanhoozer, Kevin J. *Biblical Narrative in the Philosophy of Paul Ricoeur: A Study in Hermeneutics and Theology*. Cambridge, UK: Cambridge University Press, 1990.

———. *First Theology: God, Scripture and Hermeneutics*. Downers Grove, IL: InterVarsity, 2002.

———. *Is There a Meaning in This Text? The Bible, the Reader, and the Morality of Literary Knowledge*. Leicester, UK: Apollos, 1998.

———. *Remythologizing Theology: Divine Action, Passion, and Authorship*. Cambridge Studies in Christian Doctrine 18. Cambridge, UK: Cambridge University Press, 2010.

Vermes, Geza. *The Dead Sea Scrolls in English*. 3rd ed. London: Penguin, 1987.

———. *Jesus and the World of Judaism*. London: SCM, 1983.

———. *Jesus the Jew*. Minneapolis: Augsburg Fortress, 1981.

———. *Jesus the Jew: A Historian's Reading of the Gospels*. Minneapolis: Fortress, 1973.

———. *The Religion of Jesus the Jew*. London: SCM 1993,

"Welcome to the Department of History." University of Nottingham, n.d. https://www.nottingham.ac.uk/humanities/departments/history/index.aspx.

Wenham, David. "Source Criticism." In *New Testament Interpretation: Essays on Principles and Methods*, edited by I. Howard Marshall, 139–52. Rev. ed. Carlisle, UK: Paternoster, 1979. http://www.biblicalstudies.org.uk/pdf/nt-interpretation/nti_8_source-criticism_wenham.pdf.

Westmoreland-White, Michael. "An Appreciation of the Family Niebuhr." Levellers, 22 Nov. 2009. http://levellers.wordpress.com/2009/11/22/an-appreciation-of-the-family-niebuhr/.

Westphal, Merold. "Onto-Theology." In *Dictionary for Theological Interpretation of the Bible*, edited by Kevin J. Vanhoozer, 546–49. London: SPCK, 2005.

"What Is the Q Gospel?" Got Questions, last updated 26 Apr. 2021. https://www.gotquestions.org/Q-Gospel.html.

"What Was the Apollo Program?" NASA, 18 July 2019. https://www.nasa.gov/audience/forstudents/5-8/features/nasa-knows/what-was-apollo-program-58.html.

White, James R. "Dangerous Airwaves: Harold Camping's Call to Flee the Church." *Christian Research Journal* 25, no. 1 (2002) n.p. https://www.equip.org/article/harold-camping/.

———, and John Dominic Crossan. *Is the Orthodox Biblical Account of Jesus of Nazareth Authentic and Historically Accurate?* Audio CD. Phoenix: Alpha and Omega Ministries. 2005.

"WHO Coronavirus (COVID-19) Dashboard." World Health Organization, updated daily. https://covid19.who.int/.

Wilkins, Michael J., and James P. Moreland, eds. *Jesus under Fire: Modern Scholarship Reinvents the Historical Jesus*. Grand Rapids: Zondervan, 1995.

Wilson, Bryan Ronald. *Magic and the Millennium: A Sociological Study of Religious Movements of Protest among Tribal and Third-World Peoples*. New York: Harper & Row, 1973.

Witherington, Ben, III. *The Christology of Jesus*. Minneapolis: Augsburg Fortress, 1990.

———. *The Jesus Quest: The Third Search for the Jew of Nazareth*. 2nd ed. Downers Grove, IL: InterVarsity, 1997.

———. *Jesus the Sage: The Pilgrimage of Wisdom*. Minneapolis: Fortress, 1994.

Wolfe, David L. *Epistemology: The Justification of Belief*. Downers Grove, IL: InterVarsity, 1982.

Wolters, Al. "Metanarrative." In *Dictionary for Theological Interpretation of the Bible*, edited by Kevin J Vanhoozer, 506–7. London: SPCK, 2005.

Wrede, William. *The Messianic Secret*. Translated by J. C. G. Greig. London: Clarke, 1971.

Wright, D. F. "Doceticism." In *Dictionary of the Later New Testament and Its Developments*, edited by Ralph P. Martin, and Peter H. Davids, 306–9. Downers Grove, IL: InterVarsity, 1997.

Wright, N. T. "Christian Origins and the Resurrection of Jesus: The Resurrection of Jesus as a Historical Problem." *Sewanee Theological Review* 41, no. 2 (1998) 115–16, 120–21. https://ntwrightpage.com/2016/07/12/christian-origins-and-the-resurrection-of-jesus-the-resurrection-of-jesus-as-a-historical-problem/.

———. "Five Gospels but No Gospel: Jesus and the Seminary." In *Authenticating the Activities of Jesus*, edited by Bruce Chilton and Craig A. Evans, 83–120. Leiden, Neth.: Brill, 1999.

———. "Introduction." In *The Aims of Jesus*, by Ben F. Meyer, 9a–9l. Eugene, OR: Pickwick, 2002.

———. "Jesus' Resurrection and Christian Origins." *Gregorianum* 83, no. 4 (2000) 615–35. https://ntwrightpage.com/2016/07/12/jesus-resurrection-and-christian-origins/.

———. *Jesus and the Victory of God*. Vol. 2 of *Christian Origins and the Question of God*. London: SPCK, 1996.

———. "A New Birth?" Review of *The Birth of Christianity: Discovering What Happened in the Years Immediately after the Execution of Jesus*, by John Dominic Crossan. *Scottish Journal of Theology* 53, no. 1 (2000) 72–91.

———. *The New Testament and the People of God*. Vol. 1 of *Christian Origins and the Question of God*. Minneapolis: Fortress, 1992.

———. "Resurrection and Afterlife." Bible Odyssey, n.d. https://www.bibleodyssey.org/en/tools/ask-a-scholar/resurrection-and-afterlife.

———. "Resurrection in Q." In *Christology, Controversy and Community: New Testament Essays in Honour of David R. Catchpole*, edited by David G. Horrel and Christopher M. Tuckett, 85–97. Leiden, Neth.: Brill, 2000. http://docshare02.docshare.tips/files/22496/224960291.pdf.

———. "Resurrection Narratives." In *Dictionary for Theological Interpretation of the Bible*, edited by Kevin J. Vanhoozer, 675–76. London: SPCK, 2005.

———. *The Resurrection of the Son of God*. Vol. 3 of *Christian Origins and the Question of God*. Minneapolis: Fortress, 2003.

———. "Taking the Text with Her Pleasure." *Theology* 96 (1993) 303–10. http://www.ntwrightpage.com/Wright_Text_Pleasure.htm.

———. "Towards a Third Quest? Jesus Then and Now." *ARC* 10 (1982) 20–27.

Wright, N. T., and John Dominic Crossan. "The Resurrection: Historical Event or Theological Explanation? A Dialogue." In *The Resurrection of Jesus: John Dominic Crossan and N. T. Wright in Dialogue*, edited by R. B. Stewart, 16–47. Minneapolis: Fortress, 2006.

Zhai, Jing. "Jacques Derrida and Deconstruction." Not Even Past, 7 Oct. 2015. https://notevenpast.org/jacques-derrida-and-deconstruction/.

Zhou, Peng, et. al. "A Pneumonia Outbreak Associated with a New Coronavirus of Probable Bat Origin." *Nature* 579 (2020) 270–73. https://doi.org/10.1038/s41586-020-2012-7.

Zhu, Na, et al. "A Novel Coronavirus from Patients with Pneumonia in China, 2019." *New England Journal of Medicine* 382 (Feb. 2020) 727–33. https://www.nejm.org/doi/full/10.1056/nejmoa2001017.

www.ingramcontent.com/pod-product-compliance
Lightning Source LLC
Chambersburg PA
CBHW050843230426
43667CB00012B/2125